Reading and fiction in Golden-Age Spain

A Platonist critique and some picaresque replies

B. W. IFE

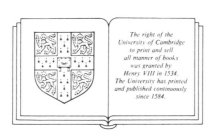

The right of the
University of Cambridge
to print and sell
all manner of books
was granted by
Henry VIII in 1534.
The University has printed
and published continuously
since 1584.

CAMBRIDGE UNIVERSITY PRESS

CAMBRIDGE

LONDON   NEW YORK   NEW ROCHELLE

MELBOURNE   SYDNEY

Published by the Press Syndicate of the University of Cambridge
The Pitt Building, Trumpington Street, Cambridge CB2 1RP
32 East 57th Street, New York, NY 10022, USA
10 Stamford Road, Oakleigh, Melbourne 3166, Australia

First published 1985

Printed in Great Britain at
the University Press, Cambridge

Library of Congress catalogue card number: 85-4199

British Library cataloguing in publication data
Ife, B. W.
Reading and fiction in Golden-Age Spain: a
Platonist critique and some picaresque replies.
– (Cambridge Iberian and Latin American studies)
1. Spanish fiction – Classical period, 1500–1700
– History and criticism
I. Title
863'.3'09   PQ6142
ISBN 0 521 30375 3

SE

IN MEMORY OF R. O. JONES

Contents

I

Introduction – first premises

To judge from the frequency with which words like 'development' and 'evolution' are used in literary studies, one might be forgiven for thinking that books were living beings subject to biological laws. Such words are, of course, insidious in the way that they equate change with improvement. They confuse quality with chronology, and – when we least expect it – they have us thinking in terms of Grand Designs and Historical Goals. The literary output of a group or a period does, however, have a habit of seeming misleadingly purposeful when looked at in retrospect. This danger is particularly acute when we consider the 'development' of prose fiction in Golden-Age Spain. The period from the 1490s to the 1650s was one of unequalled literary achievement in Spain. The enormous variety and vitality of the work produced is sufficient indication of the great importance Spanish writers attached to experiment. They tried endless permutations of form, theme and genre, and whenever they exhausted their inherited wealth they went in search of something new. They cudgelled their imaginations to satisfy the demands of a rapidly-growing reading public and in the process they tried and tested genres and formal devices which were eventually to find their way into the main body of European fiction. But the idea of Spain as a proving ground for the novel is as dangerous as it is attractive; it is too tempting to treat the writers of the period as a working party beavering away under the chairmanship of Cervantes in pursuit of the Great Tradition. Evolution simply does not happen that way.

And yet literature clearly does not stand still. No book is ever exactly like those that have gone before. If we take a page at random from a sentimental novel or a romance of chivalry and compare it with a page of Cervantes, or Quevedo's *Buscón*, or the *Criticón*, we see that there are differences and that the differences are not random. Quite apart from considerations of genre and form, we are immediately struck by differences of style, by the self-conscious attitudes which the seventeenth-century writers adopt towards their fictions, by their use of irony, and their habit of treating language as if it had a body, a weight and a life of its own. These differences are the very features which enable us to distinguish at a glance between a text from the time of the Catholic Monarchs and a text from the reign of Philip III or Philip IV, and they add up to something at once too homogeneous to be the result of chance and too contingent to be the result of necessity. However we view these changes, whether as development or decadence, they have to be accounted for. How did Golden-Age fiction come to 'evolve' in the direction it did?

Biology provides us with a model of evolution in which novelty – the chance mutations in the protein structure of an organism – is kept in check both by the requirement that it should be compatible with the system as a whole and by the pressure of natural selection.[1] The requirement of organic compatibility ensures the internal stability of the system and is responsible for its inherent conservatism, while natural selection tests the system's coherence vis à vis the world in which it has to live. This model will hardly do in anything but a non-literal sense for literature. For one thing, novelty in literature is willed and not the product of chance; for another, there is no genetic relationship between books in spite of their evident kinship. But, like life, literature is a fundamentally conservative system in which originality is hard won in the face of an often intimidatory tradition and a strongly conventional sense of what constitutes a genre, what is a fit subject for discussion or a proper style in which to treat that subject. We might easily think of restrictions such as these – conventions governing not just what may or may not be written but also what can feasibly be accepted and understood as a piece of literature – as the means by which new work is made compatible with the internal dynamic of literary tradition. All writers have to face this problem every time they decide whether and what to write.

Literature also has to live with and adapt to selective pressures from the outside world. The mere fact of communication sets limits to the scope of a piece of writing and will even determine details of form and expression. An exigent audience can effectively tie an author's hands and a hostile critic destroy his reputation. Public demand and critical response are only two of the many factors both negative and positive which contribute to the process of equilibration, of action and reaction, to which any writer is subject. It often happens that the tension between the conflicting claims of internal stability and changing external circumstances becomes so great that the system breaks down. Species become extinct and other, better-equipped forms invade the vacant spaces they leave behind. The literary arts pass from time to time through similar periods of crisis, and sixteenth-century Spain was in just such a situation. Changed circumstances in the production, transmission and consumption of books found established literary canons wanting, and from the resulting fluidity authors were forced to devise new solutions if they wished to survive. Unfortunately, the very multiplicity of factors which makes such periods of creative flux interesting also makes them difficult to grasp. In this study I want to single out one factor which compelled writers to question the nature and purpose of their art and determined to a large extent the replies they gave: the growth of private reading made possible by the printed book.

The argument of the study is basically a simple one. It starts with two widely-accepted and interrelated premises of no great originality: that the private reading of vernacular prose fiction in the early part of the sixteenth century was a new experience for most people and one which was highly distrusted by many authorities whose opinions we ought to take seriously. From these premises it proceeds to the conclusion that a number of what we regard today as the distinguishing features of mature Golden-Age prose fiction grew up as a consequence of authors taking those two factors – the relative novelty and widespread unacceptability of reading fiction – into account. The work they produced in consequence amounts to a practical defence of reading.

Immense difficulties surround any study of reading. Even if we knew exactly what books were available, where and in what numbers; if we knew who read them and under what circumstances, or even how many people could read in a given place at a given time, it could still be objected that reading is a personal matter, that no two readers are alike and that all generalisation is therefore improper. Difficulty and lack of information do not, though, invalidate the need to consider the problem. Books as such are just inert physical objects unless or until they are read. Anything we say about them will only be partly true until we can give some account of the process that brings them to life. Since this process is primarily psychological it is not so important to know who was reading what (though we can make educated deductions about such matters)[2] as to know what was happening to them while they were at their reading. On this subject the Golden Age has a good deal to say, not all of it very complimentary in that it was the harmfulness of the activity that was repeatedly emphasised. And when a reader's moral and spiritual well-being were at stake, numbers and social classes did not enter the question; one man's fate was enough to decide the issue, or so Cervantes seemed to think when he offered his remaining hand as a guarantee of the harmlessness of his work.

Accordingly, on the principle that the best way to find out about something is to ask someone who disapproves of it, in chapter 2 I offer a detailed analysis of contemporary attacks on literature in order to illustrate how much they can tell us about Golden-Age attitudes to the dangers of reading fiction. Chapter 3 takes up the most serious of the objections raised – concern at the ability of certain kinds of books to command aesthetic belief in the face of empirical disbelief – and illustrates its forcefulness in the light of current research into the reading process and the way fiction induces an almost hypnotic state of rapture in its readers. The argument of chapter 3 justifies a good deal of the readiness of the Golden Age to generalise about the effects of reading and shows that the way people read is to a considerable extent a shared experience. The remaining part of the book is concerned to show how the writers of the Golden Age attempted to deal in fictional terms with the dangers of which fiction itself was alleged to be the cause. The examples which have been chosen to illustrate how this was done are all so-called 'picaresque' novels, but this book is not about the picaresque novel in any conventional sense. It does not deal with matters of genre and is not intended to offer 'interpretations' of the works under discussion. I have chosen the novels because I feel that they best exemplify those general character-istics of Spanish Golden-Age prose fiction which bear on the central theme of this study. Picaresque novels may occupy the foreground of our attention, but in the background there lurk other figures, chief among them Cervantes, whose presiding genius will, I trust, indicate the wider reference and applicability of what follows.

We are so much a product of a typographic culture that it is impossible for us to appreciate any longer the strangeness of what we do when we go to a library, or a bookshop or to our own shelves, take down a book and read it. Yet a man (or very likely a woman: reading is essentially a sedentary occupation) who sat down to read, let us say, *Amadís de*

Gaula as recently as 1508, was doing several things, at least one of which his grandfather could not have done or would probably not have thought of doing. Reading *Amadís* meant reading from a printed book either aloud to others or to oneself in private; possession of a printed book implied that for at least part of the time its owner would read to himself, and a solitary reader would almost certainly be learning to read silently rather than aloud. Reading a novel of chivalry also meant reading a piece of fiction written in prose, not verse, and vernacular prose, not Latin. These are all things we take for granted when we read novels yet each of them was to some extent a recent development in early sixteenth-century Spain.

The possession of a printed book in 1508 was a novelty which it is historically impossible to deny, but the innovative effects of printing can be overestimated: in its initial stages, the development of printing changed the literary face of Europe to only a very limited extent.[3] For the most part the invention of printing was the child of a long-established necessity which it continued to serve for several decades after its inception. Before and after printing the market for books was predominantly a learned and specialist one. From the thirteenth century onwards a steadily-growing number of clients created a demand for books which monastic scriptoria were unable to satisfy. The monasteries lost their monopoly of book production to secular workshops in which copyists were able to improve their methods and develop the mass production of multiple copies. The systems they adopted lasted until the fifteenth century and were the direct antecedents of printing. Continued growth in demand prompted the solution of important technical problems – in particular, paper technology and the metallurgy necessary for the manufacture of moveable type – which had prevented the practical application of a technique familiar as a theoretical possibility for some time. New technology is always expensive; printers were businessmen and the new techniques had to be paid for in sales. Financial considerations encouraged printers to produce titles they knew were in demand, and ensured a conservative publishing policy which, it has been argued, may have helped to prolong the tastes of the late Middle Ages into the age of humanism.[4] In some ways, then, printing changed little. The new process was designed to duplicate old products and for several decades printers and scribes coexisted, copying each other's work and catering for a clientele with the same basic requirements, albeit different levels of income. At least as far as learned books are concerned, it was the readership that created printing and not the printers who created the readership. The figures bear this out: 77 per cent of incunabula are in Latin, 45 per cent are religious books.[5] Spanish printing in the two decades for which we have the best information, 1501–20, shows somewhat lower levels of production: ecclesiastical and religious publications account for 31 per cent of total production, while of the 1372 editions listed by Norton only 519 (38 per cent) are in Latin, and this proportion falls to 19.3 per cent in Seville and 13 per cent in Toledo.[6] But in assessing these figures it is essential to take into account Spain's dependence on the import of Venetian-, Lyonese- and Parisian-printed books to provide the majority of texts needed by scholars and the clergy.[7]

The position on recreational, that is non-specialist, literature is more difficult to assess, since this is an area in which we can be much less sure of the nature of the readership. It is clear that the readers of technical literature will be those specialists who need to refer to it in the course of their professional duties. That is why we can be fairly certain, when considering questions of literacy, that literate members of society will include those who do their work sitting down and/or need to refer to books to make their living – scholars, doctors, lawyers, theologians, merchants, teachers, civil servants, students. For these people the ability to read is a professional tool, a means to an end, but a tool which they may, if they wish, exploit in their spare time for recreational purposes. It is also apparent that others who do not actually need to be able to read have little incentive to acquire the skill if the restrictive nature of book production meant that they were very unlikely ever to set eyes on a book. But the introduction of a technique which increased the availability of books might well encourage more people to acquire reading skills for non-specialist purposes. When, and at what rate, this began to happen is unfortunately very difficult to estimate. It seems probable that in the early period of printing the market for recreational literature would be drawn primarily from those specialised readers who, already having the skills, were able most easily to diversify their interests. However, if Maxime Chevalier is right in thinking that the readership of chivalresque novels was predominantly an aristocratic one,[8] an appreciable increase in non-specialist reading must have taken place by the mid sixteenth century: reading is scarcely an essential requirement for the profession of aristocracy, and, indeed, was frequently scorned as a mark of purposeful endeavour which was quite out of keeping with true nobility.[9] The position of women readers also points to the growth of reading among non-specialist audiences: while from a strictly professional point of view women had no business being able to read unless they were undergoing religious instruction, they are, as we shall see, frequently cited by moralists as prime targets for pernicious literature.

In some respects, then, printing may well have helped significantly to bring about changes in literary tastes. The sheer quantity and availability of books – of whatever kind – was to have effects which extended beyond the satisfaction of a pre-existent demand: specialist material became available to a wider audience; students could have direct access to primary sources in philosophy and religion; and the layman, for a modest outlay, could put together a library of, say, devotional works or popular treatises on piety. The effects of such developments on the religious complexion of the sixteenth century are too well known to require further comment. As more books became available the conditions were created in which reading might become an end in itself, a pastime practised for pleasure and recreation by an audience who would not otherwise have had any use for books. As the reading public became larger so its nature gradually changed. It became less specialised and began in turn to impose its tastes on printers whose restricted traditional markets were becoming saturated. Prominent among its tastes was recreational literature, and it was this portion of the market that printers helped to develop. Thirty per cent of incunabula were works of classical, mediaeval or contemporary literature.[10] The market was slower to emerge in Spain but it was still significant. Norton lists 310 editions of vernacular literary texts, including translations, approximately 23 per cent of the total output. But when we consider that of these only 49 are 'works in substantially original Spanish prose',[11] it will be apparent that anyone in search of a good home-spun yarn would have done better at the *tertulia* or the inn than at the sign of the local printer cum bookseller. The reader of novels in early sixteenth-century Spain had very little to choose from, but within a hundred years that position had changed considerably.

Printing had one further important effect on the consumption of vernacular literature which touches on the comparative novelty of what our reader of *Amadís* was doing. It is clear that the demand for narrative literature in the early Golden Age is not a demand for a new product – sub-Arthurian romance could hardly be called that – but for an old product in a new format. There is nothing new about narrative. People have always wanted to hear stories, whether true or false or a mixture of both, but before the thirteenth century the dissemination of vernacular works for recreational purposes was almost exclusively oral. Little was read in the vernacular, though many texts must have been composed in it. Printing gave extra impetus to the long process of transformation of a hearing public into a reading one. The consequences of this shift which, again, was already in progress before the age of the printed book, are not easy to gauge, though one at least is immediately apparent. In order to listen to a storyteller or to hear a book read aloud an audience has to come together; private reading is just that, private. What an orator is to an assembled audience, an author is to a dispersed one.[12] Reading requires isolation; it leads inevitably to a loss of direct contact with one's immediate neighbours and the establishment of less tangible relationships with unknown confederates elsewhere. It is likely that a reading public consuming literature in an atmosphere of contemplative solitude will be much more individualistic in its response than a hearing public moved perhaps more readily by mass emotion. Don Quixote's approach to the novels of chivalry might have been healthier had he not read them holed up in his study beyond the protective company of his fellow men. The likelihood that he, in common with most of his contemporaries, read the books silently to himself increased the degree of his identification with the text and his abscission from his society.

Silent reading may also have been comparatively new in the Golden Age, although this is a difficult issue to decide and has given rise to a good deal of discussion.[13] The modern assumption that silent reading is the more mature form of reading while reading aloud is the sign of the learner or a mark of a low level of literacy has tended to obscure our appreciation of the fact that in antiquity and the mediaeval world it was common practice to read aloud. It may well be that the eunuch whom Philip *hears* reading Isaiah to himself (Acts 8.30) was not a very fluent reader, but there is ample evidence that even skilled readers read aloud to themselves, while silent reading was sufficiently unusual to call for comment. The Rule of St Benedict insists that monks reading after six o'clock should do so silently so as not to disturb others, and St Augustine's celebrated description of Ambrose reading silently can be taken to imply that the practice was unusual. Augustine notes that Ambrose's eyes travelled across the page while his heart sought out the sense but his voice and tongue were silent, and visitors often sat in silence, unwilling to interrupt him, before they left.[14] Bernard Knox has, however, questioned the view, which grew up on the basis of Balogh's mainly Christian and mediaeval evidence, that silent reading in the ancient world was, if not completely unknown, at least so rare as to arouse astonishment. Against the description of Ambrose, Knox has set a passage from the *Tusculan Disputations* (5.116), first noted by W. P. Clark, in which Cicero attempts to console the deaf by telling them that greater pleasure can be gained from reading songs (*cantus*) than from hearing them. If that is the case, silent reading was not only evidently perfectly familiar and acceptable in Cicero's day, but may also have been regarded as the more satisfying way of experiencing literature. This latter conclusion may also be borne out by the passage from Augustine: what he found striking about Ambrose may have been not so much the silence of the activity as the intensity of his concentration which was made all the more eloquent by the silence.

It is evident that an ability to read silently is not the same thing as the use of that ability in everyday reading. What is more important, and a better guide to normal practice, are the expectations which authors bring to their work. In spite of a good deal of evidence that readers in antiquity could and did read silently, it remains true that ancient and mediaeval books were normally read aloud simply because this method made a work accessible to the greatest number of people at a time when it was not possible for everybody to have his own copy. Authors very often composed with oral performance in view, and their expectation that their work would be read aloud is detectable in the formal aspects of the texts themselves. Yet it seems clear that by the sixteenth century expectations had changed considerably and the habit of silent reading was beginning to predominate. When Campuzano gives Peralta the *Coloquio de los perros* to read, he reads it silently although he is not alone, and there is no suggestion that he should or could have done otherwise. It is impossible to say when the balance began to tilt, but it seems reasonable to associate the consolidation of silent reading with the age of the printed book. The importance of privacy and silence in reading will be dealt with more fully in chapter 3.

While these developments were going forward, printing was also helping to crystallise important changes in the nature of recreational literature. Even such an unexceptional description of *Amadís de Gaula*

as a piece of vernacular prose fiction puts the work into a category
which would not have been accepted or even understood by the
majority of critics who might have felt themselves qualified to
pronounce on its legitimacy. Categories like fiction and non-fiction
are far from being universal and they were by no means clearly
differentiated in sixteenth-century Spain. 'Vernacular prose' to some
authorities would have been a contradiction in terms. Romances of
chivalry and sentimental novels were in many ways hybrids, bridging
the gap between the categories of History and Poetry. There had
always been some room for fiction in historical accounts, which might
incorporate the fabulous and the hearsay in the interests of entertainment or edification.[15] But, for the most part, fact, or whatever went
under the guise of fact, was the realm of History. Unashamed fiction
went under the banner of poetic truth and was the province of Poetry.
Again for the most part, the natural medium for Poetry (things which
aren't true but ought to be) was verse, and for History (things which
are true but perhaps ought not to be) the proper medium was prose,
preferably Latin prose. Vernacular prose fiction sweeps these conventions aside. The process which had begun with the *mise en prose* of verse
epic and romance saw the elevation of the end product to a new and
respectable status in the age of printing.

This seepage of Poetry into the traditional medium of History
brought with it a number of important consequences. Verse has its
own devices for building up a protective barrier between itself and its
audience. Its artificial structure, prosody, formulaic diction and
frequent use of reserved languages or dialects, all contribute towards
reminding the reader that what he has before him is a special kind of
reality, different from what he sees about him every day. Prosification
cuts down the number of artificial elements in the language and brings
it much nearer to the reader's own; and at the same time it draws on
the fund of authority invested in prose by its long association with
History. The use of prose as a vehicle for imaginative literature, a
practice which printing extended, helped to create a generation of
readers who were exposed to fiction in an unprecedentedly immediate
way. In an atmosphere of silence and solitude they recreated for
themselves the thoughts and fantasies of others in a language which
resembled their own and which they culled from what they were used
to thinking of as the ultimate source of learning, the book. If we fail to
keep these developments before our minds and allow our familiarity
with the reading of novels to dull our sense of its strangeness, we run

the risk, when studying the growth of Golden-Age fiction, of seriously misunderstanding the true nature and extent of its originality.

Originality and innovation always breed resistance, and it would be quite wrong to think that developments as radical and far-reaching as those just outlined went forward without considerable opposition. Yet the extent and the bitterness of the opposition to recreational literature in Golden-Age Spain hardly seems consistent with what we tend to think of as a bookish age. Indeed, if we are to believe the literary critics and commentators of sixteenth-century Spain, the reading of fiction at that period was a pastime fraught with hidden danger and mortal peril. In 1588, in an account of the life and conversion of Mary Magdalcne, the Augustinian theologian and Platonist Fr. Pedro Malón de Chaide wrote of the harmful effects of secular literature on the youth of the day.[16] He lamented that, as if natural inclination were not enough to bring about our ruin, writers of fiction and poetry place treacherous reefs under the fragile keel of ill-advised youth. To give the works of Garcilaso de la Vega – the outstanding Spanish lyric poet of the sixteenth century – to a young reader was, he claimed, like putting a knife into the hands of a madman.[17] All manner of other monstrous, mendacious and portentous chimeras were to accompany one of the supreme poetic achievements of the century on Fr. Pedro's blacklist. How can a toddler be expected to walk straight with a copy of the *Diana* in her satchel, or with one of those books of *caballerías*, that so-called chivalry whose deceitful villainy is waspishly anagrammed into *bellaquerías*.[18] We could cheerfully dismiss Fr. Pedro's remarks as benighted or quaint were it not for the fact that his judgments are endorsed to varying degrees by some of the leading intellectuals of the day, theologians, philosophers, humanists, and above all writers of fiction themselves, men like Cervantes, whose work constitutes the most intelligent account of the dangers of fiction for the untutored reading public and of the writer's responsibility to that public. If a less eminent figure like the Jesuit Gaspar de Astete can refer to writers of fiction as cruel, shallow, loud-mouthed, deranged, indecent and without fear of God, or say that their mouths are full of evil blasphemy and obscenity, their throats stinking sepulchres belching forth every kind of foetid putrescence and their hearts sewers of wickedness,[19] he can do so because his overwritten obscurantism is based on a long tradition and because he could rely on the support of men of learning and authority.

Behind all the apparent exaggeration these critics meant what they said; writers of fiction took them seriously, and so must we.

Attacks on imaginative literature in sixteenth-century Spain have been much anthologised but not always well understood.[20] Undoubtedly one of the major barriers to understanding has been the very virulence of the terms in which they are expressed, and the tendency to dismiss the arguments as overstated and narrow-minded, particularly when so many of the criticisms come from churchmen. The prominence of the clergy among opponents of literature is inevitable given their role as custodians of morality, and the attitude of any sixteenth-century clergyman to books can only have been ambivalence when it was not outright abhorrence. Having welcomed the press at first, the clergy soon found that by encouraging the reading of devotional literature they had made a rod for their own backs. Once set loose, the demon book could not be kept under control. The public could not be prevented from reading what it liked or from imposing its tastes on publishers and writers. Works of devotion were pushed from pride of place and imaginative literature began to impinge on areas of emotion which the Church wanted reserved for religious feeling.[21] In Spain, opposition to literature seems to form part of a general Catholic opposition to the ideals of *pietas litterata*, to the promotion of scripture in the vernacular, and the consequent elimination of the clergy's role as exegetes of the Word and intermediaries between man and God. The unacceptable directness and the individualist nature of literary experience inevitably smacked of a Protestant frame of mind, and Spanish clergymen countered with their traditional mistrust of the layman's ability to cope unaided with dangerous things like thoughts and feelings.

However, the inevitability and implicit self-interest of ecclesiastical opposition does not, of itself, invalidate the Church's case and it would be a mistake automatically to equate vigorous language with closure of mind. Even narrow-mindedness is not incompatible with being right. The clergy, after all, were not alone in their opposition to fiction and many of the strongest attacks came from men whose intellectual credentials and first-hand acquaintance with the dangers of reading it are beyond dispute. When the great hebraist Benito Arias Montano speaks of the fashionable novels of chivalry as 'monsters, the offspring of stupidity, excrement and filth gathered together for the destruction of the age' his familiarity with the power of the written word through his several roles of scholar, humanist and poet, gives authority to what he says.[22] Gonzalo Fernández de Oviedo y Valdés, the first chronicler of the New World and another uncompromising critic of the novels, had himself published a translation of one of them in 1519.[23] Yet in 1535, in the *Historia general de las Indias*, his claim to be telling the truth draws a contrast with the lying books of Amadís, and in his *Quinquagenas de la nobleza de España* he condemns these novels as means by which the devil entertains the foolish, swindling and enchanting them, and distracting them from honest and exemplary reading.[24] Juan de Valdés wasted ten years in devouring works of fiction but as his taste matured he found that, with the rare exception, he could no longer stomach their shameless mendacity and shapeless composition.[25] St Ignatius Loyola and St Teresa also confessed to enjoying, with later regret, the same childhood enthusiasm.[26]

But perhaps the most celebrated and influential criticisms came from Juan Luis Vives, the scholar and theologian and follower of Erasmus, whose knowledge of secular literature was as wide and appreciative as that of many of his contemporaries. In the *De Institutione Christianae Feminae* (1524) he complains bitterly of the modern habit of writing vernacular works about nothing but war and love.[27] Such books are written for and read by idle men and women and are nothing more than firebrands by which they may burn the more fiercely. 'What need I', he writes in Richard Hyrde's vigorous translation, 'to tell what a mischief is toward, when straw and dry wood is cast into the fire?'[28] So widespread is the reading of these novels among girls that in some cities young noblewomen are being allowed to judge tournaments and jousts, and in consequence are bending their minds in a most unchristian manner to the contemplation of the strength and prowess of the male body. 'It cannot lightly be a chaste maid that is occupied with thinking on armour and tourney and man's valiance.'[29] These women sip the poison unwittingly, leaving Vives uncertain whether he should even mention the subject, 'lest it hurts others with the smell and defile them with the infection'.[30] If it is doubtful that even a man may take up arms, what good can result if a woman, 'yea though she handle them not, yet be conversant among them with heart and mind which is worse'?[31] How can wise men allow their wives and daughters to read such wantonness; how can society overlook their practice of the pernicious habit, and do nothing about the writers, men bent on the corruption of the young and no better than those who infect the common wells with poison?

Vives cites many examples of the kind of book he has in mind, and they are not just the usual run of chivalresque novels, the Amadises, Esplandians and Launcelots. *Celestina* is included, and the *Cárcel de amor*; Pyramus and Thisbe are there, with Boccaccio, Aeneas Silvius and the *infacetissimae facetiae* of Gian Francesco Poggio Bracciolini, along with other vernacular works by idle men,

unlearned, and set all upon filth and viciousness, in whom I wonder what should delight men but that vice pleaseth them so much. As for learning, none is to be looked for in those men which saw never so much as a shadow of learning themself. And what they tell aught, what delight can be in those things that be so plain and foolish lies? . . . What a Madness is it of folks to have pleasure in these books? Also there is no wit in them but a few words of wanton lust which be spoken to move her mind, with whom they love, if it chance she be steadfast. And if they be read but for this, the best were to make books of bawds' crafts, for in other things what craft can be had of such a maker that is ignorant of all good craft? Nor I never heard man say that he liked these books but those that never touched good books. And I myself sometime have read in them, but I never found in them one step either of goodness or wit. And as for those that praise them, as I know some that do, I will believe them if they praise them after that they have read Cicero and Seneca, or St Jerome, or Holy Scripture, and have mended their language better. For oftentimes the only cause why they praise them is because they see in them their own conditions, as in a glass. Finally, though they were never so witty and pleasant, yet would I have no pleasure infected with poison, nor have no woman quickened unto vice. And verily they be but foolish husbands and mad that suffer their wives to wax more ungratiously subtle by reading of such books.[32]

Elsewhere, in the *De Officio Mariti* (1529), the romances are lambasted in similar terms along with

the works of poets, the fables of Milesius, as that of the Golden Ass, and in a manner all Lucian's works, and many others which are written in the vulgar tongue as of Tristan, Launcelot, Ogier, Amadís, and of Arthur the which were written and made by such as were idle and knew nothing. The books do hurt both man and woman, for they make them wily and crafty, they kindle and stir up covetousness, inflame anger and all beastly and filthy desire.[33]

Plain speaking of this kind was clearly not the exclusive property of the mean-minded killjoy. If men of Vives's intellectual distinction can liken writers of fiction to poisoners of common wells we may be sure that what is interesting about these attacks is not that they raise bigotry and gratuitous abuse to the level of a fine art, though undoubtedly many examples do this, but that they proceed from a serious and deeply-felt anxiety about the effects of fictional literature in general on the reading public. For we should not make the mistake of assuming that the attacks are directed solely at novels of chivalry. We have already seen that Malón de Chaide and Vives include other literary genres within the scope of their criticism. Fr. Juan de la Cerda excludes all fiction from the library of any young woman who would aspire to moral integrity, naming no one particular work, but speaking in general terms – strongly reminiscent of Vives – of 'books which waste the spirit and besmirch the soul'.[34] But the fact that the scorpion's juice (*aceite de escorpiones*) on which the young girls are weaned is compounded of tales of love as well as war shows that he is thinking, as was Vives, of the sentimental and the pastoral novel as much as the chivalresque. The prominent place of the latter in criticism of the period is easily explained: it was by far the most prolific and the most popular genre of vernacular prose fiction in sixteenth-century Spain.[35] That attacks on it of undiminished virulence continued well into the second half of the following century, when the vogue of the chivalresque was all but dead, shows that novels of chivalry bore the brunt of opposition which was directed, through them, at imaginative literature in general. Indeed, it is rare for a complainant to restrict himself to the novels of chivalry without making clear his wider reference by use of some catch-all formula embracing other equally vain and fictitious books of profanity and falsehood.

A further guarantee of the serious intent as well as the general scope of the attacks is provided by the apparent contrast between the very forcefulness of the language in which they are expressed and the common complaint that works of fiction are trivial, a waste of time and a distraction from more important matters. Critic after critic waves a dismissive hand at novels which, in Fr. Antonio de Guevara's words, do not pass the time as much as waste it.[36] And we find this point made even by authors who admit that the variety and ease afforded by light reading are beneficial for the human spirit. Jacques Amyot, writing in the prologue to the Spanish translation of the *Aethiopica* of Heliodorus, one of the few novels to gain the approval of the age as a worthwhile piece of entertainment, argues that the mind perturbed by misfortune or fatigued from much study will benefit from change as much as from rest.[37] But it is nevertheless still an *imbecilidad de nuestra natura* that we cannot concentrate for long on weightier matters, and even some learned men find history rather too austere for their taste.

The Dominican Fr. Agustín Salucio has equally worthy notions of what constitutes light reading, and would have his fellow churchmen curl up, on their evenings off, with Livy or Tacitus – or if they must read verse, then Virgil, Horace, or Ovid [*sic*!] – any of which would do them far more good than the unlettered trivia of novels of chivalry.[38] João de Barros adds others to the list of authors he would prefer to see read: Augustine, Jerome, Seneca, Valerius, Curtius, Suetonius; Eutropius, even. Instead, young people worry their heads about pointless things of no use to them or anyone else, things like the Holy Grail, or the exploits of Amadís, or Palmerín, or Primaleón, none of which serve any purpose, and all of which he would be delighted to see the back of.[39] With so much good and profitable literature written in Spanish and translated from Latin and Greek, why do people spend most of their time worrying whether don Belianís de Grecia conquered the enchanted castle or whether the battle-weary don Florisel de Niquea married the woman he desired? Such books are a waste of time for reader and author alike, and even for the booksellers and publishers, who cannot in consequence shift their stock of the morally – and commercially – more profitable lines. Only the paper mill benefits from the rising cost of paper.[40]

It is one thing to argue, however, that too much television keeps children from their homework, and quite another that television should be abolished on that account. Yet this is, in effect, what was widely contended and, to an extent, actually achieved in the Spain of Charles V, despite the Emperor's well-known fondness for novels of chivalry. A royal decree of 1531 prohibited the export to the Indies of 'romances, de historias vanas o de profanidad como son de *Amadís* y otros de esta calidad', on grounds of their unsuitability as reading matter for Indians.[41] The prohibition was reaffirmed in 1543 in a decree published in Valladolid on 29 September, and extended to include the printing, selling and possession in the colonies of 'romances que traten de materias profanas y fabulosas e historias fingidas', as well as their reading by Indians and Spaniards alike.[42] It was also, it should be said, frequently ignored.[43] Twelve years later, in 1555, Philip II heard a petition from the Cortes at Valladolid which sought to have the ban extended to the peninsula, and its scope broadened to include 'todos los libros que después de él [sc. Amadís] se han fingido de su calidad y lectura, y coplas y farsas de amores y otras vanidades', a formula which was clearly intended to cover virtually all the genres of secular literature.[44] The submission argues that young people are distracted by such things and grow to love the violence and the passion of the tales they tell to such an extent that when they are faced by similar temptations in real life they are less likely to resist them than if they had not read about them. A ban backed by stiff penalties would, it was argued, stamp out the reading of books of vanities and force people to read edifying and uplifting religious books. The King's reply to the petition, given in his absence in the following year by Princess Juana, states that the drafting of the appropriate legislation was in hand, though the bill itself was never published.

We can only guess why it was felt necessary to take additional steps to stop the growth of a popular literary genre at a time when all books were in any case required in principle to be submitted to scrutiny before a licence for publication could be issued. The vetting system had been in operation since the reign of Ferdinand and Isabel, and was administered by agents of the crown not the Church. The inspectorate was not always clerical. Lay authors were often included in the appointments, and even if the censors had all been from the clergy there is no guarantee that fewer licences would have been issued to works of fiction: very few such books appeared on the Spanish Index until well into the seventeenth century.[45] It is possible, then, that those who called for the banning of vernacular fiction were fighting an additional battle against an ecclesiastical establishment which they saw as being too liberal in its attitudes, or too narrowly concerned with doctrinal matters to be alert to other dangers. The strength of feeling is, in either case, beyond question. We have only to imagine the amount of lobbying which was necessary before the 1555 proposal ever got as far as the Cortes, or – to take an example from a later reign – the weight of opinion which led to the recommendation of the Junta de Reformación in 1625 that no licences be granted for the printing of novels or plays in Castile.[46] Yet it cannot have escaped the attention of lobbyists that in attempting to ban something so apparently trivial as stories about knights-errant and poems about shepherds, they were according them more importance than they would otherwise have wished to. If something has to be banned it cannot be trivial, and to take the opposition so seriously is to recognise and even emphasise its strength.

There was, of course, a precedent of great authority and antiquity for seeking to do away once and for all with fiction: Plato's banishment of the poets from the Republic.[47] By taking such an extreme measure – possibly the most celebrated and most questioned piece of censorship in the history of literary criticism – against the products of the imagination Plato showed just how seriously he took the power of art, and, as Iris Murdoch has argued, his attempt to put literature beyond the bounds of the completely stable society pays the arts the compliment which they now receive in Eastern Europe.[48] Sixteenth-century book-burnings were an equally eloquent tribute to the power of the written word. Behind Plato's banishment of the poets lay a conviction that their work caused positive and not just negative harm, and his analysis of that harm and detailed theoretical justification of his decision provided Renaissance critics with all the ammunition they needed. Scarcely one of the critics who ran down fiction in sixteenth-century Spain does not rely directly or indirectly on arguments that derive from Plato.

At first sight it seems extraordinary that this should be so. There is, after all, no Art of Poetry by Plato, no central treatise containing a total theory: the Platonic critic is a man without a text.[49] Yet in spite of this and in spite of the relatively late reavailability of the Platonic corpus, Plato's views on art contrived nevertheless to form a major stimulus to critical thinking about literature in the Renaissance, as Bernard Weinberg makes clear:

all Renaissance theorists felt themselves obliged to deal with Plato's banishment of the poets, either by way of accepting it or – much more frequently – by way of rejecting it on grounds of other criteria. The defence of poetry in the Cinquecento is largely a reply to Plato.   (I, 250)

When ideas are as commonplace and widely-diffused as were Plato's remarks on poetry it is not always easy to establish direct textual links between the ultimate source of the ideas and the writings of those who subscribe to them. One might have equal difficulty tracking down one man's sense of good and evil to Genesis 3.6. A number of Golden-Age critiques contain allusions to Plato but it is difficult to see exactly what their sources were. Both Vives and Fr. Marco Antonio de Camos refer specifically to the institution of censorship in the Republic and the expulsion therefrom of Homer and Hesiod;[50] Alonso de Ulloa also alludes to the expulsion;[51] Diego Gracián twice mentions Plato as a source of opinion on poetry;[52] several authors evidently knew – or knew of – the passages from the *Ion* and the *Phaedrus* on poetic frenzy,[53] while Amyot's prologue to the *Aethiopica* attributes to 'un gran filósofo' Plato's injunction to nurses to be careful about the tales they tell the children in their charge.[54] By way of contrast, Diogo Fernandes, in an apologetic dedication of the third part of the Palmerín cycle, refers to

Plato, along with Homer, Pythagoras and Xenophon, as a writer of fictions that conceal precepts and examples of good custom.[55]

None of these references, allusions and veiled quotations proves that the authors mentioned had read a word of Plato, and it would be surprising if they had. It was not until the dissemination of Platonic ideas by the Florentine Academy and the publication of Ficino's complete Latin translation (1463–82) that Plato became at all familiar at first hand to scholars in Europe, and Spanish interest in Plato was both late in developing, and much less influential than the enthusiasm shown for him by the French academies.[56] Only two dialogues, the *Symposium* and the *Timaeus*, were available in Spanish-printed editions in the sixteenth century:[57] access to the complete Platonic corpus had to be via one of the editions, mostly French or Italian, printed abroad. It should also be borne in mind that a scholar in the Golden Age who went to the trouble of consulting the corpus at first hand was more likely to have done so in search of Plato's views on more strictly philosophical issues than his opinions on literature. Herrera's *Anotaciones* (1580) are strangely, perhaps wisely, silent on the expulsion of the poets although he quotes from Book x of the *Republic* and familiarity with Plato's thinking on other matters is evident throughout.[58]

On balance, then, it would be wise to assume – at least for the first half of the sixteenth century in Spain – that a knowledge of Plato circulated, as it had done in the fifteenth century, in the form of digests and collections of *obiter dicta*,[59] and that such knowledge would vary in consequence from the sketchy to the downright misleading. Even then, late mediaeval anthologies are silent on Plato's literary views, although one collection which achieved a wide circulation in both manuscripts and printed form, the *Bocados de oro*, recounts by way of anecdote Plato's early prowess as a poet and subsequent repudiation of the art at the instigation of Socrates.[60] But anecdote has a way of ensuring the survival of ideas which otherwise might have suffered the same eclipse as the texts that contained them; the Middle Ages did not know the text of the *Phaedrus*, yet the divine fury of the poets remained common currency.[61] The very idea of expelling Homer from any society, let alone an ideal one, is at once so unthinkable and so intriguing – why not add Mozart and Leonardo and do the thing properly? – as to ensure the survival and the propagation of Plato's point of view. Provided the contention remains alive the supporting arguments can always be reformulated from first principles; and there will always be those who, impressed by the authority of Plato, will seek to refute a thesis which, had it come from a lesser figure, they would have dismissed without a second thought. So that when Scaliger tackles the 'slanderers of Agen' and their anti-literary attitudes he opens the attack with a bow in the direction of Plato: 'Now, although those critics are not worth my trouble, nevertheless because of the weight of Plato's authority I must say a few words.'[62] And inevitably, in the defence of poetry which follows that remark, the views of the 'poetices calumniatores' receive as much exposure as the defence. It should not be forgotten that a significant source of knowledge of Plato's attitudes to art is provided by those many neo-Aristotelian critics who, like Scaliger, incorporated in their defence of literature restatements of the very case they were seeking to refute: in this respect Plato's best Spanish representative is undoubtedly El Pinciano,[63] who, as will emerge, not only presents what is in some ways the most coherent and intelligent account of the Platonic argument, but underlines its particular relevance to a culture which was increasingly consuming its literature by private reading.

In Golden-Age Spain, then, knowledge of Plato as a critic of literature was not likely to have been very great or very detailed. Vives probably did know the texts at first hand, but his position at Louvain and his professional interest in philosophy make him exceptional. Many Spaniards evidently knew Vives's writings on secular literature and drew on them both for their ideas and for their colourful rhetoric.[64] Others either picked up Plato's attitudes through the anecdote about the expulsion of the poets and built their own case around that, or merely allied themselves to traditional ecclesiastical opposition to poetry, which itself had been founded on arguments of a markedly Platonic cast. However, the main purpose of relating Spanish attacks on fiction to their Platonic antecedents is not necessarily to establish the existence of direct historical and textual links – though in certain cases these undoubtedly exist – but to devise a framework within which the attacks can be analysed and properly understood. Spanish Golden-Age attacks on fiction constitute a large and rather amorphous body of material which needs to be sorted, and by assembling the apparently random snipes into clearly-defined Platonic categories, I want to show that they are consistent and coherent in ways which can be overlooked if their common origin in Plato is overlooked. Arguments against the arts and in favour of censorship have always fallen into fairly well-defined categories, many of which are still in use today. The case put forward by the National Viewers' and Listeners' Association against certain aspects of television and cinema entertainment is entirely consistent with Plato's contention that poets set bad examples by celebrating the disruptive and passionate side of mankind and encourage the vicarious experience of shameful emotions. The authority of the *Republic* may not be acknowledged by most modern supporters of censorship, but their arguments are nevertheless congruent with Plato's and with those of Spanish Golden-Age critics, and this congruence is a measure of the universal nature of the concern caused by the power of literary art. Referring the debate about the legitimacy of fiction to its source in Plato also ensures a degree of comparability between prosecution and defence, that is, ensures that both sides conduct the argument in the same language and with the same concepts in mind. By analysing the opposing points of view into the same categories we may better appreciate which aspects of which argument are most tellingly put and which points have been overlooked, misunderstood or deliberately fudged by opponents.

In the following chapter, therefore, I shall be concerned predominantly with a more detailed study of the second of the two premises outlined above: that the reading of fiction was completely unacceptable to a large number of Spanish Golden-Age critics. In placing the apparently parochial criticisms of the novels of chivalry within their Platonic context I shall be trying to show that not only do they add up to an attack on all forms of imaginative fiction, but more, they collectively represent Spain's contribution to the general Renaissance restatement of the traditional assault on poetry as a whole. When they laid into the novels of chivalry with such venomous delight the critics were subscribing to a long-established topos as well as indulging in ritual card-showing in an effort to capture the serious reader's sympathy. The fact that anti-literary attitudes were traditional – and may even have contained an element of the formulaic – is not a reason for overlooking or undervaluing them.

There is, however, a second and more important reason for emphasising the central position of Platonic arguments within the Golden-Age debate about fiction, a reason which concerns the interrelatedness of the two premises which form the basis of this book. In one sense there is a clear quantitative relationship between opposition to fiction and the extent of its availability. Although opposition to fiction was not new, as its Platonic antecedents attest, the degree of its virulence in Spain and elsewhere in the sixteenth century certainly was. But it should not surprise us to find that hostility is intensified at a time when the growth of printing meant that more people were exposed to the effects of literature – and in a potentially more dangerous way – than ever before. The greater the number of books, the greater their supposed harmfulness, and the greater the opposition they provoke. The fact that the Platonic texts which enshrined the case against fiction were beginning to be made available at the same time – and through the medium of print – makes the quantitative relationship between books and critics that much stronger and even provides it with an element of irony.

The relationship between book production and the popularity of fiction on the one hand and hostility to fiction on the other, is not, however, solely a matter of quantity. As I have argued already, printing not only increased the number of books available, but significantly altered the way in which audiences were to consume their literature, making private reading a much more familiar aspect of a recreational interest in fiction. It is my contention that opposition to fiction grew up only incidentally in response to the increased quantity of books available in the age of printing, but found its primary stimulus in changes which took place in audience response as listeners were gradually outnumbered by readers. The fundamentally Platonic cast of the arguments offered by opponents of fiction has, therefore, an important part to play in this contention, for one of the aspects of literary art which most concerned Plato was the ability of fictions to convince in spite of their untruthfulness, and, as I shall go on to argue in chapter 3, it is through reading that the ability of a fiction to convince is found at its most effective. Our two premises are related rather more closely than at first may appear: more books mean more readers, that is, more people exposed in the most compelling way possible to the blandishments of fiction; and in such circumstances those concerned about the effects of convincing lies on the minds of readers will wish to espouse arguments, and in particular Platonic arguments, which pay most attention to the harmfulness of those effects.

When Plato banned the poets from his ideal state his two main criteria were moral and metaphysical. The Aristotelian defence of poetry tackled these two points by stressing the universality of literature – what Spingarn[65] has called 'the reality of eternal probability' – and the need for verisimilitude, for writers to maintain a convincing appearance of reality and to avoid the incredible. They also argued that because poetry was an ideal representation of life it must be moral even when it has no specifically moral aim, because it represents reality in its moral aspects. But Plato went further, and tried to give an explanation of how art makes its effect. This was essential because, underlying the assumption that art is morally harmful and metaphysically illegitimate, there lies the further assumption that art is those things because it exerts a special kind of influence over its public, and that its harmfulness comes about primarily not because its content might be morally or metaphysically objectionable, but because of its power, its ability to move, to persuade, to convince. To claim, as Spingarn does,[66] that Plato's attack on art is based entirely on unaesthetic criteria is to join the neo-Aristotelians in missing the important point: art is dangerous not for what it says or what it represents, but for the fact that it does represent, and does so convincingly. Plato knew and responded to the pull of great art as well as anyone and that personal experience is what gives the strong aesthetic basis to his moral and metaphysical case;[67] the better the work of art, the more dangerous it is. Until poets could answer this objection, they would remain beyond the pale. Spanish and European neo-Aristotelians may have missed the point, but there is a substantial body of writers – including the authors of the picaresque novels we shall be dealing with in later chapters – who do appear to tackle Plato's arguments in Platonic terms by giving an important place in the novel to the psychological problems raised by the reading of fiction. When the full weight of Plato's case against poetry has been understood, we may see how the writers of these novels might be said to have tried in their work consciously or unconsciously to make a proper response to his contention – repeated time and again by Spanish Golden-Age critics of fiction – that there is something about the very nature of art which makes it inevitably harmful.

2

The case against fiction

In this chapter, the case against fiction will be considered under two main aspects, one moral and one metaphysical. They are not mutually exclusive and often overlap, but they are best kept separate in the interests of clarity. Each aspect consists of two arguments. The moral aspect concerns the way literature a) sets bad examples and b) encourages vicarious experience. The metaphysical aspect involves the objection that c) fiction is a counterfeit form of reality and d) the existence of convincing fictions undermines the authority of truth. This chapter offers an account of each of these arguments and illustrates how each is congruent with and in many cases originates in Plato's justification of his banishment of the poets from the Republic. At each stage of this account brief mention is made of the counter-arguments which in Spain, as elsewhere, were for the most part Aristotelian in form. Since the predominantly Aristotelian cast of Spanish Golden-Age literary theory is already adequately documented no attempt has been made to give a full account of these arguments here. It is, in any case, axiomatic in what follows that in certain important respects the Aristotelian defence of poetry is not at all an adequate reply to Plato, and leaves his most fundamental objections untouched.

The moral aspect

The first, that is, the most common and least subtle argument made against fiction concerns the immoral examples which it frequently offers to its readers, particularly to its young readers. Indeed, the moral case against poetry begins, in the *Republic*, with Plato's censorship of literature for school use. The telling of fictitious tales which nevertheless contain some truth is recognised as an important teaching aid in the education of Athenian youth. But the practice has

24

inherent dangers, implicit in the word Plato uses (*pseudos* – 'fiction', 'falsehood' and even 'lie'), and cannot be allowed to go unchecked; otherwise, children will be exposed to any story anyone may happen to make up and so be subjected to ideas which are the very opposite of those they ought to have as adults. A watch must be set over the makers of stories, and nurses and mothers persuaded to tell only approved and selected tales (II, 377). This will mean discarding most of the stories now in use, including the staple diet of Homer and Hesiod, since they misrepresent the nature of the gods. Plato takes as an example the myth of Uranus, Cronos and Zeus, which even if it were true should not be 'lightly told to thoughtless young people' but revealed only in a mystery:

we shall not tell a child that, if he commits the foulest crimes or goes to any length in punishing his father's misdeeds, he will be doing nothing out of the way, but only what the first and greatest of the gods have done before him.

(II, 378)

If the citizens are to be prevented from quarrelling then they must not be subjected to examples of warfare and intrigue among the gods, even if the stories are taken to be allegorical. A child cannot distinguish the allegorical sense from the literal, and the ideas he takes in at that age are likely to become indelibly fixed; hence the importance of seeing that the first stories he hears are designed to produce the best possible effect on his character (II, 378).

The complaint that literature sets bad examples when it might be better employed in setting good ones was common enough among Spanish critics of the Golden Age. Vives, in the passage quoted earlier from *De Institutione Christianae Feminae*,[1] laments that fathers and husbands should allow their womenfolk to become accustomed to evil in their reading or to 'wax more ungratiously subtle' by the example of books which are no better than manuals of seduction based on other people's love affairs. Alonso de Fuentes asks what value there can be in books which – quite apart from all the lies they peddle – tell us that so-and-so ran off with someone else's wife or fell in love with someone else's daughter, how he wooed her and what he wrote to her and 'other advice for those who chance to be unwary'. There is a ban on the import of infected bed linen from Brittany because it may spread contagious diseases, but no steps are taken against books which in themselves set such bad examples and from which so much evil ensues.[2] Benito Remigio Noydens recalls reading of a man who, on falling in love with a woman and finding himself unable to break down her resistance, gave her a chivalresque novel to read and thereby so filled her head with thoughts of love that the seduction was achieved that he had previously been unable to effect.[3] Pedro Mexía, too, comments sadly that such books are not just a waste of time but that they set very bad examples and endanger public morality.[4]

Three main objections to this argument occurred to Renaissance defenders of poetry. In the first place, it requires only minimal perspicacity to see that the case against poetry on the grounds that it sets bad examples is not a case against poetry at all, merely against the uses to which it is put. For if it is able to set bad examples it is equally capable of setting good ones; Plato himself states as much (*Republic*, II, 378) and Pico della Mirandola was forced to concede the same point when he argued in support of Plato that poetry is not useful for life, nor does it lead to happiness, 'for men derive from the poets occasions for evil not less significant for vice than for virtue'.[5] This was a point which Renaissance critics in general brought to the defence of poetry, and it is not difficult to see why. For the one thing they could not accept about Plato's banishment of the poets was that, with the exception made in the case of ceremonial poetry in praise of the gods and of good men (x, 606), the ban was total and unconditional.[6] It is true that, if certain passages of the *Republic* are taken out of context, there do appear to be qualifications in respect of those who would 'make their poetry the express image of noble character' (III, 401), or those who can show good reason why dramatic poetry is 'no mere source of pleasure but a benefit to society and to human life' (x, 607). Plato does promise to listen favourably but gives every indication that his open-mindedness is merely formulaic: he is prepared to hear what they have to say but he does not expect to be convinced by it (x, 606). Sixteenth-century apologists for poetry who took him to mean that only bad poets were excluded seriously misread the drift of his argument. Basing themselves on dictum without reference to text, they concluded with an ill-founded sense of relief that Plato was not banishing poetry at all, merely poets who abuse it: 'Platón no reprehende en el dicho lugar [sc. Book III of the *Republic*] a la arte, sino a los artífices que della usaron mal'.[7] Such a misunderstanding goes some way to explaining why Renaissance Aristotelians held so firmly to the notion that the good poet had to be a good man and concentrated on the moral status of the writer as much as the moral effect of his writing. In this they based themselves not only on Plato's praise of the philosopher, and Cicero's and Quintilian's praise of the orator, but on the

celebrated passage from Strabo's *Geography* on the moral excellence of
the true poet: 'the excellence of a poet is inseparably associated with
the excellence of the man himself, and it is impossible for one to
become a good poet unless he has previously become a good man'.[8]
Scores of Renaissance critics saw in this passage the basis of an appeal
against Plato's ban on grounds of the good character of the good poet.
In Spain, López Pinciano emphasises the discipline of writing and
cites the example of Horace, for whom poetry demands hard work,
long hours, abstinence and dedication. His conclusion is as illogical
as it is well meant: the work that issues from such abstinence must
be good since excellence in poetry can only spring from moral
excellence.[9]

The implications that follow from Plato's censorship of teaching
texts lead some way from the nature of poetry itself although they have
everything to do with the way poetry is used in society. But there are
two other problems arising from the censorship of bad examples which
also did not escape the notice of Renaissance critics who sought to
defend poetry. If it is conceded that poetry is potentially useful, as it
must be if we are to attribute harm to it, then why is it necessary to
exclude it altogether? Why not just submit it to the control of
censorship? By banning it completely its potential for good is lost. The
defenders of poetry were greatly exercised by Plato's uncompromising
stand on this issue and often had recourse to a solution first proposed
in the second century AD by the eclectic precursor of neo-Platonism
Maximus of Tyre. In the twenty-third of his *Dissertations*, 'Whether
Plato acted properly in expelling Homer from his Republic',[10]
Maximus stresses that the Republic was above all a theoretical
construction, not based on any particular model. It is intended to be a
perfect specimen of its kind and bears little relationship to the ways of
men (23, iii), the clear implication being that anything Plato says
about it can therefore safely be ignored.

López Pinciano puts the same line of argument in the mouth of
Fadrique. The Republic is an ideal and not a real place, and where
men are good there is no need for poets to have recourse to fictions in
order to persuade them to follow virtue. This puts Plato alongside St
Paul and St Augustine who find all fables reprehensible, arguing that
mankind should not need the condiments of fiction to find virtue
palatable.[11] The identical argument is found in the *Institutioni* (1541)
of Mario Equicola,[12] although the contradiction which this argument
attempts to resolve is not really present in Plato's own. At first sight

there does appear to be a clash of priorities in the *Republic*, since a complete ban certainly involves sacrificing a potential good in the cause of eradicating a potential evil. But, taken as a whole, as we shall see, Plato's argument is of a much higher order than a mere squabble over whether or not the matter of poetry can be ethically advantageous; he prefers to enquire instead into the nature of the effects produced by poetry irrespective of whether the examples it sets are felt to be good or bad, and concludes that even when the effects are supposedly good, the way they are produced makes the position of poetry morally and philosophically untenable.

Even so, Plato must have been alive to the possibility that in placing a total ban on poetry he was repudiating the use of an effective exhortation to virtue on grounds of ontological squeamishness. There is, after all, much that the arts can achieve by their example:

We would not have our Guardians grow up among representations of moral deformity, as in some foul pasture where, day after day, feeding on every poisonous weed they would, little by little, gather insensibly a mass of corruption in their very souls. Rather we must seek out those craftsmen whose instinct guides them to whatsoever is lovely and gracious; so that our young men, dwelling in a wholesome climate, may drink in good from every quarter, whence, like a breeze bearing health from happy regions, some influence from noble works constantly falls upon eye and ear from childhood upward, and imperceptibly draws them into sympathy and harmony with the beauty of reason, whose impress they take.[13]

We can imagine other legislators and statesmen, plagued by the search for an effective yet acceptable way of enforcing order and imposing virtue, who would doubtless have been tempted to retain poetry for that reason; not even Christianity, for all its emphasis on free will in salvation, loses the chance to persuade and guide men toward that end. But it remains true that the more effective a weapon the greater the risk of its misuse, and by refusing to be trapped into arguing on the one hand that poetry is *per se* evil while conceding on the other that if we are to have poetry it may as well be put to the best possible use in the Republic, Plato shows how firmly set were his priorities and how insignificant he considered his losses as pragmatist and statesman compared with his gains as seeker after wisdom and truth.

Plato's philosophical scruple clearly made him proof against the charge of sacrificing the good with the bad, but he might have been more exercised by a remaining objection, encapsulated in Mario Equicola's observation that the bad moral examples which poetry sometimes provides are no worse than those found constantly in life, in history or in the laws.[14] It was, indeed, often claimed that they are so. Vives, as we have seen, held that it was worse for a girl to read about and therefore think about jousts and tourneys than actually to take up arms herself. Gaspar de Astete also claims that in many ways books are a worse encouragement to sin than the temptations of the world, which at least carry with them fear of parental chastisement or social ostracism: no such checks exist on the untrammelled fantasies promoted by fiction and exposure to 'fábulas y patrañas'.[15] We may fairly ask how it can be that evil represented in literature is any worse than real evil in the real world which has never of itself been considered an insurmountable obstacle to virtue? Evil in literature may be no encouragement to a good life and it may even be true that, as Plato says, when artists imitate what is bad they add to the sum total of evil in the world. Yet can there be any real difference in terms of moral consequences between reading or hearing of a real crime and reading of an imaginary one? The existence of evil men in books does not prevent any particular man from being good any more than does the existence of evil men in real life. One wonders why so many sixteenth-century Christian opponents of literature either implicitly or explicitly supported this argument even though they could so easily have been driven into the position of being required to ban evil from life as well as from books, a position which would have involved them in severe doctrinal, not to say practical, difficulties. Their defence, however, would have rested on Plato's point that the evil of literature lies less in the work itself than in its effect on the audience. The bad examples set by literature consist not in reading *about* evil but in actually experiencing evil in the act of reading.

When Plato comes to explain how bad examples make their effect, an important shift of emphasis is made in the moral case against literature. In a passage of the *Republic* (III, 387) Plato defends the excision from Homer of passages describing the horrors of Hades, on the grounds that fear inspired by those passages might cause warriors to prefer captivity to death in battle. The bad examples of literature derive their power from the disturbing impression made by great poetry on the mind. The passages which Plato finds most offensive are rejected not because they are not poetic nor because they are not enjoyed by most people, but because the more poetic they are, the greater the reason for keeping them from those who should fear slavery more than death. The greater the effect of the poetry the more harmful is its example. Plato would by the same token strike out all terrifying epithets 'the very sound of which is enough to make one shiver', the fever consequent upon such shivering being likely to melt the fine-tempered spirit of the Guardians of the state. Similar treatment would be accorded to descriptions of heroes bewailing the dead, such exhibitions of emotion being reserved for women of low character and cowardly men 'so that the Guardians we are training for our country may disdain to imitate them'. This picture of Greek warriors as gentle giants with the finely-tuned sensibilities of the samurai, fearing the lash of an Homeric epithet more than the enemy battle-cry, may not accord with the modern image of the professional soldier, but anyone who has read Wilfred Owen, say, will see what Plato is getting at. Some kinds of horror stay in the mind longer than plain ordinary fear.

The origin of this extraordinary evocative quality of Homeric poetry lies in the concept of *mimesis* which is so basic to Plato's attack on poetry in the *Republic* that Paul Vicaire has been moved to describe it as 'une sorte de vice originel de l'art dramatique'.[16] The term *mimesis* is used in the *Republic* in a bewildering variety of ways, but in the discussion of the moral and psychological effects of poetry it has the same sense as that sketched out by Socrates and Hermogenes (*Cratylus* 423ab) in their discussion of the origins of language, that is, 'active representation' ('active' because it is the representation and not the object represented that is the direct object of the verb *mimesthai*). Used in this sense *mimesis* covers both the recitation or acting of the work by the rhapsode or actor and the purely formal aspects of first-person narrative in epic verse. The first kind of representation belongs properly to the drama, in which passions are represented or embodied so vividly that we might think that the characters actually exist and actually experience the feelings they appear to. The same thing happens to a lesser degree in epic verse declaimed by the reciter. Here again the rhapsode becomes a kind of actor assuming a character created by the poet. He is enabled to do so by the poet's formal device of changing from third-person narrative to first-person. It is in this dramatic representation or 'imitation' that one of the main dangers of literature lies, for the poet stops speaking in his own voice, the voice which the audience recognises as that of the omniscient intermediary, and gives priority instead to the voice of the character. His, the poet's, protective mask of conscious artistry and controlling authority is drawn aside to reveal the impassioned features of what by contrast appears to be real life. Golden-Age prose writers were to reap rich rewards from the interplay between partial and omniscient points of view.

This exposure of the first person and promotion of a too-vividly recreated and too-convincing emotion involves dangers for performers – whether actors or reciters – and audience alike. For the spectator the danger lies in the fact that identification has its basis in an empathy which is primarily emotional. Bereft of the guidance and critical (or at any rate distancing) focus of the poet's narrative, the audience is left to bear the full force of a direct appeal to its sense of fellow-feeling. But the emotions, like the senses, are subject to illusion, and whereas illusions of the senses can be corrected by the application of the higher powers of reason, by measuring, counting, weighing and so forth, the poet or dramatist is interested in arousing the emotions rather than checking them, strengthening and stimulating the inferior part of the soul in order to undermine the reason. The essence of human life is that it is never lived with an entirely undivided mind (x, 602). Man is always subject to internal conflict which sets him at odds with himself and Plato recognises that this fretful temper gives much more scope for diversity in dramatic representation than does the calm, wise and constant character, whose steadfastness is not so attractive nor so easy to represent (x, 603). 'Artists are interested in what is base and complex, not in what is simple and good.'[17] The nature of the poet's skills and his search for richness and variety of material naturally attract him to human types in whom the highest part of the soul, the reason, has given way before the chaos of emotional upheaval. When the audience enters into the joy and sorrow of such a character its reason is also held in abeyance, with equally harmful results.

When we listen to some hero in Homer or on the tragic stage moaning over his sorrows in a long tirade, or to a chorus beating their breasts as they chant a lament, you know how the best of us enjoy giving ourselves up to follow the performance with eager sympathy. The more a poet can move our feelings in this way, the better we think him. And yet when the sorrow is our own, we pride ourselves on being able to bear it quietly like a man . . . to enter into another's feelings must have an effect on our own: the emotions of pity our sympathy has strengthened will not be easy to restrain when we are suffering ourselves.   (x, 605)

The crux of Plato's case against the immorality of art is therefore that the sympathetic indulgence through art in emotions which we would be ashamed to admit to in real life has an adverse effect on the character by undermining resistance to adversity and temptation.

And it is a case seconded by a large number of critics of literature in sixteenth-century Spain, in spite of the long-lived Aristotelian justification of the arousal of the emotions in tragedy. The neo-Aristotelian defenders of literature looked for the morality of poetry not in its teaching role, but in the fact that it offers food for thought and removes the experience of the reader from the restrictions of fact and personal circumstances. Through poetry we have examples of every kind before us,[18] and some would claim that far from being obliged to represent only worthy instances, the obligation was rather that the poet should put before the reader the whole gamut of human behaviour and experience without altering or interfering: 'for evil must be made evil, just as it is, and must not be made good, which it is not'.[19] The justification of this approach to the subject matter of literature lies in an almost homoeopathic view of the purging of the emotions through poetry. By means of fears and injustices represented in tragedy, fear and injustice are driven from the heart of the spectator.[20] Instead of starving the emotions, the object was to excite them and to allay and regulate them by means of the ennobling and purifying effects of catharsis.

The question of whether passions are best repressed or best expressed is debated in the *Philosophía antigua poética* by Fadrique and Hugo.[21] Commenting on El Pinciano's account of what happened to his friend Valerio when he read a copy of *Amadís de Gaula*, Fadrique notes that anyone may melt under the heat of compassion and that Plato was quite right to have nothing to do with an art which causes such harm and brings so little benefit. But Hugo objects that the turmoil produced by poetry is the means to a greater good and more peaceful ends. Fadrique is left wondering why, if poetry is so good and so useful, Plato banishes it as 'perturbadora y mentirosa': he was right, and yet he was wrong. The paradox is only resolved when El Pinciano argues that it is possible for a short-term upheaval to be justified in the interests of long-term peace: a king may take up arms against a rebellious faction with the stability of the whole kingdom in mind although this might involve a temporary increase in unrest. So too with poetry: the very tale that produces a brief though violent emotional trauma produces thereby an enduring quiescence of spirit.

But El Pinciano's analogy would not have convinced all of his contemporaries, and even today the attempt to draw a parallel between what is expedient in politics and what is morally justifiable in literature seems more than a little strained; and, crucially, it fails to give any indication of how poetry does what El Pinciano and Aristotle before him claimed it does. Impressive though the endorsement of Aristotle undoubtedly was, the Platonic case had throughout the Middle Ages been championed by figures of at least equal authority whose views on the effects of literature on the emotions and thence on the moral fibre were much more of a piece with the anxieties of sixteenth-century Spanish critics of fiction. Isidore of Seville had forbidden the reading of the figments of the poets because they excite the mind and inflame the desires with their idle tales. Tertullian claimed that literature, particularly dramatic literature, enervates men, destroys the calm of the soul and leads to spiritual agitation: clearly he had in mind the view – endorsed by Aquinas – that in the face of real beauty desire is quietened, not awakened.[22] In the fifteenth century even a humanist like Francesco Patrizi, although more kindly disposed towards literature for its teaching of a proper way of life and knowledge of customs and its provision of examples of elegant and beautiful language, consents to the banning of tragedy, 'for it has within it a certain excessive violence mixed with despair which changes stupid men into madmen and drives the unstable to frenzy'.[23] Comedy too 'corrupts the mores of men and makes them effeminate and drives them towards lust and dissipation . . . for the plots of comedy for the most part concern adultery and rapes, and the habit of seeing them affords to the spectator the licence for changing for the worse'.[24] We recognise in the singling out of the dramatic forms Plato's own concern with the effects of *mimesis*, of imitating in an intense way disturbed minds, as well as a foretaste of the modern argument that exposure to violence on television and in the cinema has a brutalising effect on the audience and desensitises the viewer, increasing his tolerance of violence in real life. It is an argument which Pico della Mirandola might well have supported if we are to judge from what he says about the effects on him of his own reading of the poets. He says that he felt his soul to be softened by them, and goes on to support Isidore, who banned Christians from reading them because they excite the mind to the provocations of lust.[25]

Pico's remarks encapsulate both the positive and the negative aspects of the moral argument against poetry, positive because of the provocation and incitement to base desires, and negative because of the solvent effect of poetry on the best of intentions and the firmest of resolutions. In Spain this two-pronged attack was supported by critics like Antonio de Guevara who calls for the prohibition of novels of chivalry and such like 'porque su doctrina incita la sensualidad a pecar, y relaja el espíritu a bien vivir'.[26] Here we recognise on the one hand Vives's complaint that books 'kindle and stir up covetousness, inflame anger and all beastly and filthy desire' and, on the other, Pico's description of the softening effect of poetry on the soul. Because books break down a hard-won disinclination to sin, we find the ideas of melting, dissolving, decaying (*desvanecerse, corromperse, disoluciones,* etc.) occurring again and again, but two other metaphors, both originating in the comments of Vives, were equally popular among moralists who wished to convey the destructive effects of imaginative literature on the moral fibre of its readership. Where Vives had likened books of fiction to kindling, Alejo Venegas sees them as a taper which touches off the volatile sensuality of young women left unsupervised to indulge their craving for Amadises and Esplandians.[27] The undercurrent of prurient wishful-thinking which characterises this and other writings of the anti-literature lobby explodes into a positive slavering in Fr. Francisco Ortiz Lucio: the tinder which young people manufacture from the reading of 'portentous lies' is fanned by the bellows of iniquity 'with which they stoke the fires of their desire and appetite for wickedness, becoming more and more inflamed so that they experience in deeds what they read in words'.[28]

Other critics fastened on to a second metaphor in their attempts to give expression to the full extent of their abhorrence: Vives's comparison of works of fiction to deadly poison. Fr. Juan de la Cerda, Luisa María de Padilla Manrique, Benito Remigio Noydens, Juan Sánchez Valdés de la Plata, Alejo Venegas all make use of the poison topos in their critiques, speaking of books variously as sweet venom driving young girls to evil thoughts,[29] moral suicide gradually and almost imperceptibly administered, a diversion mingled with deadly poison,[30] pleasant tales with poisonous plots,[31] and a savoury and secret bane with which the devil ensnares the tender souls of young girls.[32] Perhaps Malón de Chaide makes the most effective use of the topos in painting this picture of the gradual, imperceptible and irreversible progress of the poison through the body of the victim:

But the authors of the first group [books of love stories] reply that they are love affairs which are dealt with decently and with great propriety; as if that made them stir the promptings of the will any less powerfully, or made them any less prone slowly to spread their deadly poison through the veins of the heart, until it takes hold of the quickest and purest part of the soul, where with furious ardour it dries up and desiccates the greenest and most flourishing part of our activities. You will find, says Plutarch, some tiny animals as small as certain species of mosquitos, hardly visible, yet which for all their insignificance sting so gently that although the bite does not trouble you at the time, soon afterwards you find that the area which was stung has become swollen and painful. So too with these books on such subjects that, without feeling when they inflict their harm, you find yourself stricken and damned.[33]

This is good, strong stuff and typical of the polemics of a contentious age. But what is interesting about these variations on the theme of poison is not so much the ability of one man, in this case Vives, with a few images to mould and shape if not actually dictate the critical vocabulary of a whole generation, but rather the paradox that the constant recourse to a central image, albeit ever more vigorously expressed, betrays a manic inarticulacy on the part of writers who are unable to express their loathing for the pernicious books or account for the damage they do.

It is with relief, then, that we find someone like Francisco Cervantes de Salazar who is prepared, in his additions to his translation of Vives's *Introducción y camino para la sabiduría*, to subordinate his use of the topos to an attempt at analysing the various stages by which vicarious experience brings about a lowered resistance to the call of the flesh. Careless parents, he writes, lock their daughters away from men but allow them to have access to books from which they learn evils that even the company of men would not have taught them. From knowledge comes desire once the taste for iniquity has been acquired. Girls spend their time longing to be a second Oriana courted by a second Amadís and in seeking ways of effecting these desires.[34] It is clear from this account – one which is seconded by the ever-indignant and ever-voluble Malón de Chaide – that the real villains are the twin promptings of sympathy for and identification with the characters, even though sympathy, at least, is a natural and in many respects worthy motive. Jacques Amyot finds it perfectly natural that the human heart should be stirred by reading of or witnessing the deeds and fortunes of others,[35] and the fact that this defender of fiction does not distinguish between the witness of fictional events via the written word and that of real events by actual attendance, or subsequent participation via the reports of others, suggests that the fatal urge to be moved by the sufferings and triumphs of our neighbour is part of human nature and nothing to do with books. Fr. Luis de Granada also puts the delight of fiction down to a perfectly normal, non-literary instinct, that of *admiración*, an instinct so basic and so enjoyable (when we see, for example, the death-defying feats of warriors in tournaments) that people seek to indulge it not just with real events, but with fictional examples.[36] But at this point in the argument the theologian regains control. Since the lives of the martyrs provide everything one could wish for in terms of wonderment, and (what is more) they are true, why bother marvelling at falsehood?[37] And Gaspar de Astete gives a more plaintive note to the same argument: a girl will read a book all day and all night and shed tears of sympathy for the death of a knight or the rejection of a lover, but her eye will remain dry and her heart unmoved by the thought of her own sinfulness, or by compassion for the sufferings of the Saviour.[38]

It is clear from the discussion thus far that Plato's moral case against literature was supported explicitly and implicitly by a very large number of critics in sixteenth-century Spain. Whether in whole treatises or in side-swipes, whether calmly reasoned or hysterically voluble, whether from first-hand experience or from blinkered bigotry, they all seem to have taken Plato's point that literature sets bad examples by causing its audience to experience feelings of a range and intensity which they might never have experienced otherwise in their own lives; that it does so by promoting sympathetic emotional identification between the audience and characters and so encourages vicarious indulgence of feelings which would normally be subject to rational control; and that the undermining of the reason excites and disturbs the soul and leads to the stimulation of base desires and the breakdown of the character. Any writer of fiction wishing to make a case for his wares will clearly have to come to terms with these criticisms. But as many of our examples show, the critics also held to the view that the stimuli of literature were more dangerous even than those of real life and that one of the dangers of fiction lay in its greater attractiveness even when truth seemed on the face of it to be the stranger and the more compelling. If the products of the imagination carried more conviction, and readers responded more readily to fiction than to fact, then serious doubts might be cast on the status of truth, and falsehood might take on a complex mode of existence as an alternative reality. That Golden-Age Spain felt the need to enquire into these issues shows that the metaphysical aspects of fiction were given just as much attention as the moral ones. And, once again, it is to the authority of Plato that the arguments of the critics invariably remit.

The metaphysical aspect

To the charge that the charms of poetry endanger the established order of the soul, Plato added a second count that poetry has no serious claim to be valued as an apprehension of truth.[39] Put simply, the fact is that a poet cannot hope to educate men in virtue or wisdom because wisdom depends on knowledge of the real world of Forms and that world is disclosed by dialectic not by poetry. Like any artist (*mimetes*), the poet is always at at least two removes from reality, and condemned by the very nature of his art to remain there. The basis of this permanent disqualification from contact with truth is to be found in a second meaning given to the term *mimesis* in Book x of the *Republic*. Apart from active or dramatic representation, *mimesis* also has a wider sense which is closer to the English 'imitation'. It is a very fine line that separates dramatic representation from slavish copying: the actor 'represents' Orestes whom he has never seen but he does so by imitating the behaviour of men whom he has observed. Once that line is crossed, and Plato is very prompt to abolish it altogether, art is reduced to a form of realism characterised above all by fidelity to a model. Drama is nothing but mimicry and fine art is no more than the copying of external appearances, a mirror held up to nature (595de). The artist's job is to reproduce his original as faithful y as possible and his ability to imitate so many different things is due merely to the fact that he addresses himself to only one part of each thing, its appearance, and leaves its real nature untouched. Quality in art, then, is a simple matter of measurement, in each particular case, of the distance between the image and the original it represents. Two important consequences of this view – that an art object is a likeness (*eikon*) of an original – form the basis of Plato's initial attack on the metaphysical legitimacy of art.

The first consequence is that because an art object is a copy of an original or model, the artist is in a sense out to dupe his audience, to pass off the copy as the real thing – the very criteria for excellence in art outlined above ensure that he must do so. The danger is therefore proportional to the artistry. The man who most successfully creates an illusion of reality is the one who is most likely to lead the uninitiated astray: 'poetry of that sort seems to be injurious to minds which do not possess the antidote in a knowledge of its real nature' (x, 595). Those who cannot see the unreality of art are most at risk, and the greater the skill of the illusionist the greater the risk that his audience will lose its bearings. Conversely, the more a work of art draws attention to its artificiality, the less harmful it is likely to be, a motto that might almost have been adopted as their own by the prose writers of the Golden Age.

The second consequence lies in the fact that in the hierarchy of creation the model is always truer, more 'real', than the copy, and because the art object is defined not in its own terms but in terms of its relationship with something else – the 'original', or 'model' – art is flawed by its very nature and rendered incapable of giving anything other than an impoverished image of reality. Inasmuch as the art object is a copy of anything it is necessarily an unfaithful one. Plato illustrates this argument for consigning art to the lowest rung of reality with the celebrated example of the painter and the bed. When the carpenter proceeds to make a bed he has before his mind the Form of the bed (x, 596) and what he manufactures is not the reality but only something that resembles it. When the painter then proceeds to produce a painting of the bed, he creates something even more unreal because he is reproducing only its appearance. The artist is thus 'third in succession from the throne of truth' (x, 597). The painter who paints the bed does not understand it, does not measure it, and could not make it; but his real fault is that, in Iris Murdoch's words, he 'evades the conflict between the apparent and the real which stirs the mind toward philosophy. Art naively or wilfully accepts appearances instead of questioning them.'[40]

It is Plato's poor opinion of the philosophical status of art that helps to explain his rigorous attitude to the expulsion of all but the ceremonial poets from the Republic, in spite of their potential moral usefulness and exemplarity. Even when art sets its face against the bad examples, even when it eschews images of wickedness that induce the soul to relax its guard against the surge of base emotions, even when its simplicity and harmony of design encourages harmony in our minds, art is still bad for us simply because it is mimetic, because it purports to be other than it is. It is a representation of something else and therefore not itself real.

Golden-Age critics of literature do not appear to have been at all perturbed by the fact that, on the face of it, Plato's position on art leads on the one hand to the contradiction that art is bad for us even when it is good for us, and on the other to the tautology that the trouble with fiction is that it is false. Indeed, the complaint that we meet more often than any other in the work of Spanish sixteenth-century critics is that works of fiction are all lies. On the whole, they refused – as Solon did[41] – to distinguish between lying as deception and lying as something other than historical truth, and asserted quite simply that fiction is a lie and that a lie is *per se* evil. The critical vocabulary of the period is laden with words associated with falsehood (*mentiras, ficciones, fábulas, apócrifos*, and their cognates) or with vanity and worthlessness (*vanis ac fictitiis rebus*,[42] *vanae nugae ab hominibus fictae*,[43] *vanas e fingidas*,[44] *disparates*[45]). Jacques Amyot describes some works of fiction as the ravings of a man sick with fever,[46] and others rant against the palpable lack of a basis of truth in these books. Camos can find in them no point of contact with anything that actually happened[47] and Francisco de Vallés sees them as suspended in mid air, completely without foundation.[48] Accusations of falsehood inevitably have their moral as well as philosophical side, and Spanish critics were also disturbed by the danger that, even for those who can distinguish the true from the false, exposure to lies can be habit-forming. For Juan Sánchez Valdés de la Plata the young derive nothing from their reading of books of vanities other than allowing lies to become a habit of mind,[49] an opinion which even Jacques Amyot is inclined to support if we are to judge from his advice to people of mature age and understanding to be wary of fabulous books 'de miedo que sus entendimientos no se acostumbren poco a poco a amar mentiras y vanidades'.[50]

That works of fiction are by their very nature mendacious clearly disconcerted an age which was still used to the authority and trustworthiness of the writer, and which could not see how anything that was not true could be said to exist at all. Moreover, it was the shamelessness as much as the mendacity that offended. Valdés, particularly, could not understand why authors told such barefaced lies, so obviously false that they could not possibly be taken for true,[51] thereby supporting the neo-Aristotelian preference for the life-like lie that preserved a semblance of truth. This sense of discomposure, of anxiety in the face of packs of lies that lacked even the decency to masquerade as true, was clearly as prevalent among critics of fiction as were misgivings about the morality of failing to tell the truth. What worried the unsympathetic reader of these books was not so much that they were palpably untrue but that they abandoned the pretence of truth and asked to be accepted on their own terms. A work of fiction which claimed to be true yet which obviously was not had at least the virtue of acknowledging the authority and primacy of truth; a work which no longer seeks the protection of truth is in effect making a bid for freedom, and its attempt to stand on its own feet inevitably undermines the authority of truth by claiming that we can do very well without it. And at the same time such a work deflates the moralist's case against the telling of stories. If the story is told for true its author can reasonably be brought to task if he is found out. But if he makes no claim to truth he may well argue with Cicero or Plutarch that he does no harm in leaving matters of truth or falsehood to those who understand them best, the writers of history.[52] Like his work, the writer of fictions becomes a slippery creature, difficult to pin down, inhabiting a no-man's-land of his own making in the gaps between tried and tested categories and values.

The charge of shameless mendacity against fiction is not, though, without its defence, and may even prompt the counter-charge of naivety. If a fiction cannot be said to exist at all it is difficult to see how it can be capable of offending against morality. The author knows the story is untrue, we know it is untrue; it is a convention for the sake of argument, just something to write about. The only deception is a playful one practised by the skilled writer on an audience which is momentarily persuaded to suspend disbelief. A man who can find any harm in that merely advertises his want of humour and common sense. This rather evasive attitude of sweet reasonableness between men of the world underlies otherwise attractive defences of the amorality of fiction such as Lionardo Bruni's in the essay *De Studiis et Litteris* (*c.* 1405) addressed to Baptist Malatesta:

When I read the love of Aeneas and Dido in the Aeneid I pay my tribute of admiration to the genius of the poet, but the matter itself I know to be a fiction, and thus it leaves no moral impression: and so in other instances of the kind, where literal truth is not the object aimed at.[53]

But the lack of absolutes in this approach – something is harmless provided it is known to be harmful – is unlikely to appeal to the moralist, and open-mouthed incredulity was never a proper defence against a strict if misplaced pursuit of the peccadillo.

Equally fruitless is the converse of the previous argument: if the trouble with fiction is that it is false, then the value of truth is that it is true. Christian emphasis on the example of the Bible as the archetype of the truthful narrative enabled clerics to press on the reading public the value of their own kinds of literature and place greater emphasis not just on the truthfulness of biblical stories but also on their value as sources of wonder and excitement. Both Francisco de Vallés and Malón de Chaide find the popularity of the chivalresque a source of shame when there is no lack of creditable examples and when devotional books have curiosity, variety and truth enough for any reader.[54] Fiction pales before the truth of Christ. No matter how vivid the play of the imagination, no matter how versed in the ideals of chivalry and service to the weak and defenceless, what writer, asks Fr. Pedro de la Vega, could possibly have dared to feign the example of a Man who dies not for the deserving but for the undeserving?[55] The main point here is a theological one – who will dare, then, to lay down his life for the good man? – and the literary aspect is incidental, but it illustrates how important for some theological writers was the defence of the wonder and variety of biblical truth against the pathetic search for novelty among cramped worldly imaginations. Fr. Pedro's plea is part of a generalised advocacy in the sixteenth century of the chivalry of Christ. Fr. Luis de Granada urged his Portuguese readers to set aside the books of chivalry for a 'liuro de caualaria celestial', and as Edward Glaser has noted, the use of the word *caballería* to refer to the exploits of biblical characters and to the works of Christ himself is by no means uncommon.[56]

One could not hope to find a more attractive nor more compelling argument in favour of the readability of the Bible, its value as literature as well as a source of precept and example, or even its literary superiority over the fictional genres of post-Renaissance Spain. But arguments against fiction which are based quite simply on the primacy of reality over the recreation in art of the illusion of reality can never be wholly satisfying, whether that primacy is measured in moral or metaphysical terms; that is, whether we object to fiction on the grounds that it is all lies or that it is simply not real and therefore not worth consideration. In either case proponents find themselves faced with a strong defence: either that deception is not the artist's purpose and the claim that this is what he actually achieves is scarcely credible; or that art's claim to be a special kind of non-literal truth, far from disputing the pre-eminence of truth, actually serves to under-write it. This is why the undisputed verity of the Bible is of little use as a weapon against fiction. It is hard to think of any Golden-Age writer who could not have replied in all sincerity that the value of truth was not in dispute and had little or nothing to do with the legitimacy of the products of the imagination. Quevedo was only one writer of fiction who asserted, nevertheless, that the words and deeds of Christ leave the human imagination standing.

Defenders of fiction in the Golden Age also had a powerful ally in the traditional distinction between the fraudulent lie which attempts to deceive and the artful lie which masks a hidden truth. The view that a fable consists of a nucleus and a cortex, and that while the latter may not be truthful the former most certainly must be, is a commonplace of Western thinking about the nature of allegorical and mythical discourse. Whether to enhance sanctity through obscurity, or provide instruction and pleasure through the deciphering of its mystery, or even self-satisfaction with the knowledge that the vulgar are excluded, a mask of artful untruthfulness has always been regarded as an essential ingredient of fable or parable. William Nelson has shown how in the post-Christian era, the considerable latitude allowed classical writers in the matter of truthfulness in the interests of making their tales edifying or amusing came under scrutiny as the unquestionable verity of the Bible increasingly placed other kinds of narrative within the realm of human uncertainty.[57] But at the same time an increased sense of obligation towards truthfulness in writing did not prevent post-classical pagan and Christian authorities such as Macrobius, Lactantius and St Augustine from recognising the value of certain invented tales presented in figurative language as rhetorical significations of truth, provided that they could not actually be mistaken for truth.[58] It is not surprising, therefore, to find the same arguments used in the sixteenth century in a defence of fiction which saw it as not just ethically neutral but positively useful. Fr. Juan de Pineda in the first part of his *Agricultura cristiana* (1589) reminds us that poets never intended to be feigners of lies, but rather to veil truths.[59] The 'lying' of the poets is only word deep, and does not extend to the meaning which the words are intended to convey. If it were not so, poets would not deserve their reputation as wise men, but would be time-wasters, like the composers of novels of chivalry. Feigning is not lying but the protection of great truths from the scorn of the unlearned.

The inadequacy of this defence lies in the onus it places on the understanding of the audience and the restriction it places on the verisimilitude of the fiction. We have already seen that Plato doubts the ability of the child to distinguish the allegorical sense from the literal; in fact, Pigna interpreted Plato's ban as essentially a vote of no-confidence in the perspicacity of audiences, particularly the common and ignorant people, and concluded that the poets were being punished for the shortcomings of their clients.[60] For the great majority of sixteenth-century Spanish critics the vulnerabilty of the simple-minded was the key to the downfall of the lying poets and they were quick to spring to the defence of those whom they thought incapable of defending themselves. People were taken in by what they read and while that possibility remained, the risk of writing verisimilar fiction, or at least anything that was not obviously figurative or untrue, could not be taken. What is more, the requirement of irony, of deciphering figurative language, of knowing that when we read that there was once a man called don Quixote, we are required to understand the writer to mean that there was not once a man called don Quixote, raises philosophical and linguistic problems of a completely different order from the fear that some simple-minded fellow may actually come to believe in the existence of don Quixote. The difficulty of the nucleus/cortex approach is that it presupposes a relationship between language and truth of a kind that raises more problems than it solves. St Augustine may well write that we lie 'when we make up that which signifies nothing', but if we are to play fast and loose with words and use them to mean whatever we want, how are we to know what signifies what?

As the preceding section has shown, a number of difficulties face anyone wanting to sustain a case against fiction on the grounds that whereas fiction is by definition not real, reality most certainly is, and has in consequence the greater claim on our time and attention. Such an argument fails because it presupposes a correlation between fact, truth and reality on the one hand, and fiction, falsehood and unreality on the other. Neo-Aristotelian critics were unable to accept such a simplistic formulation of the problem and invariably indicated their disagreement whenever they claimed that literature constituted a special kind of non-literal truth, a claim that disarmed their opponents in several important ways: if, as Plato says, physical existence is itself a low-grade form of reality, it is unreasonable to criticise art for its unreality and at the same time demand that it exist in the same way that the world exists; if appearance does not represent the true nature of reality, then art does well not to reproduce the surface appearance of things but to address itself to the essence; by doing just that art actually serves philosophy and promotes truth by being *true to* the world, the human condition, or whatever, rather than *true of* those things.[61] The fact that neo-Aristotelian critics called this process 'imitation' – *mimesis* – gives a satisfying and slightly ironical edge to what is essentially an anti-Platonic stance.

There was also a second major difficulty to be met by those who attacked fiction for being shadow rather than substance: that of circular self-contradiction. To equate fiction, falsehood and unreality with each other meant in effect arguing the opposite of those who pointed to the particular intensity of the experience of reading, since it makes little sense to attribute intensity of feeling or conviction to something which does not exist. Vives's 'plain and foolish lies' hardly seem consistent with his own assertion that it was worse for a girl to read about jousts than to take up arms herself. The acceptability of saying, therefore, that fiction should be stopped because it peddles unreality is once again denied, this time by the everyday experience of readers who found that the self-evidently fictitious books they read took on a compelling reality in their imaginations, a fact which was not only admitted by critics of fiction but which formed the basis of a good deal of the case they put forward. This apparent contradiction does raise, however, a question from which the final and most telling argument against fiction derives: what kind of existence can a fiction be said to have?

In the *Philosophía antigua poética* El Pinciano points shrewdly to an apparent discrepancy in Plato's argument in Book x of the *Republic*.[62] Plato illustrates his assertion that poets are at the third remove from the truth with the example of the painter who likewise 'dista tres grados de la verdad'. Why, then, asks El Pinciano, banish the poets from the Republic and not the painters, since they were both equally guilty of manufacturing unreal semblances? In what sense did the poets offend more than other types of imitators? Fadrique's reply is that painters do not disturb the soul as much as poets do; their lies are not as harmful as those of the poets who can arouse the minds of men with 'una ficción que jamás pasó y tan distante de la verdad', something that never happened and is so far removed from the truth. El Pinciano is quite right to remind us of an important point which is obvious but easy to overlook: that the particular danger of poets over other imitators lies in their use of language as the medium with which they work. The deception of the painter will always be limited while the onlooker is able to walk up to the work, touch it and satisfy himself that what he sees is not a real bowl of fruit but a skilfully-executed semblance. A semblance executed in language is not so easy to detect. As there is nothing in language to guarantee its veracity, the only test of a statement is outside reference; and as there are no facts to which a fiction can refer, what might be termed the 'irresponsibility' of the poet is so much greater than that of the painter.

Fiction shares with lies, then, not just the relatively incidental property of being untrue but, more importantly, the fact that both depend for their existence on the formal properties of language. As Keith Whinnom has put it, literature is a 'disease of language – a product, like foie gras, musk or pearl, pathological in its origins'.[63] The analogy with an organism in a state of abnormal procreation is particularly apposite. There is an infinite generative ability in language which is kept in check only by the conventions of usage which enable it to function efficiently and intelligibly in everyday life. Lies and literary language systematically abuse these conventions in order to tap the anarchic creative potential of the medium. It is an open question whether this 'misuse' of language by liars and poets has a damaging effect on the fabric of language itself. Pedro Mexía felt that it does: a man who has once lied can never be believed again.[64] Diego Gracián, too, felt that 'los libros de mentiras' detract from the credibility and authority of true histories about real events.[65] The point is surely that untruths undermine people's faith not just in the veracity of an individual but in the credibility of the medium as a whole. Just as the liar demonstrates, along with his own lack of moral principle, the fragility of the conventions which govern linguistic usage, so too the convincing fiction questions what it is that makes one arrangement of words true and another false. In matters of language the Emperor's clothes are scanty indeed; if there is nothing in a false statement which reveals its falsehood there is equally nothing in a true one which guarantees its truth. From here it is but a short step to the position that any statement may be true if one can persuade people to believe it. One may judge how disturbing these implications might have seemed to the sixteenth-century mind and appreciate how closely writers and thinkers were to examine, in consequence, the grey areas where truth and falsehood overlap.

Spanish Golden-Age critics, worried about the possible effects on established values of systematic falsehood in literature, might have turned, had they wanted an authoritative confirmation of their views, to another of the dialogues of Plato, the *Sophist*. This dialogue represents in several important ways the keystone of Plato's attack on the literary arts and the goal towards which the rest of his arguments are directed. His main target in the dialogue is the deception practised by the Sophists, who pass off their counterfeit wisdom as the real thing and defend what they do with the claim that, as it is impossible to speak of something which does not exist, everything that can be said must be true. Plato clearly indicated, though, that his purpose was wider. The Sophist is defined, alongside the politician and the artist (266d–267a), as a maker of images (*eidola*), inhabiting a world which is neither wholly real nor wholly unreal. He, like the poet, is an illusionist or puppeteer (*thaumatopoios* 235b, 268d)[66] using the 'shadow-play' of discourse to create and disseminate falsehood. The analogy with the literary artist is too carefully drawn to be overlooked. The writer of fictions may practise his deceptions without intending any harm and may claim no greater degree of reality for his images than the average reader would willingly concede, but there is no substantial difference between what he achieves through art and what the Sophist perpetrates through rhetoric.

In his attack on the Sophist, Plato is concerned with the nature of images and false statements: what is an image and what kind of existence can it be said to have? Is false statement possible, and if so, how is it possible? An image has a kind of double life: it is something which is not wholly real but which does have some kind of existence; it is not the thing it purports to be, but it is at the same time presumably not nothing; if it is something, what is it? Plato would say that, inasmuch as an image does exist, it owes its existence to deception, for the Sophist, like the poet, like other image-makers, does not limit himself to the making of images, but goes on to persuade people of their reality. For the Sophist, persuasion is everything: 'there was no truth over and above what a man could be persuaded to believe'.[67] If we were to concede the reality of the Sophist's images we would also have to revise our view of the sensible world as Calderón's Segismundo was obliged to do when his 'dreams' became as vivid as his waking experience. If we deny the reality of what the Sophist says, we lay ourselves open to the retort that it is impossible to speak or think that which is not. The existence of persuasive image-makers such as poets and novelists brings such ontological problems urgently to our attention.

In the *Sophist* Plato worked out a logical basis for his overall attack on poetry.[68] He attacked the Sophist, and through him the verbal artist, for bringing about deception by false statement, and he exposed the Sophist's major line of defence, that if what he says makes sense it must refer to something and that something must be true. Plato also succeeded in heading off two possible inferences which might be drawn from the Sophist's position: that the referents which the artist constructs in the mind are just as real as the objects of the real world; and that the reality of the real world is made questionable by the vivid yet unreal constructions of the artist. For critics of fiction, moreover, Plato's arguments in the *Sophist* are of considerable significance, for the dialogue provides an essential link in the case against the imaginative artist by giving a non-trivial, non-tautological meaning to the charge that fiction is false. The purveyor of falsehoods commits a gross philosophical impropriety: his discourse does not correspond to the structure of reality. He treats language as a toy or game, shuffling the pieces around to make alternative anagrammatical worlds of the imagination. Such a language, in which words are grouped and regrouped almost at will, is, Plato argues, metaphysically ungrammatical.

Few, if any, Spanish Golden-Age intellectuals could have known the text of the *Sophist* (none, at least, appears to quote from or refer to it), and if they did know it, it seems unlikely that many appreciated its significance for the case against imaginative literature. The arguments of the *Sophist* are not necessarily to be excluded from our consideration on that account. As we have seen, the case against fiction is a complex one, consisting of several interlinked strands of argument, some of which are less sophisticated, and, it must be admitted, less powerful than others. By the very nature of things some aspects of a manifesto will appeal more readily to its supporters than will others. No critic in Golden-Age Spain, to my knowledge, put forward a totally comprehensive account of the case against fiction. Even Plato himself worked only gradually towards a position which has to be painstakingly reconstructed from a variety of texts. The attack on works of fiction in Golden-Age Spain was in many ways a corporate effort, each critic adding his own contribution to a set of arguments whose outlines were in general both well-known and widely accepted. My purpose in this chapter has been to piece together these contributions using as a framework Plato's own discussion of the principles involved. The result is something which is inevitably much greater than the sum of its parts, but something to which all the contributors could have nodded eager assent and recognised as belonging to their intellectual tradition and expressing their system of values.

In the *Sophist* Plato raised the case against fiction on to a plane of significance which was quite beyond the reach of the neo-Aristotelians, and the central position of language in his argument with the imitative artist provides the strongest link with his followers in Golden-Age Spain. The text of the *Sophist* may have been unknown to them, but the issues with which it deals were matters of urgent concern. For it is in this dialogue that Plato points to the key assumption which underlies and unifies all parts of the arguments examined above: the recognition that works of literature have the power to convince in the face of rational disbelief. Without that power all four counts in the case against fiction lose in forcefulness: the bad examples are no longer so dangerous, nor the vicarious experience so disturbing, nor the lies so deceptive, nor the existence of images so likely to undermine our grasp on reality. In the following chapter I shall be looking more closely at this assumption, and asking how literature carries off its remarkable feats of persuasion and how much of its achievement is directly attributable to aspects of the reading process itself.

3

Reading and rapture

In his emphasis on the persuasiveness of fictional texts, Plato's case against poetry inevitably shifts attention from the nature of the texts themselves to the effects that they have on their audience. This chapter follows this shift of focus. Spanish Golden-Age writers and intellectuals held the view that in an important, powerful and in-explicable way a well-wrought fiction commands attention and demands acceptance of what it says; in short, it makes us believe in it. This chapter discusses some ways in which readers respond to works of fiction and suggests that the basis of literary belief lies in the reading process itself. It is out of their understanding of the rapture of reading that writers evolved their practical defence of fiction in the Spanish Golden Age.

Literature and aesthetic belief

When most readers approach a work of fiction they do so in the expectation that they will find it convincing. They expect to find the characters and situations credible and true to life and the narrative compelling. They do not, however, expect literally to believe in what they read; indeed, to do so would not be in the spirit of the game and would deny the author the scope to exercise his skill. Readers expect to be convinced in spite of their rational disbelief and will judge ill any writer who gives cause for that disbelief to intrude on their pleasure. When we speak, then, of belief in the context of imaginative literature, we mean by the word two rather different kinds of belief, one rational, the other aesthetic. For sixteenth-century readers and critics, how-ever, the distinction between rational and aesthetic belief was much less clear-cut than those terms imply. For some readers the two kinds of belief were one and the same. Don Quixote was by no means the only Spanish Golden-Age reader who believed everything he found in

books. Pedro Mexía notes that there are some people who think that
the things in books actually happened,[1] and Simón de Silveira is said
actually to have gone as far as to swear on a missal that the contents of
Amadís were true.[2] Melchor Cano tells of a priest who refused to accept
that anything in print could be untrue,[3] an attitude satirised by both
Lope de Vega and Cervantes who pay a wry tribute to the power of the
medium, particularly when the book is 'impreso con licencia' and
endorsed by civil and religious authority.[4] Maxime Chevalier has
recently questioned the validity and usefulness of some of this
evidence.[5] Such examples are undoubtedly exceptional, but only
because they are extreme, not because they are improbable. We may
laugh at those who put their faith in the licence printed in a novel,
while at the same time judging a man's credibility by the elegance of
his letterhead. Nor should the evidence of contemporary culture, and
in particular the power of radio, be overlooked: is there anything in
the behaviour of these Golden-Age readers which is not perfectly
consistent with the impact caused by, say, the death of Grace Archer?

If some readers – and listeners – were not entirely sure about what
was true and what was make-believe, some Renaissance literary
critics were scarcely more successful in distinguishing rational from
aesthetic belief. It was generally conceded by literary theorists that an
element of belief was essential for the audience's proper enjoyment of
the work, and great stress was laid in consequence on the need for
poetry to have an appearance of truth – to be plausible – for the
reader's spirit will remain unmoved unless he can believe what he
reads.[6] The idea originates in Horace's warning that 'Quodcunque
ostendis mihi sic incredulus odi' (*Ars Poetica*, 188).[7] The view that
pleasure in literature is dependent on the credibility of the subject
matter, based in part on the purely practical consideration that
readers will not waste their time on things they do not find convincing,
helps to explain the widespread commitment in the Renaissance to the
need to temper fiction with verisimilitude. In their endorsement of the
central importance of verisimilitude Renaissance neo-Aristotelians
were saying in effect that rational belief was an important part,
perhaps even the major part, of aesthetic belief. But as Forcione has
shown,[8] Cervantes took issue on several occasions with this
oversimplification. Whereas the Canon of Toledo argues that belief is
a function of truth, don Quixote's rejoinder (*DQ*, 1, 49) suggests that
the reverse might very well be true: the reality of both historical as well
as fictional characters may depend on our willingness to accept their

truth. Cervantes's attitude here is an interested one to an extent, since he is, as a writer, keen to show that if truth in literature consists in the last analysis in what an audience can be induced to believe, the writer might then receive a greater share of the credit due to his persuasiveness. When don Quixote goes on to evoke with such vividness the pleasure with which he relives in his reading the sights and sounds of the adventures of the Knight of the Lake (1, 50) he is demonstrating Cervantes's point that if the audience actually feels it is witnessing the events described – no matter how incredible they may seem – it is surely believing them in the only way which matters, aesthetically. Here as elsewhere in his work Cervantes seems to be saying that anyone can deceive with the semblance of truth; but to conjure aesthetic belief from empirical disbelief, that takes real skill.

Apart from ensuring that fictions conformed to the probabilities of the real world in the interests of credibility, the doctrine of verisimilitude had another important role to perform in the eyes of neo-Aristotelian theorists, that of allaying the misgivings of moralist critics about the untruthful nature of imaginative literature. If fiction were to conform more closely to what was probable or compatible with human experience of the world, the Platonic prejudice against the lie would, they supposed, be disarmed: if we are to have fictions they should at least be 'realistic'. But a moment's thought shows that this attempt to compromise with plausibility is irrelevant to the Platonic case and ultimately self-contradictory. Juan de Valdés was only one critic who found himself expressing doubts about the legitimacy of lies in fiction while saying that they should be so written as to approximate, as far as is possible, to truth.[9] Valdés's suspicion of the fictitious on the one hand and preference for the plausible lie on the other is not unique and it illustrates the central paradox of the neo-Aristotelian position on fiction. When the Canon of Toledo (*DQ*, 1, 47, 482) states that the more life-like a lie the better it is, he does not say, and probably does not know, whether by 'better' he is thinking in terms of the protection of the reader or the efficacy of the fiction. If the greatest danger of the lie is that people might believe it, and that is, as we have seen, one of the central issues of the anti-fiction platform, that danger can only be exacerbated by lies which approximate to truth. The more life-like the lie, the greater the chance that it will be believed. It is clear that, far from producing an adequate reply to the Platonic case, those who recommended the observance of verisimilitude actually played into the hands of the opposition. The restrictions they tried to place on poetic illusion actually intensified the power of the illusion by making it seem more real. In fact, neo-Aristotelian critics never did address themselves to the fundamental issues raised by the existence of falsehood in literature. The late arrival of the *Poetics* on the Spanish critical scene merely caused the issue to become sidetracked into arguments about proper degrees of plausibility. The attempt to determine permissible kinds of fiction and minimal standards for verisimilitude merely assumed – but did not by any means justify – the acceptance of fiction as a proper mode of discourse. Verisimilitude was little more than a diversionary tactic: by agreeing to stop saying that a knight defeated a million other men in battle (*DQ,* I, 47, 481) we gloss over the greater lie that he ever existed at all. Giving lies an 'apariencia de verdad' (*DQ,* I, 50, 499) does not make them any less mendacious. As far as the arguments of the *Sophist* are concerned, plausibility is merely a restriction on the way in which the counters of language may be moved; it is not what Plato required, a complete prohibition of the game, nor does it help to show how fiction can have a value of its own.

The neo-Aristotelian attitude towards verisimilitude may be seen, then, to be grounded in a somewhat imprecise understanding of the nature of aesthetic belief and how it is induced. It remained unclear whether verisimilitude was a necessary condition for a fiction to be credible, or whether a proper regard for the probabilities of empirical reality was required simply to reconcile the pull of the imagination with the dictates of reason and experience. In either case the greater efficiency claimed for the life-like lie fails to satisfy the Platonic objection that to encourage belief in the untrue is to blur the edges of reality. What is more, the importance attached to verisimilitude was inconsistent with the widespread recognition that readers are convinced by the most unlikely things. The Canon of Toledo runs into precisely this problem. He says that the novels of chivalry are 'fuera del trato que pide la común naturaleza' – that is, they do not conform to verisimilitude – and then blames don Quixote for believing them. He thereby admits, or so it would seem, that belief is not a function of verisimilitude; one cannot reasonably call something incredible and at the same time complain that people believe in it. But by throwing the books across the room in disgust whenever he catches himself enjoying them in an unguarded moment the Canon makes an even more telling admission: they are infuriatingly attractive in spite of their lack of truth. He may well feel that to have been duped by something less obviously incredible would have saved his blushes. Forcione's shrewd analysis of the Canon's debate with don Quixote supports the view that there is more to Quixote's credulity than most neo-Aristotelians were prepared to admit:

As don Quixote had intimated in his humorous thrusts at the canon's doctrine of verisimilitude, the conditions for audience belief are far more complicated than the empirically minded theorists of the neo-Aristotelian movement preferred to believe. In the last analysis belief depends simply on the audience's willingness to accept as true what the narrator offers . . . the fundamental misfocus in the neo-Aristotelians' approach to the problem of belief lies in their concentration on the objects of imitation rather than on the reader's apprehension of those objects . . . Here Cervantes comes as close as he ever does to making the aesthetic discovery that managed to continue eluding literary theorists for the next two hundred years – that aesthetic belief is of an order entirely different from that of empirical belief. (pp. 253–4)

It is precisely with the reader's apprehension of the objects of his reading that this study is most concerned.

The Canon's debate with don Quixote is undoubtedly useful for exposing the contradictions implicit in verisimilitude and for demonstrating the difference between empirical and aesthetic belief, but don Quixote's commitment to the reality of the romances and the Canon's inhibiting fastidiousness are, and are intended to be, exceptional in degree if not in kind. Few people believe that what they read in novels is literally true yet few stop reading on that account, and many a reader accepts in reading tales he would dismiss with a wry smile if he were told them in a pub. When we are reading a novel not only do we cease to be aware of the literal non-existence of the characters and situations before us, but we also cease to be aware of what we are doing, of our physical position – provided we are sitting comfortably – and even of the material substance of the book. Georges Poulet has described this absorption of the reader in the work in terms of the falling away of barriers between the self and the book: 'You are inside it; it is inside you; there is no longer outside or inside.'[10] The material nature of the book evaporates and takes on a new existence within the self. The book is reconstituted in the mind and the opposition between self and other becomes so attenuated that for once the consciousness is made satisfyingly and pleasantly compatible with its objects.

The accounts we have of readers' and listeners' responses to fiction in the Golden Age suggest not only that this intimate mental intercourse with literature was a common experience but also that its nature was quite well understood. To illustrate his contention that poets are more dangerous than painters because their fictions perturb the soul to a much greater extent, El Pinciano tells the story of his friend Valerio in whose company he was invited to a wedding.[11] After dinner Valerio retired early to read in bed while the celebration continued. After a time the festivities were interrupted by a maid who announced in great distress that Valerio was dead. Upon investigation the news turned out to have been exaggerated; they found him emerging from a fainting fit caused by his reading of the death of Amadís de Gaula. The anecdote is a particularly good illustration of the power of fiction and the inner disturbance it can cause, illustrated in this case by the outward circumstances of Valerio's swoon and the disruption caused to the assembled company whose evening's fun had been spoiled. The story is also interesting for the way it highlights the mental and physical imbalance associated with an over-active imagination. Don Quixote suffered from the same problems: lack of sleep and too much reading dried up his brains and constant physical hardship prevented him from regaining his sanity. The heat of Valerio's emotion was such that he completely lost consciousness and became dead to the world. And like Tomás Rodaja, Cervantes's other cachectic intellectual, he becomes 'blando de carona', thin-skinned, delicate and hypersensitive.

In El Pinciano's account of Valerio's fit, loss of consciousness is merely a symptom of something more important, a complete loss of the mind's grip on reality. El Pinciano's background – from the general basis of the theory of the humours to the specific observations on physiology and temperament of Juan Huarte de San Juan – would have been enough to have taught him to see a physical condition as an outward manifestation of a mental one. Other observers would have confirmed the view implicit in Valerio's experience that reading induces a state in which the rational operations of the mind are temporarily suspended. The mental passivity of the reader when he is reading is emphasised by critics of fiction such as Fr. Juan de la Cerda who likens the mind to a wineskin which is tainted by whatever is poured into it,[12] and precisely the same attitude lies behind the arguments of those critics who urge the reading of worthwhile literature in preference to profane things like fables and books of chivalry. When Fr. Marco Antonio de Camos recommends a book like Luis de León's *De los nombres de Cristo* he is subscribing to a behaviourist attitude to books and readers:[13] put the right book in the right hands and the result is instant virtue. The value of a book like the *Nombres* resides in its being the product of the author's understanding and a restatement of his wholly exemplary values, as well as being a symbol of his spiritual worth and intellectual probity. Good men produce good books and a good book in turn produces a good reader, but a reader whose role remains essentially passive. He is to benefit, of course, but only by gaping at what he is offered, while the amount of benefit he derives depends on the degree of perfection of the finished book, as if the pupil's learning depended entirely on the learning and intelligence of the teacher. Censorship is essential while readers are so susceptible. Against this must be set the claim of many writers of fiction that there is no book so bad that some advantage cannot be drawn from it.

While some critics emphasised the passivity of the experience, others found reading a more passionate activity, yet they were equally unable to conclude that readers might safely be left to their own devices. Minturno saw the poet's task as to impel certain passions in the reader or listener and incite the mind to admiration of what is described.[14] But the mind's ability to discriminate is not endorsed, rather the opposite: if the good poet can persuade us to be like the good man of whom he writes, the evil but persuasive poet can inspire in us the desire to be just as evil as he. Much the same is implied by another Italian humanist critic, Ludovico Ricchieri, when he describes the violent passion excited by reading which 'forces itself upon the very reason and after having trod upon it succeeds in extending its dominion even further'.[15] For Ricchieri, reading is a battle between reason and emotion in which reason must be given every possible inducement and support if it is to remain in control. How to achieve this seems to have been a major concern for Spanish Golden-Age writers of fiction, and in the later chapters of this book we shall be examining some of the practical solutions they proposed.

One way of overcoming the mental passivity of the reader is suggested by Fr. Pedro de la Vega in what is perhaps the most intelligent account of the harm done by works of fiction to suggestible audiences.[16] Authors should be prepared to engage their readers above all at an intellectual level. Religious authors have erred in the past, he feels, by attempting to stimulate the will rather than exercise the intellect (*entendimiento*). His own piece – the *Declaración de los siete psalmos penitenciales* – is aimed at correcting this imbalance. A book that does not appeal to the intelligence of its readers leaves the mind unoccupied, and an idle mind is attracted by the enchantment of novels of chivalry and the like. 'It is not easy', he comments, 'to explain why the human intellect, having a natural predilection for the truth, should be content with things which it knows itself are not true, but merely the empty imaginings of him who wrote them.'[17] The only answer which occurs to Fr. Pedro is that the mind abhors a vacuum, and likes to be kept occupied if only to shake off, as it were, 'la calambre del demasiado sosiego' – the cramp of inactivity. There is undoubtedly a certain vagueness here, but Fr. Pedro's is an honest attempt to understand the craving for fiction in order to make religious literature into a more effective antidote. A mind left unoccupied is an open invitation to squatters: only signs of life and proper furnishings will deter undesirable elements from taking up residence.

As the foregoing examples illustrate, attitudes to the reading of fiction in the sixteenth century have that element of inconsistency and tentativeness about them which one might expect to find among commentators who are seeking to account for an unfamiliar experience. But underlying them all is one basic idea, that the reading of fiction is – almost literally – a mindless occupation. Mindless, not just in its shallow frivolity (which Francisco de Vallés scathingly likened to a woman's love of dressing up[18]), but mindless in the sense of non-rational or even irrational. In stressing this aspect of literary experience the critics were not only basing themselves on the evidence of their eyes, on what they knew of their own responses and what they could deduce of others', but were recalling consciously or unconsciously those passages of the *Ion* and the *Phaedrus* in which Plato discussed the alienation of the mind during poetic creation.[19] As was noted in chapter 1, the *topos* of the divine fury of the poets survived in the Middle Ages in spite of the widespread ignorance of Plato at anything other than an anecdotal level, and the idea makes frequent appearances in the discussions of Spanish literary theorists of the Renaissance and after.[20] It was a popular notion because, like so much of Plato's thinking on the nature of art, it rang sufficiently true to command the respect of the great majority, yet has enough of the paradox about it to provide support for those who defended as well as those who attacked the legitimacy of poetry. By speaking of inspiration as *enthousiasmos* and *theia mania* ('divine madness', *Phaedrus*, 245a) Plato serves those who would point to the divine origin of poetry as evidence of its worth and dignity, but at the same time feeds the prejudices of others who claimed that the irrational nature of poetic insight was incompatible with true knowledge. The divinity of poetry did not alter the fact that the work of the poet is intuitive and unconscious, and as long as poets are unable to account for what they produce, they can hardly expect to rank alongside the philosopher.

If there was good authority, then, for regarding the author as being 'out of his mind' when he is writing,[21] there was also good reason for supposing that the reader's response to the work had its equally irrational aspects. In Plato's other, earlier, discussion of *theia moira* ('divine inspiration', *Ion*, 536c, *Meno*, 99e) in the *Ion*, Socrates describes Homer as a great magnet which transmits its magnetic qualities to the things that it touches. The rhapsode Ion and his audience are both magnetised by the poet in this way:

> This stone not only attracts iron rings, but also imparts to them a similar power of attracting other rings; and sometimes you may see a number of pieces of iron and rings suspended from one another so as to form quite a long chain: and all of them derive their power of suspension from the original stone. In like manner the Muse first of all inspires men herself; and from these inspired persons a chain of other persons is suspended, who take the inspiration . . . (533de) Do you know that the spectator is the last of the rings which, as I am saying, receive the power of the original magnet from one another? The rhapsode like yourself and the actor are intermediate links, and the poet himself is the first of them. (535e–536a)

The poet has the ability to hand on his inspiration, and with it his madness, to others, and to produce in his audience irrational behaviour of the type that Ion willingly admits to, both for his own part and his spectators': tears for a tale of pity, fear and shaking for one of horror, and even panic in the presence of twenty thousand friendly faces. Like don Quixote before the Knight of the Lake, the rhapsode and the audience are taken out of themselves, their souls in an ecstasy among the persons or places of which the poet speaks, whether in Ithaca, Troy or wherever (*Ion*, 535bc).

We have to look no further than Vives to find these two ideas – the irrationality and the rapture of literary art – encapsulated in one sentence: 'Quae insania est, iis duci, aut teneri?'[22] What madness is it to be possessed and carried away by the self-evident lies in books of chivalry? With one noun and two passive infinitives Vives sums up a whole critical tradition. Yet the same ideas underlie a good deal of the critical vocabulary of the Golden Age. Words like '*encantar*', '*maravillar*', or '*embelesar*' constantly recur in accounts of the way books make their effect. Fr. Pedro de la Vega speaks of the idle mind which is taken over – literally 'occupied' – by fiction as *embelesado*[23] and

Cervantes conveys the same idea of rapt attention with the rather less flattering *embobado* when the innkeeper's wife comments that the only time she gets any peace and quiet is when her husband is listening to a book being read and is so enthralled that he forgets to pick a quarrel (*DQ*, I, 32, 321). But the innkeeper, for all his abstraction and vacant reverie, is at least not enough of a booby to believe that the characters in the books are real, and thereby confirms the Canon's experience that complete absorption in a piece of fiction is by no means incompatible with rational disbelief, whose temporary suspension does not constitute a complete mental collapse.

Suspender is in fact one of the words most frequently used, particularly by Cervantes, to express the non-rational aspects of imaginative literature. This verb, especially in its participial form '*suspenso*', does duty for many aspects of the reading process, conveying both the rapture which fiction inspires in its audience, and the willing or unwilling suspension of the rational and critical faculties which is what ultimately brings that rapture about. Only rarely in the Spanish Golden Age is the word '*suspender*' used to mean what we now understand as 'suspense'. Amyot's prologue to Heliodorus uses it that way,[24] but more often it means 'surprise', as it does in Cervantes's prologue to *Don Quijote*,[25] or in *La española inglesa* when it is used to record the crowd's astonishment at the sudden arrival of Recaredo to claim his bride on the steps of the convent of Santa Paula in Seville.[26] Elsewhere its meaning is more like that of the adjective in the English phrase 'suspended animation'. Don Fernando praises the Captive's tale for its ability to 'suspend' the listener, to absorb the interest of the audience to the extent that they lose all awareness of the passage of time in their enthusiasm (*DQ*, I, 42, 433). Both don Quixote and the Canon, in their different ways, regard an ability to hold the mind in abeyance as an essential requirement of a good story well told (*DQ*, I, 50, 504; I, 47, 482), and the dueña Dolorida attributes to the same ability the emotional power of those verses that penetrate to the very soul (*DQ*, II, 38, 817).

The prominent place occupied by the verb '*suspender*' in Cervantes's critical vocabulary reflects the importance of the idea of suspension in Golden-Age attitudes to reading as a whole. Not only does it stand for the surprise and delight which were so much sought after by writers of the period, but it also accounts for the way those effects are achieved. The events of the story 'suspend' the senses and the reason of the reader or listener who, *suspenso*, bereft of the faculties which enable him to make empirical judgments, is manoeuvred into a state of rapture in which the fiction can bring its full effect to bear on a mind at its most impressionable. English usage echoes the Spanish by speaking of the 'suspension of disbelief'. Suspension of disbelief is often thought of as something which an audience either wills into being or at least submits to willingly. When Poulet says of his reading that he says farewell to what is, to feign belief in what is not,[27] he implies with that word 'feign' that he retains conscious control. Forcione, similarly, speaks of the 'courtesy' of an audience which can 'decide to believe'.[28] Yet there is every indication that such control is illusory. An audience can decide to listen or a reader decide to read, but once they have agreed to play along with the author for the sake of argument they will quickly find it difficult to resist the enchantment of the tale. When Peralta settles back to read the Dogs' Colloquy he undoubtedly does so out of courtesy, but by the time he has finished it is clear that it is not just his good manners that have led him into the position of refusing to admit that dogs can talk while conceding the artistry and invention of what they said. The example of Peralta illustrates, as does that of the gaping innkeeper, as does that of Quixote himself, the aptness of Gabriel Josipovici's observation that the phrase 'suspension of disbelief' is a misnomer because it suggests effort;[29] the effort is to emerge from rather than fall under the spell of the story. To become absorbed in a story and at the same time remain consciously aware that it is a fiction is a sophisticated achievement, beyond the capability, even, of the Canon of Toledo. The fact is that fictions have a power of persuasion which flatly contradicts their unreality, and that, beyond an initial decision to participate in the event, the audience may find that it has little or no control over its own responses.

The *Coloquio de los perros* is a key text for the study of the relationship of reading to aesthetic belief. Not only does it portray a character reading but it also contrives to make that character's reading coincide exactly with that of the real reader: they both read the same text at the same time. For the duration of the Colloquy we and Peralta become one, and when we have finished it, we express our appreciation just as Peralta does – or so Cervantes would hope. This is a daring enough attempt at manipulating the reader's literary appreciation, but the audacity of the story does not stop there. A striking feature of the Colloquy is the way that Campuzano repeatedly draws attention to its implausibility.[30] Much is made, both before the reading and in the Colloquy itself, of the unlikelihood of dogs being able to talk. There is a long tradition of animals speaking in literature (two obvious examples, Aesop and Apuleius, are actually mentioned) which would have enabled the contemporary reader to accept unhesitatingly the convention that moral satire can come from the mouths of animals. Yet Cervantes chooses not to take advantage of this convention. In spite of what he overheard, Campuzano still doubts that dogs can talk; Peralta certainly doubts it;[31] even Cipión and Berganza doubt it.[32] Moreover, the suggestion that they might actually be men who have been changed into dogs[33] is merely the old Cervantine trick of parodying rational explanations by explaining one implausibility in terms of another: those giants only look like windmills because they have been changed into windmills by sorcerers. That kind of explanation only fools fools like Sancho, and far from dealing with the problem of verisimilitude, the explanation offered by Berganza serves only to draw attention to the issues raised by the patent lack of verisimilitude in the Dogs' Colloquy.

What Cervantes seems to be doing in the *Coloquio de los perros* is asserting with particular eloquence the independence of aesthetic and rational belief, and illustrating in the process the fact that literature is little more than an organised form of language depending almost entirely for its impact on inherent properties of language. The form in which the Colloquy is cast makes this point particularly well. The text which Peralta is given to read is, as Campuzano points out, entirely composed of speech.[34] There is no narrative, no linking passages of prose in which the writer can gain the confidence of his reader, no scope for persuading him, independently of the events themselves, that what he is reading is perfectly plausible. Nor have the dogs, who are after all merely passing the time of night unaware that they are being overheard, any need to indulge in persuasive rhetoric. And yet somehow, we, like Peralta, accept what they say. Faced with perhaps his most daring literary challenge, Cervantes abandons conscious artistry and the manipulation of the reader's credence and allows speech to exert its own mysterious power, in the knowledge that dogs who talk sense will get a more sympathetic hearing than men who don't. The artless directness of the Colloquy is the product of Cervantes's awareness that as an author he is in the final analysis dependent upon the power of words and the effects they can have on the listener: his skill lies in choosing them, but once he has made his choice he has a very limited control over their efficacy. This *novela* seems less concerned with the process by which reality is turned into fiction, as Ruth El Saffar has suggested,[35] than with the turning of a self-evident fiction into a convincing literary reality. To do this, and to show at the same time how it is done, Cervantes has his character and his reader sit in each other's laps and read over each other's shoulders, and shows them that words can do rather more than just represent the real world.

The persuasive potential of language is particularly well characterised by the fifth-century sophist, Gorgias, in a passage from his *Encomium of Helen*.[36] Gorgias sets out to exonerate Helen by examining several of the ways in which she might have been obliged against her will to act as she did. One of the *forces majeures* which he discusses is the seduction of speech. 'Speech', he says, 'is a powerful lord, which by means of the finest and most invisible body effects the divinest works.' So powerful, indeed, that poetry ('speech with metre') causes its hearers to experience fearful shuddering, tearful pity and grievous longing, and, through the agency of words, the soul, faced with the sufferings of others, experiences a suffering of its own. In this description Gorgias clearly anticipates Aristotle's own discussion of fear and pity in the *Poetics*. But the *Encomium* is also notable for a fine image with which the orator characterises the effects of his own skill:

> The effect of speech upon the condition of the soul is comparable to the power of drugs over the nature of bodies. For just as different drugs dispel different secretions from the body, and some bring an end to disease and others to life, so also in the case of speeches, some distress, others delight, some cause fear, others make hearers bold, and some drug and bewitch the soul with a kind of evil persuasion.   (p. 14)

Gorgias's view of *logos* as a potion evidently had considerable influence on Plato's own understanding of the power of rhetoric and ultimately on his attacks on poetry. One recognises in Plato's frequent criticisms of rhetoric several themes which derive from Gorgias's admirably detached understanding of the workings of his craft: the equivalence of rhetoric and poetry; their indifference to the moral and ethical values at whose service they are put; and their ability to work their magic against the will of the audience. The poet, like the orator, is a *psychagogos* (*Phaedrus*, 271c), a man who tries to influence the psyche and uses language as a bewitching tool of illusion and empty virtuosity, respecting not the truth but the appearance of truth, and impressing as if by magic the minds of the unwary with all manner of falsehoods.

The *Coloquio de los perros* has, though, a good deal more than this to say about the potency of words. The Colloquy is, as we have seen, written speech; it succeeds as a written text by virtue of its directness and of that rhetorical potential in language that Gorgias so effectively describes in the *Encomium of Helen*. Yet, at the same time, it is questionable whether the Colloquy, though constituted of speech, could have succeeded in any other than written form. Campuzano admits as much when he baulks at recounting the dogs' conversation himself. On the face of it this seems strange. He has just told Peralta another, only slightly less tall, story face to face, and the change of tactic is surprising. Yet, having led with the raconteur's favourite card, 'You'll never believe this, but . . .', he gives Peralta a written record to read for himself. Also surprising is the fact that he – Campuzano – does not (as he might well have done, and as the priest did with the *Curioso impertinente*) read the piece aloud. He prefers, instead, to rely on Peralta's silent reading to make its effect, and he was well-advised to have done so. The point of the Colloquy is to accomplish a daring sleight of hand: to use the credibility and plausibility of what the dogs allegedly said as a guarantee of the fact that they did actually speak. Campuzano's remark that he omitted the business of 'said Cipión, replied Berganza'[37] in order to keep it short is, as we might expect, deliberately misleading. He omitted all traces of third person so as to bring Peralta closer to the dialogue and to tempt him away from the objective safety of his scepticism. In the process Peralta is put in a position where anything he says about the Colloquy as a piece of literature – and he is fairly complimentary about it when he finishes his reading – can only serve to reinforce the illusion that Campuzano is trying to create: to talk about the Colloquy is to talk about what the dogs said, since there is nothing in the Colloquy except what the dogs said. By having Peralta read the dialogue silently to himself, Cervantes is suggesting that there are some kinds of persuasion that only the written word is capable of carrying off. Cervantes shows here, as he does in *Don Quijote*, that if an assembled audience will fall under the spell of a skilful narrator so that it will lose all track of time and space, how much more easily will a private reader, stripped of the protective company of his fellows and locked away in a solitary world of his own imaginings, how much more easily will he succumb to the rapture of a book.

The evidence of the *Coloquio de los perros* helps to set don Quixote's delusion in a wider context and points to the underlying seriousness of the niece and the housekeeper's superstitious attitude to his library and their gleeful participation in its destruction (*DQ*, 1, 6). They were not, of course, alone in their fondness for book burning: theirs was an age which destroyed as many books as it read. An attitude of reverence towards the book as a sacred object – an attitude which the Greek world significantly did not share – can so easily turn sour when the books in question are sacred to those of a rival persuasion. Post-Christian reverence for the Book endowed other books, by association, with something of Its special status as a token of man's relationship with the spiritual world, a repository of wisdom and a key to social and political power. When books come to symbolise in this way the values of the societies which produce them, they inevitably suffer the fate of any insignia: they are prime targets for capture and destruction by the enemy who feels that by hitting at the emblem he can undermine the regime or the ideology which it represents. For these two women, however, the Scrutiny of the Books was less a political gesture, or even an exercise in practical criticism, than a blow struck against the almost supernatural enchantment of literature. With their aspersions – both liquid and verbal – and their talk of *autos de fe* they signalled their belief that there is something profoundly demonic as well as enchanting in books and that literature is powerful in ways which are not easily understood.

Looking back over the discussion thus far, we may conclude that the Spanish Golden Age recognised the persuasiveness of literary art but was unable to agree on how it is achieved or whether or not it is a worthwhile achievement. We find, on the one hand, neo-Aristotelian critics who stress the relatedness of aesthetic and empirical belief, but do not specify whether the relationship is one of cause and effect – the reader or hearer will not be duped unless the lie is plausible – or merely one of desirable contiguity in the interests of literary decency. On the other hand we find a practising writer like Cervantes who not only asserts and illustrates the independence of the two kinds of belief, but stakes his reputation on his ability to make, to the reader's gratified astonishment, the most unlikely things seem perfectly convincing. We also find a general agreement with the view of the artist as *psychagogos*, one who 'leads the soul', entering the mind and gaining control of it in a mysterious and rather sinister fashion, holding reason in abeyance and very often cutting off all awareness of surroundings, physical sensations or whatever. The audience is almost literally seized by an alien spirit – a reflection, Plato would say, of that fury which first possessed the poet in the act of creation – and mesmerised into a state of suspended animation. Intense though awareness of this phenomenon was, and Cervantes's frequent portrayal of enraptured readers and listeners is in itself eloquent testimony to the fact, no really satisfactory account of it was forthcoming. The evident similarity between the persuasiveness of spoken and written words is an important reminder of Keith Whinnom's point that literature is above all a by-product of language, as well as a clue that the persuasiveness of literature is best sought in the nature of language itself. But in *Don Quijote* and especially in *El coloquio de los perros* – the best working model we have of Golden-Age attitudes to reading – Cervantes asserts the special capability of a written text to persuade where spoken words would fail. What he, along with other Golden-Age writers, tells us about aesthetic belief confirms the view that classical opinions of fiction and rhetoric were rehearsed in sixteenth-century Spain as a direct response to the spread of fiction in printed form and that private reading raised the persuasive potential of fiction to its highest degree. In the remainder of this chapter I want to suggest some reasons why this should be so, why we do find fiction convincing in spite of our rational disbelief, and to argue that the rapture of reading is so involuntary that the Golden Age was justified in its alarm at what it saw as the mindlessness of the activity and in its search for ways of loosening the grip of the book on the reader's psyche.

Language, reading and persuasion

We have seen that Campuzano's trust in the persuasiveness of the written word, and the niece and the housekeeper's almost primitive horror of books are complementary attitudes; an awareness of the drug-like power of words goes hand in hand with the deep-seated distrust of them which permeates even the most literate of societies. This distrust – the preference for deeds over words as tokens of good faith – undoubtedly originates not just in the disastrous aftermath of persuasion, be it the sublimity of the Trojan war or the folly of tilting at windmills, but in the very nature of words themselves. Since our perception of them is synonymous with our understanding of them, and because that understanding is necessarily a mental act, words cannot really be said to exist at all until they have taken shape in the mind of the hearer, and by then the damage is done; we cannot unhear what we have heard nor unread what we have read. There is no defence against language; the words are in the room before we have answered the knock at the door. That language has this inherent capacity for infiltration is by far the most potent weapon of the literary artist.

It may at first sight seem unhelpfully obvious to attribute the power of literature to inherent properties of language, yet if we ignore Hamlet's warning that the matter of books is words we are bound to overlook the essentially linguistic nature of literature – that which, for El Pinciano, made poets candidates for expulsion from the Republic while painters were not – and, what is more significant for the subject of this study, fail to understand the basis of literary persuasion. When an artist trusts to words he is relying on his audience to use the same abilities in reading his text as they would bring to the business of coping with language in daily life. What he says may be quite different from the things that they are used to hearing or reading and he may see his purpose as being in some way separate from and superior to that of everyday discourse; but inasmuch as literature is a means of communication it is not substantially different from any other kind of language.[38] We use the same skills to read a novel as we do to read a letter from a solicitor, an advertisement for gas-fired central heating, or a notice to keep our dog off the grass. It is likely that the persuasiveness of fiction owes a great deal to the amount of overlap that exists between literary and non-literary language: novels and instruction manuals draw on the same vocabulary, are constructed from the same grammar, and the information they provide flows through identical channels and is deciphered in exactly the same way. It is hardly surprising, then, that some readers have had difficulty in telling fact from fiction. Just like a hoax telephone call, a novel exploits the language and the equipment of honourable transaction, yet without allowing of verification by simply going to the scene and looking for oneself.[39] That literary language is in some ways a parasite, claiming distinction yet feeding its separateness on the vigour of its parent, accounts for a large part of the suspicion it met with in the Golden Age.

Two points of central importance underlie these remarks. Once we admit, in the first place, the 'pathological' origins of literature we are nearer to understanding its ambiguous nature, that is, nearer to tempering a writer's or a critic's awareness of the special status of literature with a wider sense of the relatedness of literary and non-literary language. In the second place, it is clear that while writers will always treat literature with perfect justification as a unique form of expression, readers can only approach it, if they are to begin to understand it, with the equipment they have developed to handle less hallowed forms of discourse. It is only the linguistic conventions of the real world, deeply ingrained by constant use, that make fictional language possible. Without these conventions, and the sense of trust and security which they bring to a speech community, the exhilaration that comes from their temporary and playful misuse in fiction would be impossible, and an alternative imagined world could have no meaning.

One of the most telling of the linguistic conventions drawn on by writers of fiction is the way in which we commonly use words *as if* they were directly connected to the objects of the real world. We know, when we stop to think about it, that our language is merely a set of signs which symbolise our mental concepts, and that the objects to which we think our words refer are merely exemplars of those concepts.[40] Whereas the relationships that exist between symbol and concept, and between concept and referent, are causal, the relationship of symbol to referent is only an imputed one. When we say that a word 'means' something we are in effect speaking elliptically and using the word 'means' as a kind of shorthand to imply a simple and direct relationship between words and things. Daily life would inevitably be much more complex without this linguistic short circuit. While signifier and signified may be distinguishable in theory, in practice they are as inseparable as the head and tail of a coin, or the recto and verso of a sheet of paper.[41] Simple activities like phoning a plumber would become even more perilous if neither party could be sure that the words 'leaking tap' referred to a particular leaking tap or, indeed, referred to anything at all. In other respects, however, our harmless ellipsis can create more problems than it solves. It very easily leads, in particular, to the unthinking assumption that because we have a name for a concept, that concept must have substantive existence, and this assumption in turn leads ultimately to the practice of reification. And it is here that the writer of fiction is able to step in: if words refer, his words must also refer, and if they do not refer to things, people, places and events in the real world, then something must be brought into being to which they can refer. He writes on one side of the paper and leaves it to his readers to write on the back.[42]

The creativity of the novelist, then, attests to the ability of language to constitute reality. In asking us to imagine an unreal world a writer is making no greater conceptual requirement of us than we make of each other whenever we speak and, by speaking, ask each other to imagine the real world. The intervention of the concept between the word and the world (created or real) is of paramount importance in either case. Furthermore, in requiring us to imagine an unreal world rather than describing a real one, a writer is exploiting those aspects of language use which are, to use Austin's terms, 'performative' rather than 'constative'.[43] In this respect, too, literary language can be seen as no different from non-literary. Both are a way of *saying* something which is also in effect a way of *doing* something, or getting something done.

Getting things done, however, requires cooperation. Quite apart from its propositional content, every utterance also has a point – what Searle calls its 'illocutionary' force[44] – and if the utterance is to be fully understood that point has to be grasped,[45] even though it will not always be apparent from the form of words used. 'I'm going' may be a statement of fact, or a commitment to a form of action, or a warning not to try my patience further, or an attempt at emotional blackmail. How this or any sentence is interpreted depends on our being alive to intonation, context, convention and all the other clues, many of them non-verbal, which we use to decipher what people say to us.

The concept of illocutionary acts, together with the observation that the illocutionary force of an utterance is not always self-evident, are useful contributions to our understanding of literary as well as non-literary language.[46] They go some way towards solving the main problem of fiction – that of lack of strict reference – and they help us to understand the peculiar power of untrue statements if their meaning lies less in what they say than in their purpose in being said, and especially so if that purpose is deliberately obscured, as when special pleading, say, masquerades as a statement of fact. The lover who swears undying love in order to effect a seduction is no more guilty of untruthfulness than is the girl who says she believes him so as not to appear cheap. They are both engaged in the age-old language games of persuading, creating impressions and getting their own way.

To illustrate these points let us take the example of an insult. Like literary language, an insult is a particularly powerful form of performative language. It is designed to provoke a strong emotional response in the person insulted and leaves aside all considerations of truth and fact. If I call a man a bastard it is not necessary for him actually to be illegitimate for us to come to blows, though if his legitimacy does happen to be in doubt the insult may, for special reasons, touch off a particularly violent reaction. The point is, though, that my observation produces – just as a literary fiction does – its impression in spite of the facts; we may both know that his parentage is beyond reproach and in any case acknowledge that illegitimacy is no reflection on a man's true worth. Wherein does the forcefulness of my insult lie? Not, surely, in its truth (it has none), but in his awareness of my intention to offend, an awareness that stems as much from paralinguistic factors – my tone of voice, the look on my face and the circumstances of our meeting – as from his understanding of the propositional content of the words 'You bastard' and the role they conventionally play in the personal antagonisms of speakers of English; I could equally well have slapped him on the back with a smile and conveyed with the same words my admiration for his latest amatory conquest. If he chooses to rise to my insults he does so because he has understood my intention to produce an effect in him and because he is willing to provide the intended response. Without his comprehension and cooperation there can be no insult. It is this distinction between what we intend *in* saying something and what we achieve *by* saying something that led Austin to add another class of acts to his theory: perlocutionary acts.[47] In the example in question my intention to give offence constitutes the illocutionary force of my remark, and his actually taking offence gives my words an extra, perlocutionary force. I would argue that a reader's successful grasp of and collaboration with the intention of a literary text gives it a similar perlocutionary force.

The problem of the literal untruthfulness of fiction is eased by a model of language which is not representational but performative, in which language is given by mutual consent of author and reader the power to create the circumstances to which it refers. When a writer embarks on the construction of a hypothetical reality he enters into a collaborative partnership with his reader. Between them they set up a double-ended process of implying and inferring, encoding and decoding, meaning and understanding. Language is not a simple matter of input at one end of the system and output at the other: for there to be meaning there must be input at both ends. The suggestiveness of language, particularly literary language, depends on the suggestibility of the listener or reader, and credibility and credulity go hand in hand.

The reader's role in the exchange is two-fold. Firstly there is his 'courtesy', his willingness to listen and readiness to act on what he hears. Campuzano introduces his tale with the hope that Peralta 'se acomode a creerlo'.[48] Mostly, however, what the reader supplies is his comprehension, with which he signals his consent to the contract. The reader's unconscious act of understanding gives the words their meaning and supplies the context of shared assumptions and values which enables the linguistic code to be deciphered. A great deal more information goes into deciphering a sentence than is actually expressed in it. The speaker communicates more by tapping his listener's fund of knowledge and experience, by activating his comprehension, than by expressing his own. The listener, however, always has the advantage of the reader, the greater grasp of the speaker's intentions which come to him in ways other than strictly verbal. The reader has less information on which to work and must in consequence supply a greater proportion for himself. The particular suggestibility of literary language lies precisely in the amount that the reader himself has to supply.

Linguistic comprehension will always be a difficult matter to discuss. For one thing, the comprehension of our own language is, for the most part, 'rapid, automatic, and effortless'.[49] It is so close to us that it is not readily susceptible to introspection and is usually so instantaneous that we tend only to notice its presence when we are deprived of it and have, in consequence, nothing we can study. For another thing, comprehension is not monolithic. Understanding a short sentence of half a dozen words will clearly draw on different cognitive skills from the absorption of a long text that might be read in nightly instalments over a period of weeks. In the latter case memory and other synthesising procedures will obviously play a more important role. Comprehension of a literary text, then, takes place at several levels, and in the discussion that follows an attempt will be made to discuss only the extremes of the spectrum. At the same time I shall want to move away from general properties of language and the relatedness of literary and non-literary language (though these will continue to form the background of the discussion) and look more closely at two specific problems raised by literary fiction, namely, reading as distinct from listening, and the nature of a text. The first of these will be related to questions of comprehension at the sentence level, while the second will entail some consideration, if only in the most general terms, of how we are able to understand lengthy stretches of text. My overall argument will, however, remain that the key to aesthetic belief lies in linguistic comprehension since language by its very nature demands that the reader furnish the text with meaning. At whatever level comprehension is operating, whether at the purely mechanical level of decoding printed symbols and the recognition of words, or at the much more sophisticated level of reading and understanding long stretches of text, the requirements on the reader are essentially the same. He has to supply information from a store of public and private knowledge in order to interpret what is written in front of him. And the more of himself that he has to provide the greater will be his sense of identity with the text and the greater the tendency to regard it as in some sense his own work.

We have already seen how the resurgence of anti-fictional attitudes in Golden-Age Spain appears to have coincided with a period of increase in the consumption of literature by private reading. Although it is by no means our sole access to literature, private reading has become so familiar to us that we have ceased to regard it as anything but normal. Yet the mechanical and conceptual skills involved in reading even the simplest of sentences have complex and far-reaching effects on our approach to what we read. One obvious place to begin a discussion of reading is with the eyes. Although in some ways the most basic and most mechanical part of the reading process, the purely visual aspects of reading can serve nevertheless as a model for the rest. The eyes are our primary contact with the object of our interest, the book, and it is they who do our looking for us, even if it is the brain that strictly speaking does the seeing. While we are reading, the light-sensitive cells in the retina are continually converting electro-magnetic radiation into neural energy which travels along the optic nerve to the brain. During this process the movement of the eyes across the page is not at all as smooth as we might imagine it to be, nor is it unidirectional. The eyes move in a series of jerks or 'saccades' interrupted by pauses or 'fixations' when the visual information on the page is transmitted to the brain.[50] The proportion of time during which the eyes are moving is very small, about 6 per cent of reading time; for 94 per cent of the time they are at rest.[51] The eyes take in information very quickly: about 50 msec is sufficient for them to take in all the visual information that can be absorbed in one fixation. The time taken between fixations and hence the speed at which we read is governed not by physical constraints but by the speed at which the brain works. When the brain has processed the information from one fixation it then instructs the eyes to move on, or if necessary back, to the next. How quickly it does this depends on how much sense it can make of what it sees.[52] A typical subject will be able to report only four or five random letters from a 50 msec exposure, 10–12 letters from unrelated words, but up to 25 letters if the words make up a meaningful phrase.[53] Now since a reader can see four times as much when reading a text that makes sense to him as he can when reading a string of random letters, it is clear that in normal reading a great deal of use is being made of information which is not visual: the reader is supplying four-fifths of the information in the form of his knowledge of the distributional and sequential redundancy of English letters and words.

We can illustrate our knowledge and use of redundancy in reading very easily. Consider the following two sentences:

Th s s nt nc is nt ll gi le lt ou h e er th rd et er s m ss ng.

This sentence is intelligible although half of the letters is missing

Three complementary types of information, orthographic, syntactic and semantic, are used to interpret the examples, leaving aside the substantial trade-off between them, and we are not aware of how much we are drawing on our knowledge of such things as letter distribution, grammatical structure and meaning until, as here, a substantial reduction is made in the amount of redundancy in the sentence. Redundancy is what we already know and do not need to be told, but which is there to complete a pattern. The relationship between our prior knowledge, the non-visual information supplied by the brain, and the information supplied by the eyes from the text is reciprocal – the more we have of one the less we need of the other.[54] It is this fact that makes, for example, the proof-reading of one's own work so difficult. We are so familiar with the sense of the text that the brain pays very little regard to the printed words which merely act as intermittent reminders of the meaning.

Although what has been said about the eye–brain relationship in reading concerns the more mechanical aspects of decoding a printed text, the implications to be drawn apply to higher levels of the reading process. Reading and understanding go hand in hand. The brain is very selective and samples only the most important features of the text, and it can afford to do so because most of the information on the page is already known to us in one of several ways. Without that prior knowledge of the structure of English words and syntax, and the ability to predict probable sequences of words in terms of their likely meaning, reading would be a slow, laborious and painfully difficult task. But the decoding of printed symbols is only a small part of reading. The primary activity, the decoding of language, illustrates equally well the reciprocal relationship which exists between the information contained in the words and their structure and our understanding and prior knowledge of what those words are likely to mean. Few people, if asked where the meaning of a sentence lay, would suggest that it lay in the words. 'The dog bit the man' and 'The man bit the dog' contain the same words but mean different things. A venetian blind is by no means the same thing as a blind venetian. Most people would in consequence want to relate the meaning of a sentence more closely to the syntactic structure, but even this presents difficulties. The ambiguity of the sentence 'The trees were planted by the farmer' is not obvious until we compare it with 'The farmer was seated by the trees'. Most people instinctively interpret the first example as a passive sentence since it contains three passive markers, the auxiliary 'was', the participal ending '-ed' and the preposition 'by'. But the second, which appears to contain the same markers, shows that we understand the first as much by judging what it is likely to mean as by assessing fully the grammatical and semantic information it contains. In other words, when we understand what people say, and hence when we read what they write, we are bringing meaning to the text as well as deriving meaning from it. How else do we know that the man in the green hat has it on his head while the man in the green canoe does not?

Towards the end of Plato's *Phaedrus* Socrates prefaces a discussion of the superiority of the spoken word over the written with the celebrated myth of the invention of writing.[55] The god Theuth approaches the Egyptian king Thamus with a device which will 'make the people of Egypt wiser and improve their memories'; a recipe, he calls it, for memory and wisdom (274e). Thamus is horrified. If men learn this art they will cease to use their memories, 'calling things to remembrance no longer from within themselves but by means of external marks'. Writing is a recipe, not for memory but for reminder. The distinction is an important one and what Socrates has to say about the myth underlines the superficially mnemonic character of written texts: a man must be truly ignorant if he imagines that written words can do anything more than remind him of what he already knows (275cd). Socrates's main purpose here is to make the standard point about the superiority of speech:[56] you can cross-examine a man and get him to explain, refine or retract his views. In that direction lies true knowledge and wisdom. If you ask a question of a book it goes on telling you the same thing for ever. Socrates's predictions have substantially come true: men have lost the use of their memories and books have become a substitute for true wisdom and understanding. But his comments on the myth are also interesting in that they support the view put forward that reading entails prior knowledge of some kind if the words are to be fully intelligible. This does not mean that we cannot learn anything from books, merely that what we learn will be constituted of what we already know. A recipe for, let us say, shortcrust pastry will assume, by its very use of the words, a familiarity with the notions of measurement, the blending and kneading of ingredients and their behaviour at high temperature. Recipes, like other forms of written instruction, merely organise previous knowledge in new ways, and without some knowledge of cookery and its terminology on the part of their users they could not be written. In the same way authors who describe to us people and places we have never seen and could not see must rely on our readiness to recreate them in terms of people and places we already know.

Before pursuing the use a reader makes of his prior knowledge when reading fiction, one other significant physiological aspect of reading should be discussed, namely the alleged silence of silent reading. We have seen that reading and understanding of necessity go hand in hand. This means that reading must to some extent be done rapidly: a rate of less than 200 words per minute means that the reader is suffering from tunnel vision, is treating words as separate entities, and that his comprehension is likely to be low.[57] On the other hand there is a physiological limit to the speed at which it is possible to read aloud since the visual information from one fixation requires about one second to be analysed by the brain. The brain thereby imposes a limit of about four to five words per second (about 250 words per minute) on the speed at which it is possible to read aloud. Above that rate the reader is not pausing to identify every word, which is essential for reading aloud, and some form of silent or semi-silent reading therefore becomes necessary. The boundary, however, between audible and silent reading is by no means clear-cut and there is considerable evidence that some form of inaudible speech takes place even during what appears to be silent reading.[58] This aspect of the reading process, known variously as inner, silent or subvocal speech, or 'subvocalisation', has a considerable interest for the study of the relationship between reading and aesthetic belief.

The existence of some form of internalised language has long been recognised and the tendency generally has been to equate inner speech with thought itself.[59] In the *Theaetetus* Socrates defines thinking as discourse and judgment as statement pronounced, not aloud to someone else, but silently to oneself (189e–190a; c.f. *Sophist* 263e–264a). The idea also appears in Locke and Condillac, among others. The bulk of the physiological evidence for the existence of inner speech has come from psychologists experimenting in the motor theory of consciousness. Evidence has been adduced that thinking is difficult, if not impossible, when muscular activity is inhibited, and electro-myographic study of the vocal organs, particularly the larynx, tongue and lips, reveals the presence of micro-movements of the speech musculature during problem solving and silent reading.[60] These movements, it is claimed, are the outward indicators of inner speech. Although speech normally becomes internalised at about the seventh year, its rudiments are clearly present in adult readers. Even the most skilled readers are aware of some form of vocalisation while they are reading, from whispering, lip movements or feelings of tension in the lips or larynx at one extreme, to a form of speech at the other so implicit that no physical observations can be made. Some readers report a stream of speech running through their heads, often annoying and difficult to turn off. The level of this subvocal activity appears in many cases to correlate very closely with the difficulty of the task. In the face of especial difficulty, adults as well as children will 'think out loud' or move their lips when reading, particularly if the language is not their own. Whether or not subvocalisation is essential to silent reading, it does appear that 'the inner hearing or pronunci-ation, or both, of what is read, is a constituent part of the reading of by far the most of people as they ordinarily and actually read'.[61]

The existence of inner speech is difficult to account for. It is possible that thinking is inseparable from language, that inner speech is just, as it were, 'the noise the brain makes when it is working';[62] or it may be that we find it impossible once we know a language in its spoken form to dissociate the phonetic properties of words from their abstract symbolic function. There is, however, no doubt that subvocalisation during reading is of great help to an author, because inner speech entails inner hearing, and the inner hearing prompts the question of whose voice it is that we hear when we read. The French psychologist Victor Egger, arguing that inner speech originates not in motor but in auditory representations of a spoken language, was in no doubt that every voice is unique in its qualities of rhythm, pitch, intensity, and timbre, and that inner speech is for the most part an imitation of one's own inimitable voice.[63] In view of this, we can now perhaps appreciate a little more of Campuzano's purpose in getting Peralta to read the Dogs' Colloquy for himself. As Peralta reads, the dogs' words are articulated in his inner ear with the characteristic rhythm and timbre of his own voice. His identification with the text is made thereby all the more complete. In reading, their words become his own as their voices are obliterated by his.

In Campuzano's tactic, Cervantes shows how aware he was of the importance of a reader's identification with the work, and how the silent reading of a written text affords a unique opportunity for an author to promote that identification. It is, like so many of our automatic responses, difficult to appreciate until we are deprived of it or until our memory of another voice usurps our own. Some readers find that their enjoyment of a novel is spoiled as much by hearing it read on the radio as by seeing it adapted for cinema or television.[64] My own reading of Dorothy Sayers and John Le Carré is not unpleasantly coloured by the voices of Ian Carmichael and Sir Alec Guinness. The identification of reader and text via the reader's own voice may be one more contributory factor to the view that silent reading is a more mature and more satisfying experience than reading aloud or being read to. Even reading aloud to oneself, although the quality of voice is the same as it would be for silent reading, can seem to intrude on the intimacy of reader and text. This was certainly the complaint of Richalm of Schönthal who noted the following in a much-quoted passage of a short treatise on the distractions which devils cause to men of spiritual intention:

Oftentimes when I am reading straight from the book and in thought only, as I am wont, they make me read aloud word by word, so that they may deprive me so much the more of the inward understanding thereof, and that I may the less penetrate into the interior force of the reading, the more I pour myself out in exterior speech.[65]

His dismay is understandable. If, as we have seen, silent reading arises out of fluency, and if fluent reading depends on fluent understanding then his need to articulate is a clear sign that he did indeed lack the necessary inward understanding of the text. It was not his reading aloud that deprived him of understanding but his uncertain grasp of the sense that caused him to read aloud and to feel less than satisfied by what he read.

By contrast, no such lack of understanding or satisfaction appears to have marred Francisco de Quevedo's reading, if we are to judge from what he says in that marvellous late sonnet, written in exile and addressed to González de Salas:

> Retirado en la paz de estos desiertos,
> con pocos, pero doctos libros juntos,
> vivo en conversación con los difuntos,
> y escucho con mis ojos a los muertos.[66]

In the peace of desolation, Quevedo pores over a few books that inspire and comfort him, listening to their dead authors with his eyes. This is a *conversación* in more ways than one. If he feels that they speak to him it can only be his own inner voice that he hears as he reads. He speaks, in a sense, *for* them. But he would also have felt the need on occasion to answer back, to speak *to* them. In doing this he would have been doing no more than we as readers ordinarily do whenever we read a text with understanding, bringing not just linguistic knowledge to the elucidation of the words, but an understanding, however rudimentary or tentative, of life and the world in which we live. These wider frames of reference become more important as we move from comprehension at the word or sentence level towards a consideration of comprehension at the level of the text. For, as Quevedo's sonnet also testifies, reading is not an instantaneous activity but one that takes place over a considerable – and for a man in exile a seemingly interminable – length of time.

It is difficult, and it is likely to remain so for some time, to be at all precise about the process by which we are able to understand a lengthy text. The jurisdiction of grammar appears to come to an abrupt halt at the sentence boundary. Beyond that lie empty stretches of wilderness ruled only by the much less tangible authority of style and convention. The analysis of discourse is in its infancy and it is only comparatively recently that any great attention has been given to the question.[67] However, it is likely that the principles of discourse processing are not unrelated to the ways in which we perform other complex cognitive tasks such as visual perception, thinking and problem solving, in which large amounts of information have to be organised and reduced in ways which make storage and retrieval possible. The fact that reading is a linear process which takes place in time means that a reader's perspective is constantly shifting. At the moment of reading the reader is in close contact with the text and with the specific propositions of the text. He will not be reading word by word, but at the same time, unless his attention falters, all the propositions of the text will at some time pass through his mind and be immediately present to him. As he reads on, each of these propositions will fade into the past and become gradually more and more distant from him. It is impossible for most people to keep a detailed account of the propositional content of a text, quite apart from the words in which it is expressed, in the mind for more than a few seconds. If we ask someone to read a paragraph and then ask them if they understood it, they may truthfully answer that they did without being able to give anything more than the vaguest account of its content unless we prompt them with questions. What, then, has happened to everything they have read? Has it, so to speak, gone in one eye and straight out the other?

An answer to the question might begin with the observation that a coherent text is constructed in such a way that at any moment it is unnecessary to have the whole of the preceding text present in detail before the mind. That is, it takes the diminishing perspective of what has gone before into account. The text is continuously summarising itself and distinguishing in various ways between information which has already been given (theme) and information which is new (rheme). The thematic organisation of the text takes into account that we will not be able to recall what we have already read except in the most general terms, and the writer uses various devices of reference – anaphoric, cataphoric, and exophoric – substitution and ellipsis to package what he has already said, or what he takes for granted, and mark it off from what he is currently saying. In this sentence, therefore, the word 'therefore' treats the rest of the paragraph as a thematic entity and conveniently incorporates it as a single unit into this proposition.

The existence of pronouns, relatives and words like 'therefore', 'however', 'and' or 'but' is direct linguistic evidence of the existence of units of meaning above and beyond the text proper,[68] units which ensure its cohesiveness from the writer's point of view and its intelligibility from the reader's. As we read we are continually looking for coherence, for pattern and order, and turning the small detail of what we read into more generalised schemes. We ignore and delete from our generalisations everything that is repetitive or synonymous with an existing scheme and everything that can be inferred from it. We select the most important parts of the text, compare them with a scheme we have built up, and either integrate them or modify the scheme to take account of new information. As the text progresses we may have to construct a new scheme out of two or more others, thereby adding another layer to the hierarchy of generalisation. It is by this construction of schemata that we are also able to understand a text before we have finished reading it. Fore-understanding (*Vorverständnis*) entails constructing from a scheme a provisional hypothesis about a number of possible outcomes,[69] just as we use the grammar of the opening of a sentence to predict its final completed structure. In the sentence 'When he ate it, Tom found the pie indigestible' the lack of anaphoric reference for 'it' is not a problem since we can work for the time being on the assumption that whatever 'it' is it will presumably be edible. The fact that the pie turned out to be inedible makes the sentence a perfect grammatical analogue of Tom's experience. In the same way we will expect the outcome of a traditional novel to be consistent with what has preceded it and will be disappointed if it is not. Only detective fiction is allowed to tamper with this convention, and even then the play it makes with defeated expectation confirms the vigour of the prejudice. All the time, then, whether we are looking back over what we have read or anticipating what is to come, we are measuring the schemata constructed from the text against the assumptions which we bring to it in the first place, and it is by means of this constant testing for congruence between our own representations of the world and the author's that we evaluate what he has to tell us and decide whether we can learn anything from him.

One of the most significant aspects of the synthesising process in reading is the importance of implicit inference.[70] We very rarely make explicit deductions while we are reading, but the drawing of inferences is an inevitable and even essential part of the business of making sense of a text or of any new situation we meet. The ability to draw inferences depends on selecting from the memory the appropriate 'frame' or structured piece of knowledge about a typical situation and applying it to a specific circumstance. Any information which is not made explicit can thereby be supplied by default.[71] Unless we are told that a character has only one leg we assume that he has two; unless we are told otherwise we may infer that he went into the restaurant to eat and not to have a haircut. This dynamic interplay between implication and inference allows considerable economy in communication. Inference is also important in the clarification of grammatical difficulties. In the notorious sequence 'Charles makes love with his wife twice a week. So does John'[72] the ambiguity can only be resolved by inference from, say, the social milieu from which the words are taken and what we know about Charles, John and Charles's wife. But inference is also present in cases where there seem to be no difficulties of reference. Consider the following extract:

> They had unchained the door to him, they had questioned him even before they took his coat: tersely and intently. Were there any compromising materials on the body, George? Any that would link him with us?[73]

At least six inferences underlie the points of reference of the two subject pronouns 'they', the two cataphoric pronouns 'him', the possessive adjective 'his' and the anaphoric pronouns 'him' and 'us'. Understanding this text involves making these inferences, whether we are aware of them or not, and although they are prepared by the author, it is the reader who supplies them. It is he who is responsible for the complex network of inferential 'bridges' by which the propositions of the author are bound together into a coherent whole.[74] This does not mean that the reader is free to impose whatever meaning he wishes on the text: the limits of his interpretation as well as his very existence (anaphora presupposes the existence of someone who will refer back) are defined by the lexical and syntactic organisation of the text. But it does mean that whatever sense the reader does make of the text will be his own work.

The role of inference in comprehension is clearly of particular interest to writers and readers of fiction, since the more an author can leave to the reader's imagination and the more information the reader can be induced to supply for himself, the greater will be his identity with the work, and the more persuasive will the work seem in consequence. That is why literary texts are often thought to be particularly rich in their use of implication. From the extract from Le Carré quoted above the reader would be able to deduce a good deal about the characters and situation even if he had not read the rest of the book. We know, though we are not specifically told, that 'they' have sent George, a man who is well known to them and whom they evidently trust (they send him on a delicate mission and call him by his Christian name), to inspect the corpse of another man who was also known to them; they are anxious that the connection between them and the deceased should not come to light as this would evidently cause them embarrassment; 'they' operate behind closed doors in an atmosphere of security or even secrecy yet either they or George, or both, must be in some official capacity in order to have access to the body; they are unable or unwilling to conduct the investigation themselves presumably, again, for fear of embarrassment; they are impatient to know his conclusions, but it seems (they do eventually take his coat) that he is able to set their minds at rest. Now this is a fairly routine example, chosen at random, of the way in which a good writer can control the inferences which he wishes his reader to draw, and to make him 'flesh out' the bare and sometimes oblique information which he presents. His purpose is clearly to promote the credibility of his narrative by using basic procedures of linguistic comprehension to make the reader into his co-creator.

The previous example shows the case of a writer exercising a high degree of control over what he wants his reader to think. Writers are not always, indeed not normally, so strict. Indeed, it was part of Plato's case against the written word that since it requires interpretation (Homer is no longer with us to explain what he meant and even if he were there is no guarantee that he would know) it is susceptible to misinterpretation. A book does not know 'how to address the right people and not address the wrong' (*Phaedrus*, 275e). Yet even if he wished to, a writer could not possibly hope to predetermine every response his reader would make. The writer cannot say everything there is to say about his created world (he could not do it if he were writing about the real world) and has to be content to leave the text indeterminate in many places. The notion that a literary text contains 'places of indeterminacy' (*Unbestimmtheitsstellen*) originated in the work of Roman Ingarden and has come to play an important part in our understanding of the reading of literature.[75] In the following passage Ingarden describes the nature of textual indeterminacy and the way it operates:

The presence of places of indeterminacy in the objective stratum of the literary work permits two possible ways of reading. Sometimes the reader tries to regard all places of indeterminacy as such and to leave them indeterminate in order to apprehend the work in its characteristic structure. But usually we read literary works in a quite different way. We overlook the places of indeterminacy as such and involuntarily fill many of them out with determinacies which are not justified by the text. Thus in our reading we go beyond the text in various points without being clearly aware of it. We do so partially under the suggestive influence of the text but partially, also, under the influence of a natural inclination, since we are accustomed to considering individual things and persons as completely determinate. Another reason for this filling-out is that the objects portrayed in the literary work of art generally have the ontic character of reality, so that it seems natural to us that they be clearly and completely determined just as genuine, real, individual objects are.[76]

Such reading between the lines is one aspect of our tendency to seek to impose order on the unfamiliar, to seek consistency even at the expense of discarding details which resist integration into a pattern. Frank Kermode, in a telling survey of attempts to explain the twin enigmas of the Man in the Macintosh in Joyce's *Ulysses* and the Boy in the Shirt in Mark's gospel (14. 51–2), has drawn attention to a deep-seated reluctance in readers to leave narrative inconsistencies alone. We are all what he calls 'pleromatists', 'fulfillment men', seeking 'to accommodate the discrepancies and dissonances into some larger scheme' and sharing a conviction 'that somehow, in some occult fashion, if we could only detect it, everything will be found to hang together'.[77] Modern writers of fiction have very often exploited this natural tendency to discover patterns in or impose patterns on an apparently disordered narrative by increasing the proportion of indeterminacy in their texts to breaking point. They have said to their readers, in effect, 'what do you make of this?'. And the nature of the answers we give tells us a great deal about ourselves. Any degree of indeterminacy in a text constitutes a challenge to our powers of 'bridging' the gaps; a high proportion of indeterminacy makes reading a novel into a form of organised introspection.

That readers use inference to build the information in the text into a picture of a fictional world raises important questions concerning aesthetic belief and the ontological status of a work of fiction, and these, be it remembered, were the central issues of Plato's most severe criticisms of literary artists. Aesthetics has provided us with a crucial distinction between the work of art on the one hand and the aesthetic object on the other. The work of art is a material analogue of the artist's mental image; the aesthetic object is a mental image constructed by the observer from his contact with and contemplation of the work of art.[78] In the case of literature, the work of art is constituted by the objective configuration of the words on the page; our comprehension of those words and the mental images we construct from them constitute the aesthetic object. The text as such is compounded of language and its dynamism depends on the essentially dynamic nature of communication and language use; it is always virtual and is realised only in the act of reading. The aesthetic object is compounded of thought; reading and understanding a text involves thinking the meaning of the text. As Ingarden puts it: 'I extract the meaning from the text, so to speak, and change it into the actual intention of my mental act of understanding, into an intention identical with the word or sentence intention of the text. Then I really "understand" the text.' But the thoughts we read are those of another person: reading entails thinking those thoughts, not as the thoughts of another, but as one's own. As with all language use, writing and reading is a type of thought transference: the fictional realities implicit in the book become predicates of the reader's self.[79] While we are reading, rational disbelief is displaced in our minds by the mental creativity which comprehension entails, and since we cannot simultaneously think something and not think it, identification with and belief in the products of that creativity are inevitable.

We saw in chapter 2 that the most sophisticated and far-reaching of Plato's arguments against literary art had to do with the central paradox of fiction, its ability to convince its audience in the face of their rational disbelief. In this chapter I have tried to suggest some reasons why this paradox comes about. Plato argued that the key to the persuasiveness of the poets lay in their misuse of language and he was undoubtedly right in seeing this as the centre of the problem. 'Misuse' may, however, be rather too strong a term for what they do. Non-literary language has within it a great potential for creativity which arises from our use of words not just to convey information, but to effect changes in the circumstances around us, to perform actions, to persuade. Moreover, there is in our everyday use of language a compression which imaginative writers have been quick to exploit: we use words as if they referred to things rather than to concepts, and are often willing to create referents where none exist in order not to break with our habit. Most important of all for the writer, though, are the requirements that language places on the listener. Without his active participation, the medium simply will not work. He has to bring a vast amount of knowledge, both of the workings of the medium and of the world, to bear on the decipherment of the spoken words. In so doing he makes the words his own and puts into effect the intention of the speaker. Reading if anything increases the responsibilities of the receiver, who has to perform the same tasks as the listener, but often over a much longer period of time and without the paralinguistic clues to assist him. The sheer weight of information to be absorbed will usually make a reader's contribution greater than a listener's even though a written text may attempt to be correspondingly clearer and more explicit. But the skilful writer of fiction will put as heavy a burden on the reader as he can, asking him not just to supply meaning sentence by sentence, but to build the text into a coherent and credible mental construct, filled-out almost *ad libitum* with all kinds of unspecified yet convincing detail. And if in the process, as seems likely, the account is credited with the reader's own inner voice, then the rapture of the fiction will be all the more complete.

Now there is, of course, a good deal more to reading fiction than this, and that significant and sizeable extra is what the authors of the picaresque were primarily concerned with. Nevertheless, an admission of the fact that good fiction is, while it is being read, often compulsively credible, and an attempt to understand why this should be so, are essential preliminaries to an account of how the creative writers of Golden-Age Spain may be said to have tackled Plato's objections to literary art. As we have seen, the neo-Aristotelian theorists' recourse to verisimilitude was completely unacceptable as a reply. At best it is irrelevant to Plato's moral and metaphysical objections to an activity that imbued the manifestly false with the vividness of lived experience, and at worst, in urging writers to bring the fictional and the plausible into greater alignment, they were merely promoting the very element of credibility in literature that the Platonist arguments were out to challenge. A proper reply to Plato has to show that the grip of the book on the reader's mind can be loosened and that his imaginative participation in fiction can be turned to good effect. For the remainder of this book I shall want to argue that this was what the picaresque authors set out to demonstrate in practice in their work.

4

Breaking the illusion

In a brilliant evocation of the rapture of reading, Wallace Stevens has described with compelling accuracy the experience of anyone who has ever come under the thrall of a powerful illusion:

> The reader became the book; and summer night
>
> Was like the conscious being of the book.
> The house was quiet and the world was calm.
>
> The words were spoken as if there was no book,
> Except that the reader leaned above the page,
>
> Wanted to lean, wanted much most to be
> The scholar to whom his book is true, to whom
>
> The summer night is like a perfection of thought.
> The house was quiet because it had to be.
>
> The quiet was part of the meaning, part of the mind:
> The access of perfection to the page . . .[1]

The absolute empathy between the reader and the book, the way in which the reader's surroundings, the quiet calm of the summer night, become part of the reality of the book and bear witness to its truthfulness and perfection, all help to recreate that ecstatic state in which the world, the reader and the book become one. We have seen that many moralists, critics and writers of Golden-Age Spain took a much less sanguine view of the captivation induced by reading, and set about ensuring that the powerful illusions of literature at least were made safe if they could not be suppressed altogether.

Part of their requirements might have been satisfied by a number of devices which appear in the secular literature of the period and which might loosely be termed 'protective'. I have already suggested that the danger inherent in the reading of vernacular prose fiction was much greater than that posed by verse, simply because prose offered 'a familiar relation of such things as pass every day before our eyes'[2] in a language which its readers could readily understand and recognise as their own. A similar distinction of credibility lies behind Matthew Prior's 'Answer to Chloe Jealous':

> What I speak my fair Chloe, and what I write, shows
> The difference there is betwixt Nature and Art:
> I court others in verse, but love thee in prose:
> And they have my whimsies, but thou hast my heart.[3]

It is in verse, then, that we might expect to find those devices which have traditionally marked off the poetic world from the real world and helped to define the aesthetic otherness of the work of art. Malón de Chaide may well complain that the poems of Garcilaso de la Vega are like a knife in the hands of a madman, but Garcilaso might equally well reply that he has done all that is required of him as a poet to ensure that his poems cannot be mistaken for reality. Four of the five *Canciones* end with the poet's invocation to the poem, the first Eclogue begins with a dedication and contains several references to the poet's creative role, and the third is almost totally concerned with the ability of art to subdue and transcend human emotion. Surely there are frames enough here? The third Eclogue is, indeed, almost entirely composed of frames, while Garcilaso's adoption of the pastoral world for his stage and the poets of classical and Renaissance Italy for his idiom shows a determined effort to maintain a proper distinction between what is said in art and what is felt in life.[4]

There is, however, little that is defensive in Garcilaso's use, or any other major poet's use, of conventional devices to frame his work and give it artistic integrity. Rather than protecting his readers from the products of his creative imagination he is, more likely, asserting his role as their originator and controlling genius. It is unlikely in any case that a poet like Garcilaso would have felt that his own readership, one that was almost certainly skilled in the arts of reading with discrimination and perspicacity, needed the protection that such framing devices might provide. For most readers, however absorbed in their encounter with the text, the real world might also be thought to constitute a more than adequate frame, once the book is closed.

Writers of prose fiction were in a rather different position from poets like Garcilaso, in that their audience was – or was thought to be – much more impressionable and their trade much more consciously illusionistic. Nevertheless, the same kinds of provisos might be attached to their use of some analogous devices in prose fiction. As Keith Whinnom has pointed out, one of the outstanding characteristics of Golden-Age prose fiction is its markedly experimental nature.[5]

Self-conscious narration, authorial intervention, the use of *admiratio* and incongruity, the play of narrative voices and points of view, all can be and undoubtedly were on occasion used to assert the fictional nature of the work and to prevent the readership from identifying overmuch with its characters and situations. Nevertheless, in the hands of a supreme artist like Cervantes, each of these techniques can equally well become an additional weapon in the armoury of self-conscious artistry, yet one more device by which the author projects himself as the skilled illusionist and manipulates his reader's credulity at will. No amount of warnings and reminders has stopped generations of readers and critics from thinking and talking about Quixote and Sancho and the rest, *as if* they really existed.

What is more important for the present purpose is the fact that, even if a writer were able, by the use of such devices of narration, to protect his readers from imaginative identification with the fiction, such protection would be unlikely to satisfy the Platonic case against literature. Simply labelling a poison POISON does not make it any less poisonous. The Platonic case strikes at the very nature of fiction as written language, as Socrates makes clear:

The painter's products stand before us as though they were alive: but if you question them, they maintain a most majestic silence. It is the same with written words: they seem to talk to you as though they were intelligent, but if you ask them anything about what they say, from a desire to be instructed, they go on telling you just the same thing for ever.   (*Phaedrus*, 275d)

Books are by nature contumacious.[6] The written word lives outside the true domain of language, the give and take of dialogue, and is restricted entirely to its declarative function. Written words only state, do not ask and cannot answer back. Writing is 'closed' while dialogue is 'open',[7] dynamic and constantly in movement. Only a text that was open and dynamic in a similar way would stand a chance of satisfying Socrates's strictures, and authors who set out further to enthral their readers while pretending to concede the groundlessness of what they are saying merely compound the problem.

Nevertheless, many of the self-conscious narrative devices used in Golden-Age prose fiction do represent a significant step in the direction of the interrogative text,[8] the text which questions itself from within and forces the reader likewise to examine his own position in the dialogue. We have seen that the illusionism inherent in the rapturous reading of fiction depends for its success on the reader's assimilating the words of the text to himself, and making them his own through his act of comprehension and the imaginative filling-out of the text that this involves. Such a collaboration is not, though, a dialogue since the words of the text are not seen as those of another but become the reader's own. This occupation of the reader's own mind by the thoughts of another forms the basis of the distraction and mental relaxation afforded by reading. Such relaxation is undoubtedly a source of pleasure, but the Spanish Golden Age also demanded profit from its reading, and profit suggests a much more critical, thoughtful approach to reading in which the reader does not 'become the book' but remains aware of the voice of the book as something other than himself. Authorial intervention could be one way of encouraging this approach. Neo-Aristotelian critics seem – not for the first time – to have allowed themselves to be led into some self-contradiction on this point. Authors intervene extensively in the romances of chivalry whereas classical authorities, including Aristotle, advocated a restrained narrator.[9] But the critics who followed Aristotle in recommending that the poet speak as little as possible in his own voice in the narration seemed to have missed the point. In this case Aristotle was an ineffective weapon with which to placate the Platonists since what interested him most was the way practising artists successfully plied their trade, and he counselled restraint on narrators because he felt from experience that that was the best way of sustaining an illusion.[10] But if the writers of the romances could intervene in their narratives and still be accused of irresponsible illusionism it seems unlikely that there is much to relate the effectiveness of the illusion to the prominence of the author's profile. As Forcione says, when Don Quixote intervenes in his narratives to comment on the events and the morality thereof, he does so not to affirm or deny the historicity of what he is saying but to 'reinforce the effect that he as author is in firm control'.[11]

A further step in the direction of the interrogative text can be seen in the requirement that the literature of Golden-Age Spain should cause *admiratio* in the reader. Wonder and astonishment result in the main from the reader's unexpected encounter with the exceptional, whether it be a surprising turn of events or *peripeteia*, the unravelling of a complex dramatic situation, or a powerful evocation of the marvellous. In all its forms, including its stylistic analogues of virtuoso writing and visual vividness (*energia*), the effectiveness of *admiratio* depends on a momentary withdrawal by the author of his words from the reader's grasp. In order to be surprised, a reader has to be made momentarily aware that the words are those of another, even if the surprise is one of recognised appropriateness. The technique is essentially one of distancing or alienating the work in order to stir[12] the reader's mind instead of lulling it or hypnotising it. *Admiratio* does not, however, depend on a total breech of illusion, but rather a sudden shift of focus which gives the reader a fleeting awareness of the work's otherness before the illusion settles in again around his adjusted scale of values. Still less does *admiratio* depend on verisimilitude: just as the spell of romance is woven quite independently of empirical belief, so too the sudden shifts of direction that provoke *admiratio* depend on shifts of the reader's attitude to the work rather than on larger or smaller doses of reality or fantasy injected into the narrative.

In some ways, then, while *admiratio* as a technique has an element of self-consciousness about it and the pleasure it gives is also essentially a conscious pleasure, the ability to surprise and astonish is one more of the ways in which authors retain their hold on the imaginations of their readership. Cases of *admiratio*, like the incongruities and inconsistencies that writers like Cervantes frequently introduced into their narratives, do, to an extent, serve as *Verfremdungseffekte*,[13] reminding the reader that what he is witnessing is art not life, but at the same time they suggest 'that the pleasures of the imagination are all the more enjoyable precisely if we are made aware of their unreality'.[14]

It may be significant, nevertheless, that alienating effects occur in prose fiction at a time when writers of both prose and poetry were increasingly concerned to make their texts more difficult to read, to put an ever greater strain on their readers' intelligence. The *conceptista* movement in Spanish poetry and prose is the most obvious example of the tendency, and at first sight this seems to contradict the received notion of what happened to reading habits and literary styles as printed books became a more familiar feature of the literary landscape. Marshall McLuhan has argued that the effect of printing was to increase reading speeds in the sixteenth century to the extent that readers could 'speed over the super-highways of assembly-line prose'.[15] This view may, however, be based on some anachronistic responses. Mediaeval manuscripts can be difficult for modern readers who are unused to them, but those who copied and commissioned them could well have read them as easily as the letter forms (which were often based on book hands) of the printed book. Standardised letter forms make very rapid reading possible for modern readers, but the comparative rarity and cost of books in the sixteenth century might well have encouraged a more reverent approach. In any case, it is difficult to imagine any reader skimming over the super-highways of, say, Quevedo's *Sueños*, nor could Alemán's or Gracián's prose style be described as 'macadamised' (p. 129).

It may, of course, be that these and other writers made their work difficult precisely because they felt that printed books had made reading a little too cursory and because they wanted to re-establish habits of close reading that they felt were in danger of disappearing. Or, and here we may be on firmer ground, they were attempting to put back into their readers' experience of literature the sense of a dialectic that private reading had taken out. Whatever the reasons, the kinds of difficulty posed by Spanish *conceptismo* do undoubtedly have the effect of slowing the reader down, making him decipher the text, making him conscious of his own acts of comprehension, and requiring him to participate actively and intellectually in solving the enigma of the text.[16] In doing this the *conceptistas* are doing two things that might be thought to help the breaking of illusion: they are drawing attention to the text as language, helping the reader to focus on its opacity, its unreliability, its contingency, helping him to see the text not as a transparent window giving access to a world beyond, but as a stumbling-block that demands to be treated on its own terms. At the same time they are making their readers aware of the extent of their own contribution to the literary process and of their ability to grow and develop as rational and creative beings.[17]

Conceptista prose writing in Golden-Age Spain takes place, however, only on the very edge of fiction. The *Sueños* and the *Criticón* do not deal in illusionism and where wit is present in fiction to any marked degree (*La pícara Justina* for example), it is wholly incompatible with illusion. Indeed, wit is used by seventeenth-century prose writers rather to expose illusion than to create it, and it is this peculiarly analytical aspect to wit that makes the *Buscón* such a corrosive piece of writing. The cultivation of difficulty in Spanish seventeenth-century prose can only, then, serve as an illustration of a general trend rather than a specific attempt to remedy the problems which concerned contemporary moralists and critics of fiction. Writers of fiction knew that there was only a limited extent to which they could undermine their own creations and remain in business. Fiction demands illusion or it becomes something else, and though Cervantes was obviously aware of developments in prose style going on around him, his use of self-conscious narration and other similar devices is kept well below the threshold at which it would seriously disrupt the reader's progress through the book. The fact remains that compelling fiction entails rapt reading and that none of the techniques mentioned above would be enough, of itself, to break the illusion that results from reading. No matter how often the reader is reminded through frames, or authorial interventions or surprises or incongruities in the text that what he is reading is not true, aesthetic belief always asserts itself by virtue of the factors discussed in chapter 3. However much the illusion is questioned from without, the spell of fiction is safe as long as it does not question itself from within. When an author intervenes in his narrative to comment on the activities of his creatures he is not intervening in but emerging from the fiction. His remarks force him to stand, with the reader, outside the fictional world, and though he may leave it in abeyance for a moment he also leaves it intact and free to reassert its hold on the imagination once he has had his say.

The problem, then, is to produce a form of fiction which will enable the reader to identify with the products of the fictional world yet at the same time encourage him to stand apart from them and view them with discrimination. Any technique that dispersed the illusion completely would not serve the purpose since it would be tantamount to taking the easy way out and banning fiction completely. Nor can the reader stand so far detached from the work that he cannot cooperate with its potential of illusion. If falling prey to the illusion is an essential part of reading fiction, then responsible fiction cannot afford to dispense with this aspect of the reading experience. Rather, that experience of reading must be made part of the book, and the reader must be able to look critically at his own reading. Making the reading of the book part of the book involves giving the reader an active and conscious role to play in it. A book that could do this would make reading into a dialectic in which the reader does not become the book nor stands completely detached from it, but is both inside it and outside it in a dynamic state of identification and alienation.

Richard Wollheim has described this state of being part of and separate from a work of art in an essay on the phenomenology of vision.[18] When we see a representation of something in art, we do not take it for real nor judge the excellence of the representation as art by the readiness with which it enables us to take it for real. 'To see a drawing as a representation of something is [not] to take it, or to be disposed to take it, for that thing: it is rather to understand that thing by it . . . we are able simultaneously to take in, or admire, a drawing as a configuration and as a representation' (p. 139). The ability to grasp simultaneously *that* something represents as well as *what* it represents is an essential part of all mature experience of art. Art engages and detaches the spectator at one and the same time,[19] and literary art is, or should be, no exception.

How the authors of some Spanish picaresque narratives attempted and achieved this simultaneous engagement and detachment of their readers is the subject of the rest of this book. All the authors go about this task in different ways but all the works have an overall strategy in common. They all seek to make the reader's relationship to the text dynamic rather than static; they all give the reader an active part to play, casting him in roles and making him adopt positions that are often shown to be untenable; they all refuse the reader a consistent viewpoint by which to make sense of the fictional world, making him question the veracity of what he is told and the plausibility of what he thinks and feels in response. Most use illusion creatively, correlating it with gullibility or unthinking states of mind, or with moral blindness or corruption. Most use the natural empathy of reader and protagonist as a snare and make this identification a prelude to an unhappy awakening. In all these works author, protagonist and reader become entangled in a web of irony from which no one escapes. Above all, these books are seeking to create a form and a language that will answer the Platonic case against literature by bridging the gulf between understanding and experience. Gabriel Josipovici has shown how this gulf is perfectly expressed in a passage from Thomas Hooker:

> There is great odds betwixt the knowledge of a traveller, that in his own person hath taken a view of many coasts . . . and by experience hath been an eye-witness . . . and another that sits by his fireside, and happily reads the story of these in a book, or views the proportion of these in a map. . . . The like difference is there in the right discerning of sin. . . . The one sees the history of sin, the other the nature of it; the one knows the relation of sin as it is mapped out, and recorded; the other the poison, as by experience he hath found and proved it.[20]

The traveller experiences but cannot express, while the map-reader understands but cannot experience. Any attempt at expression turns one man's experience into another man's map. A middle way has to be found between 'meaningless sensation' and 'knowledge devoid of feeling' (p. 187), a form of fiction which will ensure that the reader is not only unharmed by reading but, through reading, comes to understand his experience and experience his understanding.

La vida de Lazarillo de Tormes

When a novelist sets out to write a novel he is doing nothing substantially different from what we all do every day. Narrative is part of daily life, a way of remembering, of making sense of what has happened to us, of sharing our experience with others, persuading them, placating them, or taking part in a ritual social activity. Narrative is not an aesthetic invention but 'a primary act of mind transferred to art from life'.[21] In life as well as art a narrator needs an audience who not only listens but, by listening, sets in motion the act of narration and keeps it under control. The presence of the listener determines what the narrator will tell him and how he will tell it.[22] Natural oral narrative, therefore, is essentially dynamic. It cannot take place in a void and it always has a purpose – to report, to instruct, to persuade, to entertain, to cement social relationships, to lie – and that purpose is always expressed explicitly or implicitly in the narrative. William Labov's analysis of natural narrative among black American adolescents has led him to conclude that every good narrator is constantly warding off the words 'So what?'[23] A story without a point leaves the listener uneasy or uninterested, and a stranger who beards us with unwelcome accounts of his war service or his step-daughter's hernia will leave us perplexed and wanting to say 'Yes, but why are you telling me all this?'

His point, of course, is that he is trying to make contact, and his meaning lies not in what he says but in the fact of his saying it. Narrative, then, is above all an activity. When the Papago Indians gather together to hear their tribal myths recited to them they signify their participation in the communal event by repeating the last word of each sentence,[24] just as a Christian congregation adds its 'amen'. An important part of the meaning of these myths lies in the fact that the audience has gathered together to hear them and that it expresses its sense of community by so doing.

When a story is written down two significant changes come about. In the first place, a written narrative is often lacking in context. No longer is it composed or retold in a certain place at a certain time for a specific purpose; by having to be available to anyone, anywhere, it becomes, in a sense, pointless. In the second place and as a consequence of the first, a written narrative falls victim to the circumstances under which it is read, by an individual in private. The listener to an oral narrative has to proceed at the pace of the narrator.

A reader is freed from the constraints imposed by the living presence of the story-teller and the rest of the audience. A reader can control the pace and the depth of his own reading, recap and pause for thought. He can start to ask questions about the story and look for a meaning which is distinct from the story's function as an activity.[25] Printing and private reading can significantly alter the nature of the narration, rendering it much more static than oral narrative and shifting the burden of meaning from what the story does to what it says.

Any narrator composing for publication in printed form will have to take these facts into account when he is writing. If he wishes to retain the dynamism of natural narrative, the give and take that is essential if the reader is to be anything more than a passive and perplexed onlooker, then the writer has to set up a role in which the unknown reader can cast himself, conjure up a fictional person whom he can use as a sounding-board and whose anticipated responses can act as a shaping force for the narrative. As Walter Ong has put it, 'the writer's audience is always a fiction'.[26] Furthermore, the writer must ensure that his imagined reader is given a clear sense, whether implicitly or explicitly, of the point and purpose of the book and the role he is to play in it, if he is to evaluate what it says. Perhaps these considerations help to account for the rich prologue literature in Golden-Age Spain.

In the prologue to *La vida de Lazarillo de Tormes* (1554) both the anonymous author of the work and its protagonist have a great deal to say on these matters. In reality there are two prologues, one addressed by an author to his reader, one couched in the form of a letter from the protagonist to the unnamed recipient. One is set in the public domain, the other belongs to a private, fictionalised world. The two prologues overlap and are made to shade into each other with infinite skill and cunning; indeed, so skilfully made is the join that it is difficult to locate its exact position in the text. There are no protective frames here. An unwitting victim of a consummate sleight of hand, the reader begins the prologue in the real world, a punter seeking admission to a fictional world of which, by the end of the prologue, he has become one of the central characters.

The author begins with an impressive and reassuring display of the conventions of the prologue. There is no book so bad that some good cannot come of it; one man's meat is another man's poison; the travails of authorship deserve the rewards of exposure. Yet this honest aspiration is tempered with a decent amount of self-deprecation: the book is a poor thing, a 'nonada' (28)[27] written in a 'grosero estilo' by a man who makes no claim to be any better than his fellows. So self-effacing is he, indeed, that he quite forgets to mention his name. This unfortunate oversight should not, however, be allowed to detract from his evident seriousness of purpose or from the exemplary character of the story he has to tell. Lightly-worn erudition does him credit: Pliny and Cicero are there, together with an allusion to Horace. The expected antithesis of pleasure and profit, however, appears disconcertingly as a pair of near synonyms: 'pues podría ser que alguno que las lea halle algo que le agrade, y a los que no ahondaren tanto los deleite' (3–5) ('for it could be that a reader might find something to please him, and those who do not delve so deeply, something to delight them').[28] Carelessness again, perhaps, or the kind of forgivable lapse we might expect from an author capable of allowing accidental anonymity to thwart ambition.

As the first prologue developsm the safe public world of convention becomes more and more subject to contradictions and inconsistencies of this type. Does the example of the jouster unjustly praised by his lackey not contradict the previous two examples of the soldier and the preacher who perform their tasks creditably yet who are not averse to the extra spur that comes from praise? Does the fruit of the story lie in the fact that a man can live with so much ill-fortune, danger and adversity (30–31)? And if so, what does 'live with' mean? Put up with ill fortune or prosper in spite of it? This is a strange author indeed: he claims to be seeking public esteem yet omits to give his name; he alludes to conventional notions of the purpose of literature and gets them wrong; he gives an example that fails to illustrate its point and states his purpose in a phrase that contains a crucial ambiguity. All of this can hardly be the product of carelessness. Yet, whatever its purpose, one thing remains clear thus far; however much the author may play with the conventions of the prologue, the use of those conventions maintains the author and the reader in their well-defined roles. These roles become more confused with the appearance of 'Vuestra Merced'.

One of the many striking things about the prologue is the confidence with which the author begins. 'I am of opinion,' he says, 'that things so worthy of memory . . . ought by all reason to come abroad to the sight of many' (1–2; Rowland, p. 5). He is addressing a multitude of readers. He wants the book to be available to everybody (11). Writing is hard work and no one goes to all that trouble for one man alone (13–14). The book is offered 'that such as finde any taste in this my grosse Stile and noveltie, may pleasure and delight themselves therwith' (30; Rowland, p. 6). Why, then, is Vuestra Merced singled out, and why does an author who begins by writing for everybody end by writing for one man in particular? The shift from a 'yo' who has in mind an undefined plurality of third persons to a 'yo' who addresses a specific second person singular is fundamental to the way the prologue casts its spell. On the one hand, it marks the way in which the author-as-creator hands over his responsibilities to the protagonist-as-narrator. On the other hand, the shift from plural to singular is accompanied by a consequential change in the nature of the reader's role, from consumer to participant.

The double apostrophe to 'Vuestra Merced' ensures that these changes of role are carried out smoothly and imperceptibly. The first apostrophe seems designed at first sight to be little more than a flattering synecdoche, singling the reader out, but only as a representative of his kind. The author's continued modesty about the 'pobre servicio' (32) harks back to the 'nonada' (28) and continues to suggest a relationship of artist and patron, with the reader playing Dives to this Lazarus.[29]

The force of the two apostrophes is, however, cumulative and the second apostrophe of V.M. increases the feeling that our individual attention is being enlisted. The book, it seems, was written to commission. V.M. has written to its author requesting a full account in writing of something he calls 'the case' ('el caso', 34–5). The book, then, whatever the reasons for its publication as a book, was actually written initially for a specific if as yet undefined purpose. It is not an abstract piece of storytelling, but was written to explain something, or, as Claudio Guillén has put it, it is not a 'relato puro' but a 'relación'.[30] Almost imperceptibly we have slipped from the public world of the prologue into the private world of the fiction in which one man gives an account of himself to another. The introduction of V.M. enables Lázaro to make clear from the outset what his purpose is and enables the author to create a role for his reader to play. It is never made clear who V.M. is within the world of the fiction, and this seems deliberate. V.M. is a focal point of evaluation[31] rather than a specific fictional character. It may well be possible to define him to an extent. He is an establishment figure, a man of sufficient authority to call others to order, a friend and superior of the archpriest of San Salvador (7.25) ('Birds of a feather . . .'). But his main function is to give point to the narrative, to be an audience, and the lack of specific information about him makes it easier for the reader to adopt his viewpoint and grow into his role. V.M. is never anything more than a pronoun; no noun is supplied within the book for which that pronoun can stand. Only the reader can supply that missing person. Nor is it made clear, at this stage, what the 'caso' refers to. By the time we reach the end of the account it will be clearer: the 'caso' is the circumstances that obtain at the end of the account, the *ménage à trois* in which the gossips say that Lázaro and his wife and the archpriest are living. This unwillingness in the prologue to make the 'caso' specific must also be deliberate. It starts us *in medias res*, projecting us into a world where things are already happening, where the people involved know the score and where V.M.'s familiarity with the facts is taken for granted. The vagueness of the 'caso' ensures that by the time it becomes apparent to V.M. why he has commissioned this account, he has become too closely involved in the circumstances to be able to view them impartially.

Francisco Rico has shown how the 'caso' acts as the major structural principle of *Lazarillo de Tormes*.[32] It is both the beginning and the end, the pretext and the point of the narrative, and it shows that when Lázaro decides not to begin in the middle (35–6) he is mistaken. No one ever really begins at the beginning, and Lázaro is no exception. Like all good narrators he starts at the end, taking us directly to the heart of the matter, and alerting V.M. to the fact that his extensive account (extensive for a letter, but one of the shortest fictional narratives in Spanish literature), this 'entera noticia' (36), has been carefully designed to replace one set of appearances with another. For it is clear as early as the prologue that Lázaro has not done what was asked of him: V.M. has asked for an account of a set of circumstances and Lázaro has replied with an autobiography. By responding to V.M.'s request in this way Lázaro betrays his defensiveness.[33] He knows that things look bad for him. He knows that in a sense he is on trial. His tactics, then, are to divert attention from the present to the past. In so doing Lázaro will exploit the capacity of autobiography to conceal as well as reveal. Autobiography is revealing in that the act of narrating involves selecting and organising from experience: recounting one's life imposes an order on it, an order which grows out of selective memory and the thematic subordination of the past to the present.[34] What kind of order Lázaro imposes on his past life tells us something about the man he is. But there is a contract of frankness about autobiography, an assumption that it exists to promote honest self-revelation, which is open to exploitation. Selection can be used to conceal as well as to reveal, and to direct attention away from the first person. As his narrative proceeds Lázaro makes use of these diversionary tactics, sheltering his former self behind 'extensive accounts' not of himself, as he promises, but of other people, blind men, miserly priests, impoverished *hidalgos* and the like. But Lázaro's account, however sketchy it may be as a life story, will turn out to be one of the most penetrating pieces of self-analysis V.M. could have wished for, a truly 'entera noticia' of Lázaro's 'persona'.

The latter part of the prologue does not entirely supersede the more public, literary concerns with which the author began. Even after the introduction of V.M. we continue to be given apologies for the quality and the length of the book; Horatian notions of pleasure and profit are supplemented by a refusal to begin *in medias res*,[35] and the prologue ends with an endorsement of its ostensible hero, the self-made man,[36] directed provocatively at 'those which possesse great rents and revenues' (37; Rowland, p. 6). But, as we have seen, the entry of V.M. directs our attention more firmly towards the world of the book and away from the world of its author. The introduction of a second-person pronoun disguises and facilitates a shift in the nature of the first person, with the anonymous author reconstituting himself as the apologetic correspondent. In the process an equivalent change takes place in the nature of the second person, as the reader is manoeuvred from the safety of his position as patron of the arts into taking on the role of V.M. as the 'onlie begetter' of Lázaro's account. The introduction of the 'caso' gives an extra dimension to this subtle play of pronouns. Lázaro's decision to tackle the problem of explaining the 'caso' by beginning at the beginning introduces in the prologue a theme and a tactic on which the greater part of Lázaro's self-defence will be based. Lázaro's autobiography involves, as all autobiography does, a division of the first person into two distinct characters: Lázaro de Tormes the *pregonero*, the mature man, experienced and worldly-wise, and Lazarillo the boy he once was. The choice of fictional autobiography as a form by the author of *Lazarillo* was not entirely original,[37] but his exploitation of the divided self which is dramatised in autobiography and his use of a second person as a foil for each of these first persons will amount to a major breakthrough in the search for a text to carry the fight to the enemies of literature.

The division of self into speaking subject and the subject of speech has always been recognised as an important aspect of growing up and of self-knowledge. It is the linguistic equivalent of the mirror-stage of development in which children learn to distinguish 'I' from 'you' and learn to see their own 'I' as another's 'you'. The process is acknowledged in one of Lázaro's earliest reminiscences about his little black brother who runs in fear from his father because he cannot see himself for what he is (1.35–44).[38] It is no accident that Lázaro fixes on this incident so early in what will be an attempt to give a full account of himself in writing. Lázaro responds to V.M.'s request because he knows that only through language does subjectivity become possible; only language allows the subject to constitute himself as a first person by becoming the subject of a sentence.[39] But Lázaro also appreciates the corollary of this: 'I' cannot be conceived without contrastive differentiation. 'I' only exists by virtue of dialogue with 'you'. The view of himself that he wishes to present to the outside world will therefore depend not only on what he reveals of himself but on the kind of dialogue he is able to strike up with V.M. His division of himself into mature man and young boy not only helps him to present himself in his twin roles as speaking subject and subject of speech, but helps him to determine how the reader will respond to his playing of these roles.

Lázaro's division of self creates, then, two first persons, each of which becomes involved in a relationship with the same second person dramatised in the book as V.M. These relationships can broadly be characterised in terms of empathy and irony. Empathy is the relationship that establishes itself most readily, for formal and stylistic reasons. Autobiography is a first-person genre: first-person verbs and the first-person viewpoint predominate. When the reader embarks on his reading of Lázaro's account he hears not the authoritative voice of an independent narrator, but something with which he can more readily identify. As we saw in chapter 3, the inner voice he hears will very likely be his own and he will have no difficulty in associating his own self with the speaking self of the text. Moreover, he will encounter little in Lázaro's 'grosero estilo' to distract him, finding it pleasantly conversational for the most part, an 'epístola hablada',[40] skilfully written, but no more learned or literary than he might expect from a correspondent from the real world. The extensive use of characteristically oral devices helps the reader to recreate the character in his inner ear and to hear him speaking, not *to* the reader, but *through* him. But one of these oral devices is apostrophe, and this performs quite a different function. From time to time, particularly at the outset, the reader finds himself apostrophised from the text, and while it may be possible not to notice such a call in the street, where we might reasonably suppose that it is not meant for us, in the privacy of our own home it is impossible to escape the conclusion that it is we who are being addressed. One minute the reader is a first person, the next minute he is a second person thrust back into the role of disinterested observer. Such a technique seems designed to keep V.M. alert to the complex issues that Lázaro is putting before him.

There is, however, a further role for the reader to play. The first person of the narrative is in fact two people: Lázaro and Lazarillo. Because Lazarillo's experiences are retold by the mature man with the benefit of hindsight, Lázaro is often critical of his former self, commenting with a certain detachment on his exploits. To him, Lazarillo is not just 'I' but 'he'.[41] When the blind man is about to play his first trick on Lazarillo, Lázaro writes: 'Yo simplemente llegué' (1.19). The verb is first person but the adverb is third. Under these circumstances the reader's relationship of empathy with the younger man becomes overlaid with one of complicity with the older man, and Lázaro and V.M. – first and second persons singular – find themselves allies – first persons plural – in league with each other, with Lazarillo the ironic victim.

The result of this technique is a literary equivalent of the Necker cube, in which the reader sees the events of the narrative from opposing points of view almost, but not quite, simultaneously. Either he stands with Lazarillo or with Lázaro, in which case he sees his former engagement with detachment. This almost simultaneous engagement and detachment is made possible by the format and historical circumstances of the book, a fictional autobiography designed to be read privately and in silence. The true originality of *Lazarillo de Tormes*, and its importance in the evolution of a morally defensible fiction, lies precisely in the way in which it exploits the division of self implicit in autobiography – the chronological distance between the events and their narration – to produce a double protagonist, two first persons, each of which the reader assimilates to himself and clothes in his own voice. This complex configuration of relationships, of reader to narrating protagonist and acting protagonist, and of narrator to his former self, is given concrete expression in the book by the presence of V.M., which acknowledges and crystallises the reader's role, and by the peculiarly ambivalent tone in which most of the narrative is written.

The tone of *Lazarillo de Tormes* has often been commented on but not always well accounted for. I myself have described it as shifting from 'a mixture of innocence and guile to something between defensive shamefacedness and defiant self-congratulation';[42] Stephen Gilman speaks of an 'amalgamation of compassion and contempt, respect and disdain, affection and carelessness' which could only have been written by a person 'who is at once himself and another'.[43] Two things are important here. The fact that we find ourselves speaking about 'tone' rather than 'style' underlines the importance of the aural dimension of the words and the way this gives extra immediacy to cold print. In consequence the reader is less inclined to approach the circumstances of Lázaro's case with the analytical detachment of the trained judge or advocate, but rather more inclined to show the compassion and fellow feeling of the juryman, setting less store by 'evidence' than by 'character', by whether he feels able to trust the defendant and what he says. The second important point is that to describe the tone in which Lázaro addresses the reader, we have inevitably to have recourse to antitheses. As Gilman says, this account can only have been written by a man who is at once himself and another. It is both naïve and knowing, defensive and defiant, and it denies us the uniformity and consistency of approach that we might expect from a man who is trying to give a good account of himself. It tells us that things look rather different depending on one's point of view, that values are relative, that a jug may be both 'dulce' and 'amargo' and the word 'bueno' may mean anything we wish;[44] all of which is doubtless very good philosophy, but rather poor advocacy.

The ambivalence of tone which Lázaro displays in his account is not, as we might have expected, accidental or the mark of a man who does not know that confidence springs, rightly or wrongly, from a clear eye, a firm voice and courageous conviction, and not from pusillanimous relativism. At one level Lázaro's ambivalence is his own attempt at honesty: we are not always proud of what we once were, or even of what we now are, and there is no point in hiding that fact. At another level, Lázaro's exploitation of multiple and conflicting viewpoints in the language he uses is a consequence of a very sophisticated and considered attempt to defend himself against the charges which are implicitly laid against him. For there can be no doubt that he is no unconscious sinner, so depraved that he has lost sight of his own depravity: he knows that appearances are against him. The 'charges' are serious ones: 'to exploit another person sexually for the sake of material affluence is the definition of a pimp'.[45] Merely by replying to V.M.'s request Lázaro is forced to admit that those charges have to be answered. His decision to reply, and to do so at length, has other consequential effects: as soon as Lázaro begins his defence, the reader, merely by choosing to remain in the room, is cast in the role of judge. He cannot choose not to be involved. The making of the reader into a representative of establishment values will be an important factor in Lázaro's defence.

Lázaro's defence has three main strands to it, each of which is expressed by means of a stylistic strategy or a formal device in the text. At each stage of the argument the presence of the reader as V.M. is crucial. The first line of defence takes the form of an implicit plea of reduced responsibility. It consists in arguing, in effect, that Lazarillo had a deprived childhood, that he suffered great cruelty at the hands of his masters and was forced in consequence to cheat and lie in order to survive, and that he learned from their example, as well as from his apprenticeship in survival, the values of a corrupt society. Under those circumstances a man would have to be a saint to hold out against such adverse environmental conditioning and if anyone is to blame, surely it is the society represented by his successive masters who is the guilty party. This argument is put forward, at least in the first four *tratados*, by means of that relationship of empathy that is encouraged between the reader as V.M. and the young protagonist. Lázaro sets out to present his former self as a victim and to get the reader to see Lazarillo as such, to side with him against his malevolent masters. That is why he begins at the beginning, showing his life as a process, not as a completed state to be explained and analysed. The diachronic portrayal of his early life is not so much chosen because life itself is a process, but because it is the act of narrating that is a process, and it is through this act of narrating that Lázaro hopes to trap his reader in a web of sympathy. Lazarillo's ill-treatment might have been summarised much more analytically, but what he needs above all is time to work on V.M., and to gain that time he needs to take a fairly broad historical perspective, giving himself plenty to talk about, since he knows that the longer he talks, the more chance he has of persuading V.M. to his point of view.

The fact that Lázaro is conducting his own defence also works in his favour. The first-person point of view from which the narrative is focussed inevitably makes the reader adopt Lazarillo's position. It is not just the verb forms that assist this identification but the whole approach to description and the selection of topics. Lázaro constantly reminds us that what he is telling us is illustrative, not exhaustive ('contaré un caso de muchos', 1.245)[46] ('I will declare one chaunce amongst many', Rowland, p. 16), though we have ourselves to be alert to the other ways in which he manipulates our point of view, casting himself as young, frail and innocent while his masters are condemned with adjectives that encapsulate their spiritual and moral emptiness.[47] As Howard Mancing says, 'Seldom has an author so prejudiced the reader in favour of his protagonist as in *Lazarillo de Tormes*.'[48]

Lazarillo's portrayal of himself as a victim is also helped by the way in which he puts great emphasis on the power and presence of the first three masters, setting them up as adversaries and playing on the reader's instinctive indignation at the extent of the mis-match. By casting himself as an underdog he ensures that the reader will give him support in the unequal struggle and that, paradoxically, he will not just see Lazarillo as victimised and put upon, but will actually end up encouraging him to play to win. The narrative symmetries of the first *tratado*, then, are very skilfully handled. Lazarillo's final cruel trick on the blind man is just recompense and satisfying revenge. But the aesthetic pleasure that comes from an elegant symmetry is made to overlap with a different kind of satisfaction in the reader's mind, the satisfaction of seeing that two wrongs make a right.

Lázaro's campaign to enlist the sympathy of V.M. is helped considerably, too, by the fact that this document is written to be read in private and, probably, in silence. We have already noted how important the idea of 'tone' is in Lázaro's account, together with the allied notion that we can tell a man's character by his voice, like testing a bell or a coin to see if it rings true, or by 'auditing' accounts by reading them aloud. When we read Lázaro's account silently to ourselves the voice we hear is not his but our own. We are also, when reading his account, making up a good deal of it, as we noted in chapter 3. We are filling in the indeterminacies of the text, creating objects to which it can refer, and in the case of the pronoun 'V.M.' standing in ourselves for the missing person to whose presence that pronoun alludes. The kinds of inference that are a natural part of reading are supplemented in *Lazarillo de Tormes* by some specific allusions to gaps in the text. Not all of Lázaro's apostrophes to V.M. take the form of direct address ('sepa V.M.', 'huelgo de contar a V.M.', etc.). When Lazarillo tells the reader that he nearly died of hunger in the blind man's service, he anticipates an incredulous response:

jamás tan avariento ni mezquino hombre no vi, tanto que me mataba a mí de hambre, y así no me demediaba de lo necesario. Digo verdad . . . (1.132–4)

(there was never man so wretched a niggarde. For hee caused mee not onely to die for hunger, but also to wante what so ever I needed. And therefore to confesse the troth . . .)   (Rowland, p. 12)

After 'necesario' there is a gap which the reader is obliged to fill if the affirmation which follows is to make proper sense.

The most overt allusion to textual indeterminacy in *Lazarillo de Tormes* comes in the fourth *tratado*, in the very brief account of the behaviour of the Mercedarian friar, whose services he tells us he left 'for other small matters, which at this time I will not speake of . . .' (Rowland, p. 58). A phrase like that is an open invitation to the reader to supply a reason which is not stated. But we are not free to supply any reason. In fact, Lazarillo is careful to restrict our choice almost completely, by invoking the convention that a nod is as good as a wink in a context in which he had just told us that the friar associates with prostitutes, is a glutton, has a large number of secular interests and wears out a lot of shoe leather when he should be attending services. In such a context Lazarillo's reticence has to be interpreted as concealing delicate matters which are best left unsaid, the convention that requires that we lower our voices when talking about sex.

It is at points like this in the text that the reader's empathy with Lazarillo shades into complicity with Lázaro. A very good example of this divided allegiance on the reader's part and the ambivalent tone in the text which gives rise to this division comes early in the first *tratado* when Lazarillo is telling how his mother's black lover, Zaide, comes to the house to visit her:

Este algunas veces se venía a nuestra casa, y se iba a la mañana; otras veces de día llegaba a la puerta, en achaque de comprar huevos, y entrábase en casa. Yo, al principio de su entrada, pesábame con él y habíale miedo, viendo el color y mal gesto que tenía; mas de que vi que con su venida mejoraba el comer, fuile queriendo bien, porque siempre traía pan, pedazos de carne, y en el invierno leños, a que nos calentábamos. De manera que, continuando la posada y conversación, mi madre vino a darme un negrito muy bonito . . .
(1.26–34).

(So that for his part hee would oftentimes arrive at midnight to our house, and returne againe betimes in the morning, otherwhiles at noonetide, demanding at the dore, whether my mother had egges to sell, and so come in pretely without suspicion: At the beginning I was right sorie to see him make repare thither, being afraid to behold his black uncomly visage: but after that I once perceived how only by his resort our fare was so well amended, I could by no means finde in my heart to hate him, but rather beare him good will, rejoycing to see him: for hee alwayes brought us home with him good rounde cantels of breade, and pieces of broken meate, and in the Winter time wood to warme us withall. To bee short, by his continuall repaire thither, matters went so forwarde, that my mother founde good time to bring forth a yong morren . . .)   (Rowland, p. 8)

There is a good deal of skilfully recreated naïveté here: the way Lazarillo simply reports that Zaide came to the house and left in the morning, as if the young Lazarillo could see what was happening, but could not grasp its significance; the way Lazarillo's fear of the man's colour gives way childishly and understandably to affection under the blandishments of food and warmth. The naïveté breaks down, however, and the empathy becomes complicity, with the word 'conversación', with which carefully chosen euphemism Lázaro injects Lazarillo's innocent vision of bread, meat, log fires, courtesy calls and conversation, with his own world-weary and rather sniggering view of his mother's intercourse with the black man.

It is at points such as this, when we become aware of a slightly false ring to Lazarillo's naïveté or a rather knowing note of acerbity in his perceptions and comments, that we realise that a different sort of claim is being made on our sympathies as readers and judges of the facts of the case. It is on the basis of this further allegiance between protagonist and V.M. that Lázaro advances the second strand of his defence. This time the appeal is not to the reader's emotional identification with the young protagonist as victim in a cruel and heartless society but to the reader's intellectual acceptance of the conclusions drawn by the mature Lázaro from his experience. Almost unbeknown to V.M., Lázaro slips a confidential arm round his shoulders in an effort to persuade him that they have both lived, are both men of the world, both possessed of shrewdness, knowledge and even wisdom. The allegiance he is proposing now is not one of sentimental identification with a frail innocent cast adrift in a hostile world, but a union of superior intelligences, capable of a level of perception to which most people cannot aspire. The basis of this new allegiance is the ironic complicity that characterises the relationship between Lázaro and V.M.

Irony is not, of course, excluded from the reader's relationship of sympathy with Lazarillo and, indeed, irony underlies many of those occasions when the reader has to supply the thoughts and feelings that are going on in Lazarillo's head and heart without being articulated in the text. Lazarillo's account of his period of service with the squire is a case in point. (Here, as elsewhere, 'contaré un caso de muchos . . .') The first two masters had been treated as adversaries, forces to be resisted with the direct literary weapons of satire and caricature. The treatment of the squire – as befits Lazarillo's changing attitudes and greater affection for this master – is altogether gentler and less directly antagonistic in approach, if no less destructive of the man's pretence in the final analysis. Much of what the squire says, particularly about honour, his background and prospects, is allowed to pass without comment by Lazarillo. The squire's words are allowed to stand alone, naked in their lack of substance – the surrounding silence eloquent of their emptiness – while Lazarillo and the reader exchange knowing looks. At least, one assumes that that is what happens, though one might be forgiven for wondering why we should treat the squire's words with any greater or less credence than we do Lazarillo's: perhaps the hollowness of the squire's words is more audible only because Lazarillo's have been so much more thoroughly assimilated to the reader's own.

The ironic relationship between V.M. and Lázaro, however, is of a rather different sort. This time it is the young Lazarillo, rather than his masters, who is the ironic victim. The need for V.M. to have a detached as well as a prejudiced view of Lazarillo's early life springs from the fact that the young protagonist himself contributes to the process of corruption which he undergoes at the hands of his masters. His contribution must therefore be made as clear as theirs is, even if he hopes that V.M. will eventually accept a plea of self-defence. What enables the reader to have both a partial and an impartial view of Lazarillo is that technique of division of self, by which one of the first persons is reconstituted as a third. This technique also helps the narrator to get round the problems of reconciling omniscience with a partial point of view, a problem that Quevedo has difficulty with in the *Buscón*[49] and which Philip Roth alludes to very neatly in *Portnoy's Complaint*:

. . . so loud is his roar, and so convincing, that my normally placid sister runs to the kitchen, great gruntfuls of fear erupting from her mouth, and in what we now call the fetal position crouches down between the refrigerator and the wall. Or so I seem to remember it – though it would make sense, I think, to ask how I know what is going on in the kitchen if I am still hiding beneath my bed. (p. 137)

There are many occasions in *Lazarillo de Tormes* when the young protagonist recreates himself as an independent third person: when his head is clouted against the stone bull, when he falls victim to the wine jug, when he is caught sleeping with the key to the bread chest in his mouth.

For the most part, however, Lázaro uses the division of self to illustrate the corruption as well as the victimisation of Lazarillo. What emerges from Lazarillo's accounts of his services with his masters is not just their cynical cruelty, but their self-seeking, deceitfulness and cunning, precisely those values that Lazarillo has to acquire in order to survive. In many respects, then, Lazarillo becomes a mirror held up to those around him, and in acquiring their habits he enables us to see all the more clearly the faults in the others. This process is most clearly seen in the first two *tratados* where the conflict of wits and the need to survive are at their most acute, and in particular, in the exchange of roles which underlies Lazarillo's treatment of the blind man. The indifference of the final words of the first *tratado* – 'No supe más lo que Dios dél hizo, ni curé de lo saber' (1.420–1) ('I never understoode nor yet sought to knowe what God almightie did with him', Rowland, p. 23) – brings home with a shock the extent of the change wrought in Lazarillo by his experience with the blind man.

The third *tradado* shows these aspects of Lázaro's technique at work at their most interesting and most subtle. The shift of attitudes implicit in this part of the book is underlined by Lázaro himself: 'antes le había lástima que enemistad' (3.330) ('yea and I did pitie him, rather than hate him', Rowland, p. 48). The antagonism of the first two *tratados*, associated with the battles of wits between Lazarillo and his first two masters, gives way to just that kind of sympathy[50] that the reader had previously shown for Lazarillo himself. As Lazarillo is gradually ingested into the society around him it seems natural eventually to find him on the same side as his master. The enemy, in turn, has moved elsewhere, becoming less tangible and more abstract. Now the enemy lies within, within the squire's self-deceptive sense of honour and within Lazarillo's reactions to his master's fatal delusions. From Lazarillo's discussion of honour with the squire there appears at first to emerge a fairly conventional satirical view of all that honour stands for. The *escudero*'s obsessive concern for outward appearance, dress, demeanour, are ruthlessly exposed for the pose that they are, and

Lazarillo dwells with fascination on the exquisite awfulness of the squire's dispute about the raising of hats. Lazarillo expresses mock-innocent surprise (the voice of Lázaro can be heard here) that it should not be considered courteous to commend a man to the care of God (3.483–4) and there is a nice moment when, in a discussion of proper forms of address, the boy momentarily abandons the respectful 'vos' for the scornful 'tú': 'por eso tiene [Dios] tan poco cuidado de mantenerte, pues no sufres que nadie se lo ruegue' (3.493–4)[51] ('that is the cause, that hee hath so little care to mainteine thee, for thou canst abide no man to wish it thee', Rowland, pp. 53–4). What Lazarillo finds most strange, however, in the squire's position is that those who pride themselves with honour have nothing to back it up with. The *escudero's* mistake in leaving Old Castile in a huff because his neighbour would not raise his hat first lay, as Lazarillo sees it, in the fact that the neighbour was better off than the squire (3.458–60). In this respect Lazarillo falls, perhaps deliberately and instructively, into a common trap. To criticise a man for presenting a false front is inevitably to require him to back up his claims with substance. For Lazarillo, then, honour comes to consist in the ability to back up fine words with real wealth, and by extension wealth comes to confer honour. Lázaro's technique of self-division enables us to see two kinds of confusion at work here. Lazarillo rightly sees that the squire's mistake lies in his inability to distinguish appearance from reality, but at the same time he goes on to make the perhaps more serious error of making material wealth the basis of honour, and thereby confusing integrity with respectability.

Perhaps the key to Lazarillo's view of the *escudero's* self-delusion lies in what he himself says in his one main quarrel with his master:

Solo tenía dél un poco de descontento: que quisiera yo que no tuviera tanta presunción, mas que abajara un poco su fantasía con lo mucho que subía su necesidad.   (3.347–9)

(only that me thought he was to presumptuous, where I often wished that seeing hee so plainely perceived his owne povertie, hee wold something have hid his fantastical pride.)   (Rowland, p. 48)

This failure to match his image of himself to the reality of his circumstances is demonstrated at its best in the squire's account of his property in Valladolid, and it reminds us once again that one of the most effective adjuncts to the creation of a façade is the creative mendacity of language. The passage deserves detailed consideration:

Mayormente – dijo – que no soy tan pobre que no tengo en mi tierra un solar de casas, que a estar ellas en pie y bien labradas, diez y seis leguas de donde nací, en aquella costanilla de Valladolid, valdrían más de docientas veces mil maravedís, según se podrían hacer grandes y buenas; y tengo un palomar que, a no estar derribado como está, daría cada año más de docientos palominos; y otras cosas que me callo, que dejé por lo que tocaba a mi honra.

(3.495–502)

(Furthermore he saide, I am not so poore, but that I have in my countrey ground, where foundation of houses is well and surely laide, which if they were built up as they ought, sumptuous and great, and by exchange placed in *Valladelid*, sixtene mile on this side the place where I was borne, they woulde bee worth no less than a thousande Maravedis: and I have a Dovehouse, which if it were built up as it is now falne, it wold yelde me yearely above two hundred pigeons: beside other thinges which I will not nowe speake of, all which thinges I forsooke for matters which touched mine honor . . .)

(Rowland, p. 54)

This is an excellent example of the way the squire uses language to sustain the illusion of wealth even in the face of greater and greater concessions made to reality. He makes three assertions here, one about his ownership of some houses, another about a dovecote (particularly significant for its associations with feudal aristocracy)[52] and a further one about other matters on which he prefers to remain silent. At each stage of his assertions he grows in confidence. He begins with a tentative double negative ('no soy tan pobre que no tengo'), posits the existence of some land and follows up with a hypothesis about some houses that might be built, or rebuilt, on that land. As a result of this progression of ideas, from the land itself ('un solar de casas') to the existence of the houses ('a estar ellas en pie') to their condition ('y bien labradas' – this estate becomes real enough for him to be able to discuss its upkeep), he ventures an assertive conditional: 'valdrían', they would be worth 200,000 *maravedís*.[53] So real have they become that he can put a price on them. Having so successfully built something from nothing he can now go on with greater confidence. 'I have a dovecote' – no hedging with double negatives here – 'which, if it were not in ruins, as it is, would produce 200 doves a year.' The change of approach here is subtle. The double negative has been replaced by a negative in the hypothesis: 'a estar ellas en pie' becomes 'a no estar derribado' and concedes a greater measure of reality in the process, a concession reinforced by the telling phrase 'como está'. Yet in spite of this lacklustre reality he can see the doves well enough to count them, though here he overreaches himself: true noblemen count their doves in pairs. From here he can go on to his final assertion: 'y otras cosas que me callo', a phrase that brilliantly sums up the squire's whole strategy, to make something out of nothing. The silence of the phrase asserts the total lack of substance behind the squire's pose, yet its indeterminacy leaves it to the reader to take up his train of thought and construct a reality in the emptiness, just as the squire does. Reality is acknowledged completely in his silence yet his pose is made all the more impervious to that reality.

If Lazarillo needed a lesson in how to make language constitute reality, and in particular in how to make silence constitute reality, then this is surely it. But he needs, of course, no such lesson. He has already told us in this *tratado* that when the squire asked him 'muy por extenso' (3.52–3, c.f. prologue 34–5) about himself, he lied in reply: 'le satisfice de mi persona lo mejor que mentir supe' (3.56–7 – here again the echoes of the prologue are surely significant) ('bringing foorth the beste lyes I coulde frame for my selfe, I made him account what I was . . .', Rowland, p. 39). He tells us further that when he learns that there is nothing to eat, he feigns asceticism as best he can with some amusing and rather self-mocking ambiguities about eating not being something he was much concerned with (3.82–6). Here the reader knows that Lazarillo is lying with the truth and telling the *escudero* what he wants to hear. In form the words are true, in substance they are not, and the untruthfulness is made possible by the *escudero*'s readiness to interpret the words in a manner that suits him. Later, when trying to 'hacer del continente' by refusing the offer of wine, Lazarillo is discomfited to be told that the jug contains water. In these and other cases Lazarillo demonstrates how well he has learned the lessons the blind man taught him, that one can use words to create any kind of illusion, subtly using truths, half truths and untruths to build up a façade to which the observer will often willingly contribute.[54] Indeed, all of Lazarillo's lessons in the deceptiveness of language can be traced back to his first experience by the bridge at Salamanca. The blind man tells him to place his ear against the stone bull: 'Lázaro, llega el oído a este toro, y oirás gran ruido dentro dél' (1.89–90) ('*Lazaro*, put thine eare to this Bull, and thou shalt heare a terrible noise within it . . .', Rowland, p. 10). Now Lazarillo thinks, and we think that 'él' refers to 'toro', but the blind man knows that it refers to 'oído'. The clout Lazarillo gets should come as no surprise. This is the oldest trick in the book, and surely significantly placed here in a context in which pronouns are so important. Ambiguous pronoun reference lies at the heart of a great deal of popular humour ('If I say you've a beautiful body will you hold it against me?') and what Lazarillo and the blind man are doing is going through a comedy routine, like Laurel and Hardy: 'When I nod my head, you hit it.' But there are many lessons here for Lazarillo as well as the reader. Lazarillo is being taught to listen to what people say, because it is by their words that they will betray themselves; and that is a lesson which applies just as much to V.M., especially if he, too, was taken in by the blind man's crucial ambiguity. Lazarillo learns not just to listen, but to master language as well as any of his masters and, finally, he shows that he has learned the value of silence by urging it on the gossips who threaten to overturn his hard-won prosperity.

There is also something exemplary about the choice of that particular object, the stone bull, for Lazarillo's baptism, because it raises for V.M. and for the reader the crucial issue of the realism of the book. Lázaro's account is written in a *grosero estilo*, its tone aspires to the colloquial and confidential, and its matter is pitched at an appropriately low level. It is what we loosely, and confusingly, call 'realistic' – it *seems* real enough. On top of that, instead of opening a book and reading about fantastic goings-on in faraway places like France and England, a contemporary reader would have been confronted with something that allegedly happened at a place where – especially if he lived in Salamanca – he himself could go and stand and see the scene for himself. The hardness of the stone bull seems to stand for the tangibility of the reality that – we suppose – underlies the book. But behind that false equation Lázaro is at work, urging us to accept literary 'realism' as a guarantee of the veracity of what he says. Not that he is being entirely dishonest with us, as he allows the blind man to demonstrate, using the unfortunate head of his former self as an example. It is not, after all, the bull that roars; the noise is in Lazarillo's head. The words 'toro', 'puente' and 'Salamanca', for all their apparent substance, are merely words.[55] What we choose to make them mean is up to us. The incident of the stone bull is perhaps the *mise en abîme* of the whole work, showing just how radical is Lázaro's scepticism. He calls reality itself into question by reducing it to words, and exposing the illusory nature of those words. The surface realism of this book, the settings, low-life activity, names, the most palpable contemporary reality symbolised by the bridge at Salaanca, all this is there to point to a paradox: what seems most realistic is least real. What seems real – the stone bull – is an insubstantial illusion and what seems insubstantial, power, greed, persuasion, people's impressions and opinions of each other, the things that this book is actually about, they are the true realities of life.

The lessons of language, persuasion and reality will be recapped in the fifth *tratado* in the person of the *buldero*, but they pervade Lázaro's account of his early years so fully as to constitute a major part of the substance of the book. In the first four *tratados* Lázaro is putting forward two strands of his defence simultaneously. On the one hand he is portraying his former self as a victim of circumstances in order to enlist the sympathies of V.M. for his plight. In this he uses the literary techniques that are available to him as natural concomitants of his decision to narrate the process of his life: the techniques of 'retrospective subjective significance'[56] that unobtrusively masks prejudice and partiality under the appearance of frankness, together with the natural coincidence of points of view that springs from inviting V.M. to read an account written in the first person. At the same time, Lázaro is keen that we should sympathise with the kind of man he is at the time of writing. This he tries to achieve by showing us that he has learned a great deal from his experience.[57] He writes with the insight of hindsight and is ready to look as critically at his past life as he would have us look kindly upon it, and he shows us in the process a great deal about the infinitely subtle ways in which values are distorted in social life, the way hypocrisy is all-pervasive, and the way self-deception and the deceit of others go hand in hand. In this radical exposition of the process of his own corruption Lázaro paints a black picture indeed. In this world no one says what he means or means what he says; nothing is what it appears to be. The nature of the witness which the reader is obliged to give to this state of affairs is therefore one of true empathy in the sense in which D. W. Harding has interpreted this word.[58] Like any onlooker at an event in real life, the reader is both spectator and participant. He is part of the action, yet at the same time detached from it. In the same way, when the reader reads the 'I' of the text, he reads it as another 'I' as well as his own. He makes an imaginative leap into the mind of the protagonist, yet he remains separate, attending to the events of the narrative and evaluating them in the process. The thoughts and feelings of the protagonist are in the reader, but are not predicable of him.[59] Lázaro's dual technique of having V.M. side emotionally with Lazarillo and intellectually with himself produces a text which engages V.M. and detaches him at the same time, and Lázaro's frank admission to being as much a manipulator of language as any other gives his text that quality of which Richard Wollheim writes,[60] the quality of being a representation that makes us aware of its status as configuration. As for Lázaro's defence, thus far he seems to admit the charges of corruption, but argues convincingly that the fault was not entirely his and offers the depth of his intelligence, a quality in which he is ready to measure himself against V.M., in mitigation. But there is a third and more powerful argument to be advanced.

Most readers go cold on Lazarillo after the fourth *tratado*. Whatever their attitudes may be to the youthful Lazarillo, by far the majority of critics have little time for the grown man: liar, cheat, thief, hypocrite, unrepentant sinner,[61] cynical, ignorant, presumptuous, adulatory,[62] base and repulsive,[63] self-satisfied,[64] complacent,[65] scoundrel,[66] and degenerate cuckold.[67] It is easy to see how Lázaro comes to attract such adverse reactions. At the very moment when his rhetoric seems to be bearing fruit he abandons his hold on the sympathies of V.M. The third *tratado* gave us the subtle ironies of Lázaro's exposure both of the *escudero* and of his former self, and the fourth *tratado* returned briefly but deftly to the theme of the opening chapters, the problems of surviving in a wholly corrupt and alien moral environment. In the fifth *tratado* Lázaro chooses to disappear almost entirely from sight, deliberately making himself marginal,[68] relegating himself to the sidelines and concentrating our attention on the exploits of his master, the *buldero*.

Raymond Willis has drawn attention to the way in which the fifth *tratado* 'disengages Lazarillo momentarily from the process of either intensely recollected, or actually occurring, living'.[69] But even though the events which Lazarillo describes have little to do with him as a *persona* they have a great deal to do with the rest of the book,[70] and, although the empathic relationship between reader and protagonists may be put temporarily into abeyance or suspended indefinitely, there is much in the episode of the pardoner, and the way in which Lázaro presents it, that makes it a thematic recapitulation of what has gone before. Even Lazarillo's submersion into the crowd of spectators, signalled by the change from first person singular to first person plural, helps to maintain him and the reader on the same footing. V.M. no longer has to identify with Lazarillo; in this *tratado* Lazarillo will come and stand at the back with his readership and show how narrators may easily become spectators and even innocent bystanders.

What the episode of the *buldero* tells us is what Lázaro has been telling us all along: that the world is a theatre of illusions, that it is peopled with unscrupulous actors who peddle an illusory reality and blind, self-deceiving audiences who willingly allow themselves to be persuaded into accepting that illusory reality. Lázaro stresses the role that language plays in this process by telling us in advance what a mastery of language the pardoner was possessed of: when the clergy he dealt with spoke Latin he made free with an elegant and eloquent Castilian (5.14–15); if they knew none then it was he who spoke Latin, or what passed for Latin. These and other warnings, nevertheless, do not detract from the effectiveness of the confidence trick, in which a central role is played by two very eloquent prayers. Lázaro gives the text of the first one verbatim (5.86–103), but spares us the second, saying merely that it was as long as it was devout. These theatrical devices should immediately put us in mind of the blind man's techniques for feigning piety (1.114–18), but it is not until the constable and the pardoner are caught giggling together after the event that Lazarillo and, one suspects, his readers finally see the light. It is a very impressive display that reminds us of Chaucer's pardoner, who announces to the assembled company that he is going to fool them with words and then, to their intense annoyance, goes ahead and does just that.[71]

The choice of a pardoner, rather than any other confidence trickster, to occupy such an important position in Lázaro's narrative also helps to consolidate rather than disrupt his train of thought. What the pardoner is selling, and what the congregation, after the 'miracle', are so anxious to buy that hardly a soul in the town was without one (5.170–1), is pieces of paper, specifically pieces of printed paper. And this reminds us that among the many other problems caused by the spread of printing was the fact that the mass production of indulgences made their abuse even more difficult to control than it had been before printing. The earliest dated printed matter to come from the workshops of both Gutenberg and Caxton was an indulgence.[72] In May 1498 alone, eighteen thousand indulgences were printed by Johann Luscher for the abbey of Montserrat. Mass production on this scale obviously meant lucrative business for jobbing printers and salesmen alike, and gave the Reformation, the moralists and the community even greater reason to view the products of the printing press with suspicion. In the fifth *tratado* Lázaro skilfully correlates the pardoner's eloquence and the fake miracle with his previous observations on the deceptiveness of language, and by exposing the sham authority of one piece of printed matter – the indulgence – he warns us to beware of putting too much trust in another, the book that is his life. The fact that both documents have to do with the remission of sins is also, surely, significant.

In the main, however, the impression created by the fifth *tratado* is one of discontinuity rather than continuity. When Lázaro reappears in the sixth and seventh *tratados* he is a changed man. Time has passed and the struggle for survival has been replaced by more bourgeois aspirations:[73] thrift, save and prosper, a nest-egg for his old age. Four years' work enables him to save enough money to buy himself some decent clothes and his sufferings over the years are repaid with a secure, relatively undemanding, pensionable post as town crier, a job that will enable him to take it easy and put something aside for his old age (7,8). And in the fullness of time his abilities come to the attention of the archpriest of San Salvador, who evidently supplements his income with some spare-time viniculture, and Lazarillo is rewarded with what the gossips say is only a half share of one of the archpriest's servant girls for his wife.

On the face of it there is little for V.M. to complain of here. What is so terrible about wanting to be well turned out, to have clothes to one's back, shoes on one's feet; to have a little money to one's name, a secure job, the means to settle down with a good woman for company, rent a house and live a quiet life of modest prosperity? And if people want to gossip, why should Lázaro listen to the 'dichos de malas lenguas' if he loves and trusts his wife, as he says he does, and if he has the assurance of a clergyman that she enters his house 'muy a tu honra y suya, y esto te lo prometo' (7.47) ('which doing, I promise thee, shall not otherwise redound but to thy great honestie and hers', Rowland, p. 70)?

There is, nevertheless, something provocative, almost insolent, in the way that Lázaro recounts his climb up the crest of good fortune. Lázaro could hardly have foreseen the delicious irony that his own modest achievements would be howled down by twentieth-century academics from the security of well-paid, pensionable appointments in publicly-funded educational establishments. But he seems in two respects at least deliberately to provoke the disappointment of his readers. Returning from the exile of the fifth *tratado*, Lázaro decks himself out 'muy honradamente' in the very costume that the *escudero* wore to act his part: doublet and hose, cape and sword, and the caricature of his former master is made all the more telling by the fact that Lázaro's clothes are second-hand.[74] V.M. may well feel that Lázaro has let him down, has sold out to the very appearance that earlier he was able to see through so clearly. But there is worse to come. Lázaro is prepared not only to ape the manners and dress of his erstwhile enemies, but is willing to offer the thing he says he loves most, his wife, to secure his new-found prosperity. The choice of his wife as the price to be paid is particularly provocative – any kind of compromise would be better than one that strikes at the very heart of the notion that a man's self-respect resides in the sexual possession of a woman.

Something has clearly gone badly wrong. A man who considers himself on trial abandons two good lines of defence to trumpet pride in the very attitudes and behaviour for which he is being called to account. Why? The answer lies both in the suddenness with which Lázaro reappears after the entr'acte of the fifth *tratado* and the degree of change that he seems to have undergone in the meantime, and in the fact that so much of his new prosperity is shown to be an appearance, from the clothes at one extreme, to the alleged *ménage à trois* at the other. For what has changed is not Lázaro himself, but his attitude to those who are sitting in judgment on him. No longer does he court the favour of V.M. but defiantly turns the tables on him. The third and final strand of Lázaro's defence is, then, to refuse to recognise the authority of the court on the grounds of its blindness, stupidity and incompetence. Lázaro is in effect saying to the court: 'I argued earlier, and you agreed, that the world is a hostile theatre of illusion peopled by hypocrites; nothing in the world is what it appears to be. And now you judge me by appearances. You claim that I have let you down, that I have betrayed the trust between us, yet it is you who have betrayed me. You take the shadow for the substance, you see the clothes but not the man inside them, you side with the "malas lenguas", you pay heed to the lowest kind of gossip and ignore everything that I have been trying to tell you. It is not what a man looks like that counts or even how he contrives to live in and alongside a corrupt world. It is what he thinks and feels that matters. You refuse to make that distinction and prefer to judge by appearances instead. You have learned nothing from what I have been saying. How can you dare to sit in judgment on me and expect me to accept your verdict?'

With a brilliant *coup de théâtre* Lazarillo has manoeuvred V.M. into a totally untenable position. By encouraging him in his empathy, then suddenly recasting himself in the guise of the enemy, Lázaro has left

V.M. exposed and has tricked him, and with him the reader, into betraying his own false values. It is for this reason that Lázaro has skilfully introduced into the conclusion of his account so much that is a matter of judgment: is he a cuckold? does he know? does he care? does he love his wife, as he says, and does it even matter? has he sold out to the system at a price that is just a little too high to be acceptable? All these questions, like questions of guilt and innocence generally, are matters for judgment and not for knowledge, and how V.M. judges Lázaro will tell us more about the man on the bench than the man in the dock. One thing seems certain, however, and that is that the distance between Lazarillo and Lázaro, measured in terms both of the way they project themselves and the degrees of sympathy and antipathy they provoke in the reader, is so great and so consciously orchestrated as to constitute a conceit. Lázaro the *conceptista* asserts the likeness in things apparently unlike – the two persons are, after all, one man – and challenges us to reconcile the man whose intelligence we admire with the man whose behaviour we condemn. Such a reconciliation is only possible if we think in terms of a cultivated, dynamic hypocrisy on Lázaro's part, only if we see him as capable of keeping thought and action separate, as a man whose conduct is corrupt but whose mind is not.[75] There is no question of his being totally debased: if he were he could not have thought there was anything to write about, nothing to account *for*. He knows what people are saying – perhaps he even knows what we can only suspect – and he knows that, whatever the facts of the matter, things look bad for him. But he also shows that he knows that what things look like is of no importance. To call him a cuckold is to judge him by the standards of society,[76] by standards that he has shown to be worthless. Complaisant he may be, complacent he certainly is not.[77]

What emerges may seem like a cynical lifemanship but is in fact rather more than that. Unlike Quevedo's Pablos, whose analysis of social corruption is merely the prelude to a desperate attempt to beat the world at its own game, Lázaro's outlook is more defensive and much more akin to the Gracianesque heroic man who swims with the tide but keeps his own counsel. It requires a very indignant prosecutor indeed to deny that Lázaro's longing for a quiet life is an unexceptionable human aspiration which he rescues from cosiness by the hard cutting edge of his counter-attack against his detractors. He is no better than his neighbours (27–8) and his wife no worse than hers (7.73–4). Lázaro's position in the final *tratado* is a hard-won equilibrium in which acceptance of the realities of social life is counterbalanced by a cultivated moral distance from them. It is an uncomfortable balance for the reader to accept because it involves the overthrow of conventions – sexual possessiveness being the main one – so deeply-rooted as to appear to be fundamental social realities. Lázaro demonstrates that one may touch pitch and remain unsullied, and that personal integrity may be strengthened, not jeopardised, by getting one's hands dirty in the grime of social existence. He shows that since shadow and substance can never coalesce and since there will always be shadows in this world, then the best way of ensuring that they do not get confused is to keep them strictly separate. Accordingly, Lázaro's 'entera noticia' works at two levels at once: it narrates the process of his survival and prosperity in the world of shadow and at the same time bears witness to his accumulated wisdom in matters of substance. Lázaro emerges from the task that V.M. has set him as an intelligent, knowing, perspicacious and often compassionate narrator of his life. His life is not, he suggests, the way he lives. His life is his art.[78]

At the end of the book, then, V.M. is faced with a number of choices. He has either to condemn Lázaro or to accept that he himself has been exposed as inconsistent and inattentive at best, and fraudulent at worst. In one way, Lázaro has neatly trapped his reader by choosing to defend himself when invited merely to explain, by creating a role for the reader, by obliging him to fill it and by making sure that he fails to fill it adequately.[79] But Lázaro has also trapped us in another sense. By writing quite as well as this, he has also, like Cervantes in the Dogs' Colloquy, brought aesthetic values to bear on questions of credibility and truth. We have to concede that a man who can write with this degree of insight cannot be all bad, and to ask here, as in so many other cases, whether we judge an artist's work by the life he leads. And if we set artistic values above social values, do we not also, in Lázaro's case, set intellect before conduct? Lázaro may also, of course – and it is he who warns us of this – cynically be projecting a favourable image of himself. But if he is, then that image is not just what he would like us to see him as; it is also what he would like to see himself as, and that is about as close to the real man as we are ever likely to get.

Guzmán de Alfarache

From the foregoing brief analysis of *Lazarillo de Tormes* there emerge a number of points of importance for an understanding of the work whose success was to make it synonymous with the picaresque genre,

Guzmán de Alfarache. The first and most striking has to do with the difficulty which readers and critics experience in trying to grasp the true nature of either Lázaro the man or Lazarillo the boy. Lázaro's account of himself seems to deny that there exists a full and rounded character who reveals himself to the reader as the book unfolds. Instead, Lázaro presents himself problematically. He is there not to create an illusion but to provoke a response, forcing us to judge and assess him as he acts and speaks. Inasmuch as he is, or has, a character, he acquires that character from his reader's assessment of him as he narrates. *Lazarillo de Tormes* suggests, then, and herein lies only part of its originality, that the presentation of character has less to do with the unveiling in the book of a being who, we might imagine, pre-exists the book, than with the creation during the reading of the book of a being who exists solely by virtue of the responses he provokes. In sum, *Lazarillo de Tormes* promotes the idea of character as device.

Other important points follow from this. If character is a device, a means, then it must be directed to a purpose. Why does Lázaro present himself as he does? I have tried to show that he does so in order to trap the reader, first by exploiting his willingness to identify with what he is reading, then by going on to undermine the basis of the reader's objections when he finds his expectations defeated. Lázaro presents his life chronologically, and rhetorically, in order to persuade. The book in consequence becomes a dialectic, an activity, and its meaning shifts from what it says to what it does. No work illustrates better than *Lazarillo de Tormes* the truth of Kafka's requirements that 'a book must be the axe which smashes the frozen sea within us'. But this dialectic between an intangible narrator and a fallible judge is bounded by, indeed, could not take place without, a very firmly controlled narrative point of view embracing both protagonist–narrator and reader alike.

All of these points have a bearing on two longstanding problems in the interpretation of *Guzmán de Alfarache*: the nature of the relationship between narrative and commentary, and the question of the sincerity or otherwise of Guzmán's repentance at the end of the book. (I use the word 'repentance' rather than 'conversion' because, as I hope will emerge during the process of this discussion, the moral principles to which he allegedly subscribes are present to him throughout his early life: he is not forsaking one set of religious principles for another.)[80] I will want to suggest that both these issues, which have dominated *Guzmán* criticism for some time,[81] tend to solve themselves if we take into account the reader's function in the reading of the book and, in particular, the way the book's structure is determined by an awareness that it will eventually be read. For this approach, too, our conclusions from *Lazarillo de Tormes* are of paramount importance.

It is a matter of common agreement among critics of *Guzmán de Alfarache*, as of prose fiction in general, that narrative point of view is the key to interpretation. We have seen how seriously the author of *Lazarillo* took this requirement, providing a fixed point of departure for protagonist and reader: Lázaro is careful to outline the circumstances of his writing and these control the inclusion and purpose of everything that is in the book; the 'caso' is the cause of the book. At the same time Lázaro subtly shapes the reader's role by casting him as Vuestra Merced. When we come to look at *Guzmán de Alfarache* things appear nothing like so well ordered, in spite of the fact that Alemán provides the reader with a short explanatory prologue in the form of the *Declaración para el entendimiento deste libro*. On the face of it, the *Declaración* creates more problems than it solves. In it Alemán tells us for example that Guzmán is writing his own story from the galleys where he has been banished for crimes committed during his career as a famous robber. Yet when we reach the end of the book, or the end of the second part, we find that Guzmán, although undoubtedly sentenced to the galleys, has succeeded in engineering his release. Is there an inconsistency here, and if so, whom are we to believe?

If we assume that the ending of Guzmán's account as we have it is consistent with Alemán's declaration at the outset, then two solutions suggest themselves: either that Guzmán did actually write his account on the galley or that Guzmán's narrative has not yet reached the present moment at which he writes. Both solutions, it must be admitted, involve some difficulties. In the first case, while it is satisfying to imagine that the manuscript of *Guzmán de Alfarache* was part of the small bundle of effects that Guzmán must have taken with him as he left the galley on regaining his freedom, he makes no mention of writing the book at the time it must have been written. One might reasonably expect such an excursion into authorship to have been worthy of note: if not always momentous, then the writing of a book is at least an arduous undertaking. The inclusion of a coda to narrate Guzmán's disembarkation would also seem to require an explanation which it does not receive.

Furthermore, and in respect of the second solution, Guzmán's last words include a promise to keep us up to date with subsequent developments:

Aquí di punto y fin a estas desgracias. Rematé la cuenta con mi mala vida. La que después gasté, todo el restante della verás en la tercera y última parte, si el cielo me la diere antes de la eterna que todos esperamos.   (p. 905)[82]

(And heere (gentle Reader) doe I put a full point to these my mis-fortunes. I have given thee a large account of my lewd life; it is truely summ'd up unto thee. What it was hereafter, thou shalt see in my third and last Part, if God shall give me life: and that I doe not first exchange this transitorie one, for one that is eternall, which is the hope and life of the faithfull.)   (Mabbe, IV, 353)

'La que después *gasté*'. That preterite seems strongly to suggest that the future events to be recounted in Part III are already past at the moment of writing. He does not say of his as yet unrecounted life 'la que después gastare', though he does, perhaps significantly, use the future subjunctive in his expression of hope that he be granted such life: 'si el cielo me la *diere*'. Even this, however, could refer, not to that life which he has already lived, but to that which he will need if he is to tell the tale: 'I will tell you what happened next, if Heaven grants me time enough.'[83]

If we take Guzmán at his word and assume that the moment at which the fictional protagonist and fictional narrator coincide – the present moment of writing, the point at which any autobiographer has to stop work because he has brought himself up to date – lies in the future; and if we further assume that the reference to a third part is consistent with Alemán's *Declaración*, then it follows that though Guzmán may indeed write from the galleys, he is not *as yet* writing from the galleys. His freedom must therefore be provisional and short lived. His remark that he has cleared his account with his wicked life is either premature or foreshadows a third part in which a blameless and saintly existence will be unjustly rewarded by a definitive spell as a galley-slave. Either way, more and worse is to come, or at least that is the promise, though even that may be a formulaic gesture on the part of an author who wishes to close the existing work but not in such a way as to preclude a continuation should the opportunity arise.

It is difficult to know whether these issues are of genuine importance in understanding *Guzmán de Alfarache*. To the extent that they have been given importance by critics who use what seem to be incon-sistencies between the beginning and the end of the book to question the sincerity of Guzmán's repentance and point to his implied recidivism in the unwritten third part, then they are important. To the extent that the alleged inconsistencies can be explained perfectly adequately by historical means then they are not important.[84] They are not, after all, inconsistencies within the fiction. They exist, if they exist at all, between what Alemán says and what Guzmán says. Leaving aside the dangers inherent in speculation about the possible contents of a third part and their influence on a reading of the work as it stands, we know that Alemán considered the work to be finished because he said so. The *Declaración* was written for a specific purpose in a specific historical situation. It was put there to explain to readers of Part I that the work had been intended for publication in one volume. Circumstances which are not explained evidently prevented this. Alemán therefore thought that since readers were getting only half a book to begin with, a word or two of clarification might be in order:

Teniendo escrita esta poética historia para imprimirla en un solo volumen, en el discurso del cual quedaban absueltas las dudas que agora, dividido, pueden ofrecerse, me pareció sería cosa justa quitar este inconveniente, pues con muy pocas palabras quedará bien claro. (pp. 95–6)

(Having written this Poetical History, with purpose to have it printed in one only Volume, in the discourse whereof those doubts might be cleared, which now (being divided) might offer themselves; it appeared (to my seeming) a very just thing, to remove this inconvenience, beeing it might easily be done, and that in very few words.) (Mabbe, I, 19)

Had they been able to read Part II in 1599 readers would have been able to see for themselves that Guzmán, punished for his career as a celebrated thief and chastened by his experiences, takes advantage of his intelligence and his education – also fully documented in Part II – to write up his life in the time at his disposal in the galleys. Readers of Parts I and II complete in one volume do not need to be told this.[85]

As we know, however, Alemán's original plans for *Guzmán de Alfarache* were severely affected by the plagiarism of his own Part II before it could be published and the need to write a new second part. In the process his conception of the ending evidently underwent a change, though the *Declaración* was left in its original form. The *Declaración* continues to announce his first thoughts, while the text inevitably reflects a later view. Why did Alemán, even so, not recreate his original intention to land Guzmán in the galleys? Reasons can only be guessed at. When Alemán comes to rewrite Part II he has, of course, to face up to the issue of plagiarism in a way which he did not have to before. The problem is a difficult one for the writer of fictional autobiography since the death of the protagonist is not an option available to him. Yet Alemán produces an ending which is an open invitation to writers of sequels. It is possible that Alemán had other, more practical, considerations in mind. His concern for verisimilitude is evident even in the *Declaración*: he is careful to account for aspects of the work which he senses might cause his readers some difficulty. His explanation of Guzmán's ability to write 'alguna dotrina' by virtue of his theological education is a case in point. It may be that Alemán baulked on second thoughts at the inherent unlikelihood that a man could actually write anything chained to an oar in a galley, something that Alemán is somewhat defensive about in the *Declaración*:

Pues aun vemos a muchos ignorantes justiciados, que habiendo de ocuparlo en sola su salvación, divertirse della por estudiar un sermoncito para en la escalera.   (p. 96)

(Being that we likewise see many ignorant poore soules sentenced to death, who being to spend the remainder of their time in thinking on their soules health, divert their thoughts from all other worldly things, for to make a short studied speech when they come to the Ladder.)   (Mabbe, I, 19–20)

The suggestion that a convict might write his autobiography is easier to take if the convict 'escapes'. It is possible, too, that Alemán felt that a change of heart on Guzmán's part deserved a better fate than continued languishment at sea.

Whatever the reasons for Alemán's change of plan, some things are clear: he originally intended that Guzmán should write his story from the galley; Guzmán complies with this intention, speaking at one point of 'the miseries I suffer on this galley' ('esta galera', p. 391); and in spite of Alemán's change of plan at the end of the book Guzmán continues to write *as if* from the galley in the sense that his point of view and the manner of his writing remain consistent to the end. What is more, even Joan Arias, who lays some stress on the fact and significance of Guzmán's release, continues to refer to him as the 'narrator, Guzmán galeote' (e.g. p. 56), thereby subscribing to a general preparedness among readers to overlook the exact circumstances of the final chapters in favour of Alemán's original intention: though nominally released, Guzmán is really still a galley-slave to most of us.

In suggesting that the inconsistency between the *Declaración* and the end of *Guzmán de Alfarache* as we have it can be resolved in purely historical terms, as a change of plan between the first and second recensions, I do not mean to imply that the resulting clash is without interest. For one thing, the fact that we are able to practise this selective blindness to certain details of the text tells us a great deal about the relationship between narrative detail and literary purpose, between what the text says and what it means or is intended to do. The fact that generations of commentators have continued to think of and refer to Guzmán as a galley-slave in the face of the evidence suggests that readers respond more to Guzmán's conception of his life as exemplary in some way than to the precise details of the events he recounts.

For another, the absence from the fiction of any account of how it came to be written does raise questions about its purpose. Lázaro de Tormes does not actually recount the act of writing his account but he does make clear within the fiction why and how he came to write it, who it is addressed to and what it is intended to achieve. Guzmán's fortunate release from captivity relieves him of the need to be specific about such matters and deprives him of the opportunity to explain the genesis of his work. And it is this lack of definition about his purpose that has undoubtedly led critics to question the 'sincerity' of Guzmán's avowed repentance at the end of the book. If we cannot be sure exactly when and under what circumstances he is writing we cannot be sure either what his approach to his own past is likely to be. Yet some clear idea of the point of the narrative must form in the reader's mind long before the end of the book, or it would be unreadable. What, then, is Guzmán's aim in telling us all that he does?

Perhaps the clearest statement of his purpose comes from Guzmán himself in the first chapter of Part II. Much has been made of this chapter for the defensive tone in which it is written, though less has been made of the clarity with which Guzmán's intentions emerge from that defensiveness. The chapter is based on an admission that his own life has been a sinful one and an assertion that his purpose is to denounce sin. His defensiveness arises from a recognition that his own behaviour must inevitably undermine his credibility as preacher. Yet in spite of this he sees his own wickedness and the narration of that wickedness as an essential part of his didactic method:

> aquesta confesión general que hago, este alarde público que de mis cosas te represento, no es para que me imites a mí; antes para que, sabidas, corrijas las tuyas en ti.   (p. 484)

> (this generall confession that I make; this publike opening of my Packe, laying before thee all my Knacks, and my Trinkets; I doe not therefore shew things unto thee, that thou shouldst either imitate me, or my evill actions; but rather, that (when thou shalt come to know them) thou mayst learne thereby to correct thine owne.)   (Mabbe, III, 30)

The whole chapter makes use of a general appeal to the *topos* about the morality of the moralist, and asserts the validity of the moral in the face of the sinful humanity of the preacher. Quevedo often expressed the same fears that the contrast between his own life and writings would bring the latter into disrepute.[86] Guzmán does the same, as did Lázaro de Tormes before him; and all three assert that the difference between theory and practice ('video meliora proboque, deteriora sequor'),[87] though perhaps regrettable, has little effect on the validity of the lessons they are trying to teach. Implicit in this assertion is also a rejection of arguments that lay behind the criticisms made of fiction, the view that immorality has no place in the moralist's, or the artist's, sphere of interest.

There is a specific appeal, however, in Guzmán's statement, one that amounts to rather more than an invitation to do as he says, not as he does:

Si me ves caído por mal reglado, haz de manera que aborrezcas lo que me derribó, no pongas el pie donde me viste resbalar y sírvate de aviso el trompezón que di. Que hombre mortal eres como yo y por ventura no más fuerte ni de mayor maña. Da vuelta por ti, recorre a espacio y con cuidado la casa de tu alma, mira si tienes hechos muladares asquerosos en lo mejor della y no espulgues ni murmures que en casa de tu vecino estaba una pluma de pájaro a la subida de la escalera. (p. 484)

(If thou seest me falne, because I was wilfull, and would not be ordred; looke thou well to thy steps, that thou mayst hate and avoyd those occasions, that wrought my fall. Set not thy foot, where thou hast seene me slip before thee; but let my trippings and my stumblings, serve as so many markes to make thee more wary. For thou art a man, mortall as I am, and peradventure neither stronger, nor wiser then my selfe. Looke well into thy selfe; runne over very leisurely and carefully, the house of thy Soule, and see if thou have not made there, even in the greater and better part of it, Dung-hils of filth, and all manner of beastlinesse; and doe not sift and prie so narrowly into thy neighbours, to see if thou canst finde but the feather of some bird at the foot of the Stayres, whereat thou mayst picke a quarrell.) (Mabbe, III, 30–1)

Here and elsewhere in the book a common bond of fallibility is forged between protagonist and reader, and the relationship of the two kinds of experience, the first-hand and the second-hand, is brought into the forefront of our concern. He errs in order that we may, in discerning his error, correct our own:

A mi costa y con trabajos propios descubro los peligros y sirtes, para que no embistas y te despedaces ni encalles adonde te falte remedio a la salida. (p. 485)

(At mine owne cost and paines, I discover shelfes, quicksands, and dangerous rockes unto thee, to the end that thou mayst not fall upon them, and dash thy

selfe in pieces against them, or runne thy selfe on ground, where there is never
any hope of comming off.)   (Mabbe, III, p. 31)

His examples are to be avoided, but avoided on the basis of shared
experience ('no pongas el pie donde me viste resbalar') and it is
through his narration of his errors, and the reader's reading of them,
that that basis of shared experience is established.

Far from excusing his behaviour, then, Guzmán urges us to accept
its exemplary nature and his didactic purpose in recounting it. We are
not asked to overlook his own failings when considering the value of his
advice, nor are we even asked to learn from them; we have to learn
through them. Hence the importance that attaches in both Alemán's
mind and Guzmán's to the proper relationship between precept and
example, and the need to submit experience to the discipline of mind:

Haz como leas lo que leyeres y no te rías de la conseja y se te pase el consejo;
recibe los que te doy y el ánimo con que te los ofrezco: no los eches como
barreduras al muladar del olvido. Mira que podrá ser escobilla de precio.
Recoge, junta esa tierra, métela en el crisol de la consideración, dale fuego de
espíritu, y te aseguro hallarás algún oro que te enriquezca.
                                            (p. 94, 'Al discreto lector')

(Reade so, as it becomes thee to reade, and doe not scoffe at my Fable; and if it
shall receive intertainment at thy hands, accept these lines, which I give thee,
and with them, the minde wherewith they be offered unto thee. Doe not cast
them, as dust and sweepings of the house, upon the dunghill of oblivion;
consider that there may be some filings and parings of price; rake them out,
gather them into a heape, and when they come to a convenient quantitie, put
them into the crisole of thy consideration; give to them the fire of the Spirit;
and I assure thee, thou shalt extract some gold from them, wherewithall to
inrich thy selfe.)   (Mabbe, I, 17–18)

One might be disposed to shrug off such a passage as a commonplace
assertion that no book is so bad that no good can come of it, were it not
for the fact that the passage constitutes a statement in miniature of
what should happen in the mind of his reader when he is reading:
experience should give way to understanding, pleasure to profit and
the dross of life be transformed in the crucible of the mind. The
vicarious experience that reading entails is therefore an essential
preliminary to the emergence of a responsible approach to the text.

These ideas are summed up in the Latin motto that appeared on the
title page of the 1599 first part and was used subsequently by Alemán
on a number of occasions: LEGENDO SIMVLQVE PERAGRANDO. An
extensive search has failed to locate a classical or learned source for
this device, and it may reasonably, if provisionally, be assumed to be

Alemán's own. The interest of the motto lies in the choice of the relatively unfamiliar verb 'peragrare' to describe the act of reading. 'Peragrare' is, literally, to traverse or to scour a territory or the sea, generally to some purpose, but it is also used figuratively, particularly by Cicero, to mean scouring with the mind.[88] Reading, then, is a journey in two senses: it takes us into unfamiliar territory through vicarious experience, and it involves the discovery of new intellectual horizons when that experience is fired in the 'crisol de la consideración'.

Implicit both in Guzmán's avowed didacticism and in Alemán's choice of motto is the fundamental problem that runs throughout the fiction of the Spanish Golden Age, the proper relationship between experience and understanding. Alemán's motto could stand for its age. It reminds us again of Thomas Hooker's distinction between the traveller and the map-reader, and the problem of reconciling thinking and feeling. Like Thomas Hooker, Alemán realised that moral decisions are not made in the study in response to directives. They are made by reason and passion working in context. It is an attempt to supply such a context that lies behind the use of the *consejo* and the *conseja* in *Guzmán de Alfarache*. It is a widely accepted rule among writers of sermons that specific examples are more effective than abstract precepts. The translator of the Latin version of *Guzmán*, Gaspar Ens, put it thus: 'Efficatius docent exempla quam precepta.'[89] By supplying a *conseja* in didactic writing, the writer supplies a model of the context in which a particular decision was made or a particular course of action decided upon. The reader is left to infer, with or without the help of the author, the general principles which underlie the particular example. Like Cervantes in the *Novelas ejemplares*, the writer supplies a sample, a slice of life, and can either, as Cervantes does, limit himself to implying that such-and-such a course of action is likely to lead to these or those consequences, or he can drive home his point with a more explicit moral. Either way is a more sophisticated alternative to straightforward preaching.

The problem remains, however, that no matter how vivid and convincing this model or context may be, it remains someone else's context, never the reader's own, and any decision made within it can ultimately only have the relevance of a precept even if it has the narrative vividness of a real situation. It is not enough for Guzmán to say 'Yo aquí recibo los palos y tú los consejos en ellos' (p. 483) ('The blowes I shall receive, thou the good counsels. . .', Mabbe, III, 28), not enough to turn a life narrated *a posteriori* into an *a priori* example.[90]

To be 'desengañado' the reader must first be 'engañado', he must know the pitfalls by experiencing them in his reading, by experiencing them as *consejas* as well as *consejos*. Alemán's task, then, if his avowed aim of exemplarity is to be successful, is to create a work which will involve the reader at an emotional as well as an intellectual level. Alemán was sufficiently widely read in the literature of his age, and well enough acquainted with the critical and moral problems associated with it, to perceive that in fiction lay the solution to his problem. Fiction allowed the creation of an analogue personality to illustrate the reader's own by encouraging him to identify with the protagonist. Yet at the same time, if the critics of fiction were to be silenced, and his own didactic purpose was to succeed, Alemán had also to ensure that the reader's identification was controlled and channelled in an appropriate direction. Guzmán's approach to his autobiography is an analysis of these problems. As Lázaro did before him, Guzmán will find that the solution to his particular task lay in the creation of a work which would engage and detach the reader at one and the same time.

At the simplest level it is possible to see each of these two functions, engagement and detachment, carried out by the two main structural threads of the book, the narrative and the commentary. The fact that this division of the book into two not entirely distinct parts has become a commonplace of *Guzmán* criticism from Le Sage to the present day does not detract from its importance as one of the book's central rhetorical devices. The many attempts that have been made to illustrate the relevance of the commentary to the narrative and the skill with which each is integrated into the other do not deny, either, the fact that when Alemán had Guzmán choose to tell his life in the way that he does, a number of options were selected which will determine the ways in which the reader will have to respond. As Francisco Rico has made clear in an important essay on *Guzmán*, the narrative–commentary structure is not something that Alemán picked up and made the best of: it is a consciously chosen literary device.

In telling his story Guzmán tends on the whole to make a clear distinction between his past and present, between the events of his wicked past and the clearsightedness with which he seems now to view them. He sets down his life as it was lived, and rather than hedge it about with apologies, he prefers to give the raw, unedited narrative its head. When he does interrupt the narrative flow from time to time it is to deliver fully-fledged sermons and homilies which, while they grow out of and refer to the events of the past, remain stylistically and thematically distinct, as if self-consciously dissociating themselves from the surrounding morass of immorality. As a consequence the whole work often seems to separate into two distinct strands, the one an earnest palinode desperately striving to recant what the other narrates with relish. It is out of these fiercely warring voices, the first person vividly recreating the past while a predominantly third person condemns from the present, that the charges of prurience and insincerity laid against Alemán and Guzmán have sprung. Such charges can be effectively answered if account is taken of the point of view of the reader, the person for whom the whole narrative–commentary structure is designed.

As Marcel Bataillon has noted,[91] all confession – and confessing is what Guzmán claims to be doing – involves an element of immorality as the sins confessed are recounted. Confession involves reliving past sin. The issue in Guzmán's case is whether or not his sins have to be recounted in such prurient detail. Yet although Guzmán's avowal of confession would lead us to expect him to temper the excesses of the past with understanding of the present, his overall purpose, it must be remembered, is not entirely self-centred and autobiographical. He is not confessing for the good of his soul – he has none – nor is he simply writing the kind of autobiography in which the distinction between a life lived and a life recollected in tranquillity and maturity is the centre of interest. As far as the reader is concerned the distinction between the protagonist's past and his present is not one of great importance since it is telescoped to such an extent as to disappear almost entirely. Guzmán's past and present are both present to the reader at the moment of reading. Guzmán's narrative is not a way of reliving his past but a way of recreating it so that the reader may experience it as present. If Guzmán's past was a sinful one, then for the reader to experience it as such, it has to be retold exactly as it was. The cautionary aspect of the story will only succeed if the reader is given the chance to experience what it is he is being cautioned against.

The narrative vividness of Guzmán's confession, a vividness which depends for much of its effect on the skilful development of the consequences of first-person narrative, is therefore an essential part of the didactic technique of the work as a whole. First catch your reader, and do not scruple to mislead him, at least for the time being, in order to force him to acknowledge his error. The technique is an old one, an essential ingredient of *elenchos* and frequently employed by Christ.

Milton described Christ's teaching method as 'not so much a teaching, as an intangling',[92] and Stanley Fish has shown how Milton himself uses the technique of entangling his reader in *Paradise Lost*, 'recreating in the mind of the reader . . . the drama of the Fall, to make him fall again as Adam did' (p. 1). By giving Satan and his sophistry such attractive prominence in the poem Milton allows the reader to experience what it is to be enthralled by the Devil. The analogy with *Guzmán* is clear: both Milton and Alemán draw a parallel between aesthetic experience and moral experience and are prepared to allow the one to stand in place of the other in the interests of a higher purpose. In both writers the aesthetic experience is vicarious in a special sense: a living experience of sin is imitated in art by the deployment of artistic rather than moral values. In consequence, and because both writers are careful to match their readers' involvement with an equal dose of devices designed to ensure his detachment, the reader himself becomes the true centre of the work, experiencing as a conflict of artistic values the struggle of inclination and conscience that beset the protagonist before him.

In *Guzmán de Alfarache* the artistic values in question tend to group themselves around the two poles of autobiography: first-person narrative and second-person address. While Guzmán uses the 'yo' to close the gap between himself and the reader, he uses the 'tú' to make sure that the gap is maintained. The crucial difference between Guzmán and Lázaro, however, is that Guzmán does not use his second person to cast the reader in a single clearly-defined role. Maurice Molho has commented on the way the whole work can be seen as a dialogue between Guzmán and an unnamed interlocutor, the reader, who takes on any role that is required of him: notary, constable, doctor, merchant, innkeeper, etc.[93] Addressing a protean reader in these several ways both engages him since these roles are not static but are types of relationship between reader and protagonist,[94] and detaches him since underlying the various relationships is an assumption of social difference, of enmity.

It is, then, the dynamic potential of the first-person narrative that interests Alemán, as it interested the author of *Lazarillo de Tormes* though in a somewhat different way. Guzmán's 'yo' exists to bring into being another person or persons against whom he can measure himself, and since Guzmán's confession is inevitably made from a defensive position it is equally inevitable that the reader will frequently fill the role of judge. The division in Guzmán's own self-portrait (his past 'yo' accused by his present 'yo', the judge) is therefore reproduced within the reader, who identifies with Guzmán's past 'yo' recreated as present and with his present 'yo' by virtue of being apostrophised in various ways as 'tú'. It is by a dialectic of assimilation and dissimilation,[95] first person *versus* second person, that Guzmán coaxes his reader towards a proper understanding of his own experience. At one moment he cajoles him by calling him 'hermano', at another he accuses him of being the ever-critical 'curioso lector', at others he is insulting and wheedling by turns, as capable of a hostile 'tú' as a complicitous 'nosotros'.[96]

Guzmán has other antagonists than his reader, however, since the dialectic between himself and another frequently turns inwards and the dialogue becomes a dialogue with himself. Gonzalo Sobejano first noted this particular use of the 'tú' form in a footnote to an article published in 1959.[97] More recently, Francisco Rico has followed up the implications of that note, arguing that the potential incompatibility of Guzmán and Guzmanillo (how does such a wicked youth turn into such a saint?) is avoided by the fact that Guzmán's repentance is foreshadowed in the young protagonist.[98] Guzmanillo is very intelligent, 'hombre de claro entendimiento', endowed not only with a wit and intelligence that get him through life, but also with a capacity for self-analysis which enables the author to place much of the didactic commentary in the mind of the young pícaro. Guzmán not only lectures the reader, but as Guzmanillo's better judgment he lectures himself. He is always muttering to himself, or scolding himself angrily: '¡Cuánto sentí entonces mis locuras! ¡Cuánto reñí a mí mismo! ¡Qué de enmiendas propuse, cuando blanca para gastar no tuve!' (p. 340) ('How much did I then risent my former follies? How angry was I growne with my selfe?', Mabbe, II, 110). Often his arguments develop into a vigorous dialogue (here he is speaking of the corruption of law officers):

Di también – pues no lo dijiste – que si a los tales, después de ahorcados les hiciesen las causas, dirían contra ellos aquellos mismos que andan a su lado y agora con el miedo comen y callan. Di sin rebozo que, por comer ellos de balde o barato, carga sobre los pobres aquello y se les vende lo peor y más caro. Acaba ya, di en resolución, que son como tú y de mayor daño, que tú dañas una casa y ellos toda la república.

¡Oh qué gentil consejo que me das ése, amigo mío! ¡Tómalo tú para ti! ¿Quieres por ventura sacar las brasas con la mano del gato? Dilo, si lo sabes; que lo que yo supe ya lo dije y no quiero que comigo hagan lo que dices que con los otros hacen.   (p. 677)

(I could tell thee likewise something which thou hast left out, that if these men, after they were hanged, should have their causes heard, and see what they could say for themselves, even those very men would plead stiffley against them, who theretofore were in their favour . . . they are, as thou art; and worse than thou, and doe much more hurt; for thou doest but damnifie one house alone; but these a whole Country.

O what good counsell dost thou give mee! But let mee wish thee (my friend) to make use of it thy selfe. Think'st thou perhaps to save thine owne fingers from burning, to take the Cat by the foote, and therewith to rake the coales out of the Oven? If thou knowest this to be true, or hast anything else to say of them, speake it your selfe for me: for I have told thee all that I know, and I would not willingly that they should deale with mee, as thou sayest they deale with others.)   (Mabbe, III, 340–1)

It is perfectly possible, of course, to take this 'tú' as the reader, but if it is taken to refer to Guzmán himself, then the narrative–commentary structure becomes an analysis of a divided soul, a *debate espiritual* between reason and passion, culminating in the final appearance of the disembodied voice of Guzmán's conscience: '¿Ves aquí, Guzmán, la cumbre del monte de las miserias, adonde te ha subido tu torpe sensualidad?' (p. 889) ('Guzmán, thou seest heere the top of that Mountaine of miseries, where-unto thy filthy sensualitie hath brought thee . . .', Mabbe, IV, 327–8). As Rico himself notes, this use of the second-person address is an economical way of dissecting a conscience torn between the pull of instinct and the call of grace.[99] Guzmán's analytical approach to his autobiography emerges, then, as doubly significant; not only does it enable him to present his past in all its uncensored vividness, enthralling the reader in a vicarious sinfulness only to bring him up short against a revised and corrected view of things in the commentary; it helps to make the complexity of Guzmán's past more immediately available to the reader. The engagement and detachment with which the reader approaches the work springs, therefore, both from the intercutting of a naïve, sinful life and a more morally mature, retrospective view of that life, and from a recreation of that past life in terms of the warring factors which were at work in Guzmán's personality.

Such an analytical approach to the portrayal of a man's inner life is not unique in the literature of Golden-Age Spain. In *El condenado por desconfiado* Tirso de Molina portrays the interior drama of his character Paulo in terms of the devil and the shepherd boy; Lope de Vega exteriorises Alonso's death wish in the form of the premonitions in *El caballero de Olmedo*; and, later still, we find a masterly analysis of moral and mental processes in the allegories of *El criticón*. But the fact that Alemán consciously chose this approach seems clear from the way he began the work in a rather different style. He was as competent as the author of *Lazarillo* at combining a mature vision and a childlike vision in a sustained piece of irony. One might note, for example, from the opening chapters,[100] the sensitive mixture of sympathy for his mother's failing good looks coupled with a knowing recognition of what she would have done with them had she still got them:

aunque su hermosura no estaba distraída, teníanla los años algo gastada. Hacíasele de mal, habiendo sido rogada de tantos tantas veces, no serlo también entonces y de persona tal que nos pelechara; que no lo siendo, ni ella lo hiciera ni yo lo permitiera.   (p. 142)

(And albeit her beauty was not disfigured, yet her yeeres had somewhat defaced it: And it grieved her exceedingly, that having beene so many times sued unto by many, that she was not now in case to be courted: And especially of some such person, whose fethers she might have pull'd from him; for otherwise, neither would she have yeelded unto him, nor I have permitted it.)
(Mabbe, I, 88)

The highly elliptical last remark, expanded by Mabbe in his translation ('if she had not been, she would not have done it, and I would not have allowed it'), puts a great deal of strain on the reader's ability to complete the sense (if she had not been what? she would not have done what?), and in completing it (if she had not been such a faded beauty no longer sought after by men of means, she would not have sold herself on the streets) the reader cooperates in a subtle play of complicity with Guzmán, reading the truth under his denials and the reality of economic necessity under his protestations of youthful chivalry ('I would not have allowed it').

A passage such as that is worthy of, indeed reminiscent of, *Lazarillo de Tormes*, and there is much else in the early chapters of Guzmán that is like it. When Guzmán first ventures into the world he describes his many troubles, of which the greatest was that it happened to be a Friday, in a sustained piece of irony:

Hice allí de nuevo alarde de mi vida y discursos della. Quisiera volverme, por haber salido mal apercibido, con poco acuerdo y poco dinero para viaje tan largo, que aun para corto no llevaba. Y sobre tantas desdichas – que, cuando comienzan, vienen siempre muchas y enzarzadas unas de otras como cerezas – era viernes en la noche y algo oscura, no había cenado ni merendado: si fuera día de carne, que a la salida de la ciudad, aunque fuera naturalmente ciego, el olor me llevara en alguna pastelería, comprara un pastel con que me entretuviera y enjugara el llanto, el mal fuera menos.

Entonces eché de ver cuánto se siente más el bien perdido y la diferencia que hace del hambriento el harto. Los trabajos todos comiendo se pasan; donde la comida falta, no hay bien que llegue ni mal que no sobre, gusto que dure ni contento que asista: todos riñen sin saber por qué, ninguno tiene culpa, unos a otros la ponen, todos trazan y son quimeristas, todo es entonces gobierno y filosofía. (p. 147)

(There I made a new muster of my life, survay'd it over and over, and discoursed with my selfe thereupon. I was about to goe backe againe, for that I came forth ill provided, worse advised, and poorely furnisht with money for so long a Voyage, having scarce sufficient to serve my turne for a farre shorter journey. And amongst other my so many misfortunes, (which when they once beginne, come by clusters, hanging like Cherries; one at the tayle of another) it was Friday night; and withall, somewhat darke. I had neither supt, nor had any bever that afternoone. Had I gone out of the Citie upon a flesh day, although I had beene borne blind, my nose would have helped mee to smell out some one Cookes shoppe or other, where I might have bought a penny Pasty, wherewithall to entertaine my stomake, and to dry up my teares, and so my sorrow would have beene the lesse.

Then I began to perceive, how much more sensible a man is of the good he loseth then when he injoyed it; and what difference there is betweene the hungry belly, and the full-fed paunch. All troubles passe the better with bread: Where good feeding fayleth, there is no good followeth; no evill which aboundeth not; no pleasure that indureth, nor content to comfort us. All fret and chafe, and know not why, nor wherefore. No man is in fault; and yet they lay it one upon another; all runne upon the haunt, feigning strange Chimera's in their heads; all is then nothing but government; all is Philosophy.) (Mabbe, 1, 94)

Once again the childlike excuse ('poco dinero para viaje tan largo') corrected by the mature realism ('que aun para corto no llevaba') is worthy of the author of the *Lazarillo*, as is the meditation on hunger, which trivialises ('Los trabajos todos comiendo se pasan') at the same time as it makes food all important ('donde la comida falta, no hay bien que llegue ni mal que no sobre'). The lightheadedness and fractiousness that hunger brings are brilliantly conveyed by the progressive abstractions that culminate in 'gobierno y filosofía'.

Yet the fact is that for the greater part of the book, for the whole of the narrative which takes place between the two dark nights of the soul at the beginning and the end, Alemán chose an analytical rather than a synthetic approach. We see this especially in those passages where Guzmán stops talking to himself and holds imaginary conversations with others instead. At one point señora Doña claims that she sins of necessity. Nonsense, Guzmán replies, pull yourself together and do something constructive. Back comes the answer: why should I, when you won't?[101] It is hardly necessary to add that señora Doña does not exist in the rest of the narrative; Guzmán invents her *ad hoc* so that he can have that argument. She is a model, in fact, of the way he uses the reader for much of the time. The same is true a chapter later when Guzmán records what purports to be a sermon he gave to one 'otro' who was in the same cell as he (p. 611). In fact 'otro' never appears in the ensuing dialogue; it is Guzmán who does all the talking and supplies all the answers. Here, as elsewhere, Guzmán is giving himself a drubbing in the person of another. Guzmán is not always convinced by his own arguments, however; sometimes he accepts, sometimes he rejects. When he lectures himself, or is lectured at by others, he invariably rejects, sometimes quite violently: '¡Oh qué gentil consejo que me das ése, amigo mío! ¡Tómalo tú para ti!' (p. 677) On other occasions he mumbles away bitterly. 'No hay mal tan malo de que no resulte algo bueno', they say. What have I got to show? '. . . gastado, robado, hambriento, y deshechas las quijadas a puñetes, desencasado el pescuezo a pescozadas, bañados en sangre los dientes a mojicones' (p. 193) ('There is no ill so bad, from whence there doth not arise some good . . . My money spent, my Cloake stolne, my belly hungry, my cheekes buffeted, my necke out of joynt, and my teeth bathed in blood, with the bobs on my nose, and the dashes that they gave mee on the mouth', Mabbe I, 161).

Guzmán makes most headway, however, when he contemplates his own experience and finds it a living *exemplum*. One of the best examples of this takes place after he leaves prison and before setting out for Milan. Three men become involved in a game of cards at Guzmán's lodgings and he is drawn into the game as a spectator, watching the play of one of them in particular for more than two hours. The players take their changing fortunes with perfect equanimity, but Guzmán notices that he becomes emotionally involved in the game for no reason; he does not even know the men. What starts as a comment on the strangeness of human nature ('¡Oh estraña naturaleza nuestra!') turns on reflection into an expression of dismay at his own stupidity:

¡Qué pecado tan sin provecho el mío, qué sin propósito y necio, desear que perdiesen los otros para que aquél se lo llevara! ¡Como si aquel interés fuera mío, como si me lo quitaran a mí o si hubieran de dármelo!'   (p. 619)

(See what a kinde of sinne this was in mee; how unprofitable to my selfe? how foolish and to no purpose, to desire that the other two might lose, that hee might rise the winner, and goe away with their money, as if my selfe had beene interessed therein, or as if they had got it from me, or were bound to let me have it.)   (Mabbe, II, 244)

There is something in our natures that only makes us show an interest in our neighbour's affairs if it is to his detriment. We are quite happy to sit up all night to watch a man lose at cards, or to spy on who comes and goes, but would not dream of staying up to keep watch over his house for him.

In this episode, Guzmán's sermon grows naturally out of his experiences by means of the generalising *topos* of human nature: '¡Oh estraña naturaleza *nuestra*!', and by the appeal to the reader in the second person as 'hermano' or 'hermana': '¿Qué ganas o qué te dan por la mala noche que pasas?' (p. 620) ('What good doest thou get by it, or what reward doe they give thee, for that thy nights watching, so ill bestowed on thy selfe, and others?', Mabbe, III, 245). Self-contemplation and didacticism are made one and the same by virtue of the common experience of men. But there is another dimension to the episode since it hinges on the almost automatic nature of empathy. Guzmán's experience as an onlooker is that he finds it impossible not to identify in spite of the fact that he knows he should remain detached. His advice to the reader is doomed, therefore, from the outset: 'Si gustas de ver jugar, mira desapasionadamente si puedes; mas no podrás, que eres como yo y harás lo mismo' (p. 620) ('If thou take pleasure in looking on those that game, looke on (if thou canst) without passion. But thou canst not doe it; for thou art, as I am; and thou wilt doe, as I doe', Mabbe, III, 246). Guzmán, watching the cardplayers, is like the reader reading the book; he gets involved with the affairs of others when it is his own house that he should be putting in order.

It is this sense that Guzmán has of doing things in spite of his better knowledge to the contrary that makes his moments of self-contemplation so rewarding for the reader. Throughout his life *consejos* and *consejas* battle for Guzmán's attention. He resists the *a priori* teachings that come to him in the form of sermons and other narrative *exempla* because they are the results of other people's experiences and not his own: 'tómalo tú para ti'. They are the *consejos* of the book. He is more disposed to accept the teachings of his own experience, the *consejas*, since they are the results of his own heartsearchings. By having them available as the vividly reconstructed narrative of Guzmán's past life experienced in reading as present, the reader is given access to this inner struggle while it is taking place: Guzmán refuses to give him the resolution of the struggle on a plate. In reading, Guzmán's heartsearchings become the reader's own, and the reader's vicarious experience of sin is broadened and deepened in the process: not only does he know what it feels like to err; he knows error in the face of his better judgment. Like Adam in Milton's poem, Guzmán and his reader are not deceived, but see their error with 'troubled clarity'.[102]

One of the best examples of the clarity with which Guzmán sees his own mistake at the very moment of making it comes at the point in the narrative when he meets and falls in love with Gracia. Resident in Alcalá for more than seven years while reading Theology at the University, and with the reputation of one of the best students there, Guzmán visits the hermitage of Santa María de Val one afternoon. 'De aquí se levantó la tormenta de mi vida, la destruición de mi hacienda y acabamiento de mi honra' (p. 816) ('Hence rose that terrible storme of my tempestuous life, the destruction of my wealth, and the finall over-throw of my credit', Mabbe, IV, 211). This prior announcement of the impending destruction of the greatest of Guzmán's efforts at reform is important in that the tragedy of his encounter with Gracia is narrated and read with foresight as well as hindsight. Then, as if to underline the ordered calm of the steady achievement of his life that is so soon to be shattered, Guzmán sums up: 'Yo estaba ya en el punto que has oído, los cursos casi pasados, la capellanía fundada para ordenarme y tomar el grado dentro de tres meses' (p. 818). He was only three months away from the graduation when the hurricane struck. In the brilliantly written passage that follows, Guzmán tells us in horrifying and compelling detail how in an afternoon he became captivated by Gracia's looks, accomplishments and charms, and how she reduced him to an automaton, completely at the mercy of his own feelings and the women's astuteness:

Era taimada la madre, buscaba yernos y las hijas maridos. No les descontentaba el mozo. Diéronme cuerda larga, hasta dejarlas dentro de su casa. Donde, cuando llegamos, me hicieron entrar en su aposento, que tenían .muy bien aderezado. Llegáronme una silla. Hiciéronme descansar un poco y, sacando una caja de conserva me trujeron con ella un jarro de agua, que no fue poco necesaria para el fuego del veneno que me abrasaba el corazón. Mas no aprovechó.   (pp. 819–20)

(Her mother was a crafty flye subtill thing; she sought after sonnes-in-Law, and her daughters were desirous of husbands, nor did they mislike of the man: They gave me line enough, till they had led me along by the nose within their owne doores: whither when we were come, they made mee enter into their private chamber, which was very well furnisht; they brought me a chayre, and would needs have me sit downe, that I might rest my selfe a while; and taking out of a Cupboard, neere there at hand, a boxe of Conserves, they brought me with it a jarre of water, which was no more than needed for to quench the fire of that poyson which had so scorcht my heart: but all would not doe.)   (Mabbe, IV, 216)

Here Guzmán conveys his powerlessness by making himself a grammatical object: only of the verb 'no descontentaba' is he the subject.

Guzmán then goes on to describe the tortured night that followed his leave-taking:

¿Qué largas horas, qué sueño tan corto, qué confusión de pensamientos, qué guerra toral, qué batalla de cuidados, qué tormenta se ha levantado en el puerto de mi mayor bonanza? – dije –. ¿Cómo en tan segura calma me sobrevino semejante borrasca, sin sentirla venir ni saberla remediar? Me veo perdido. (p. 820)

(How long were the houres? How short the sleepes? What a confusion of thoughts? What distractions of mind? What a generall warre? What a battaile of cares? What a cruell tempest risen on the sodaine, even in the very Port and Haven where I thought my selfe so surely anchored, the sky being so cleare, the weather so faire, and the Sea so smooth, as heart could wish? This made me say to my selfe; How in so quiet a calme, could such a sodaine storme come upon me, without perceiving its approach, or knowing how in the world to provide any remedy against it? I am utterly lost, and undone for ever.) (Mabbe, IV, 217)

Here the renewed references to the idea of the storm that blows up out of nothing to destroy the calm of his life make it clear that the agitation he feels – or rather, felt then ('dije') – is not just the excitement of the *flechazo* but the despair of being able to see that, in spite of himself, he is doomed: 'Me veo perdido'. This and the paragraphs that follow are some of the most moving in the book, as Guzmán's inner struggle between passion and better judgment resolves itself in the bitter flow of tears, a mistaken sense of relief ('sentíme con esto algo aliviado') and the inevitable decision to miss a class and visit Gracia. Guzmán's simile – a course of study is like a piece of knitting: one dropped stitch and the whole thing is ruined – is both a homely and a frightening symbol of the shreds into which his life is already falling.

Guzmán's encounter with Gracia comes sufficiently near the end of the book to suggest that it might stand as a summation of all that Guzmán is attempting to do in his narrative. It is, in any event, characteristic of his technique throughout. It is, first and foremost, extremely effectively written and makes compelling reading. No one who has ever fallen disastrously in love could fail to recognise the symptoms or to experience once again the enthralling powerlessness that love entails. Yet at the same time Guzmán conveys the humiliation that is also involved. Part of this comes from hindsight. From his notional vantage-point of the galley he can see how the rock which he had so very nearly pushed to the top of the mountain had rolled once more to the bottom (p. 822). But the destruction wreaked by Gracia was obvious to him at the outset; he knew then that he was lost. In this way Alemán brings about a fine blend of didacticism and fiction. As Edmond Cros has noted,[103] the novelisation of didacticism requires at once a measure of 'verismo', that the reader enter into an understanding of the psychological truth of the character, and a measure of distance so that sympathy can be tempered by a more objective assessment of the character's actions and motives. In *Guzmán de Alfarache* this simultaneous engagement and detachment is provided by a number of interlocking relationships between author, character and reader. The author allows us to see events 'desde dentro' by having the character narrate them convincingly as they happened so that the reader can experience them as present. We also see them 'desde fuera' because Guzmán adopts a critical attitude to his past life, casting his present self in the role of judge and his past self in the role of the accused. As the reader is also invited to associate himself with the critical perspective of the judge, the dialectic of then/now, accused/accuser is transferred to the reader. However, the reader experiences Guzmán's past *and* his present as present, and the resulting complex interplay of vicarious sinfulness and better judgment emerges as a convincing reconstruction of Guzmán's own past life which had its full share of dilemma and trauma: 'no hay batalla tan sangrienta ni tan trabada escaramuza, como la que trae la mocedad consigo' (p. 599) ('There is no battaile so bloody, no skirmish so hot, and so hard to come off cleare, as that warre, which we wage with our youth', Mabbe, III, 208). Although Guzmán does not spare his former self whom he presents in all his former impenitent error,[104] he nevertheless enables us to see the young Guzmán as a rounded, complex and ultimately redeemable figure by showing that his present was there all along, foreshadowed in his past.

One further avantage that comes from presenting Guzmán's past in terms of a *debate espiritual* (inclination *versus* conscience represented fictionally by the wisdom of hindsight) is subtly to blur some of the distinctions in matters where it is very difficult to lay down hard and fast principles. Charity is one of the issues that emerge from the book as more problematical than might be supposed. There is a good example of this after Guzmán leaves Florence. He is masquerading as a beggar, made up to look ill, and he is given a substantial sum of money – all that he had on him at the time – by a gentleman who takes pity on him. The gentleman seems to be motivated by true compassion and yet

Guzmán, apparently in retrospect, curses him ironically for his charity:

Estos tales ganaban por su caridad el cielo por nuestra mano y nosotros lo perdíamos por la dellos, pues con la golosina del recebir, pidiendo sin tener necesidad, lo quitábamos al que la tenía, usurpando nuestro vicio el oficio ajeno. (p. 380)

(Such good soules as these, did (in the exercising of their Charity) gaine heaven by our hands, and we (wicked Villaines) have lost it by theirs; since, through the greedy desire that we have to receive, being still craving and begging when we have no need, we rob those thereof that are in true want, suffering this vice of ours to usurpe upon anothers Office.) (Mabbe, II, 170)

Guzmán seems to blame the man for fuelling with his generosity the error of those who seek alms under false pretences, blaming the victim of the deception for the deception itself.

There is at first sight little to be said for the unreasonableness of this attitude. It might be argued that Guzmán is not here speaking in retrospect, in spite of the tense he uses and the fact that he seems to be commenting rather than narrating at this point. He could be reliving for the reader the kind of ill-founded reasoning that Guzmán and his confederates might hypocritically have used at the time; but such an explanation is not entirely convincing. It might also be said that the passage is evidence of the continued perversion of Guzmán's values that merely demonstrates the unreliability of his avowed repentance;[105] but, as I shall seek to demonstrate, the sincerity or otherwise of Guzmán's repentance should not be the main touchstone for evaluating the book. What Guzmán is doing here is showing that charity is much more difficult an issue than it might seem. Two key questions are raised by Guzmán's remarks: what are the donor's motives and what are the consequences of indiscriminate charity? Guzmán clearly has his doubts about this man's motives as he makes clear by imagining the man's prayer with the following sub-text: 'Thank you, Lord, for making me so much better off than this poor wretch when You could have put me in his position. In token of which, witness this act of charity with which my conscience is now clear.' Furthermore, the gentleman gave no consideration to the recipient, only to the motive ('no considerando a quién lo daba, sino por quién lo daba' ('not considering so much to whom he gave, as for whose sake he gave', Mabbe, II, 170), that is, he looked only to himself. This is undoubtedly a harsh interpretation, but charity is, after all, a difficult matter, made more difficult by the fact that it is inevitably a form of exchange[106] in which the donor buys power, prestige, self-satisfaction, or whatever, with his donation: 'compra muy caro el que recibe y más caro vende quien lo da al que lo agradece' (p. 381) ('For hee buyes at a deare rate, that receives this kindnesse; and farre more dearely does he sell, who gives to him that is of a thankefull nature', Mabbe, II, 171). It is difficult to refuse charity, but should one give alms to support corrupt regimes in third-world countries or buy schoolbooks for children to compensate for shortages caused by cuts in educational provision? On the other hand, should one refuse an individual act of charity on the grounds that such acts are a disincentive to the provision of adequate social services? Should one refuse money to a beggar because it will almost certainly be used to compound his misery and inadequacy by being spent on drink or drugs? Is the mere consideration of these questions a cover for meanness? When Guzmán curses the man who gives him alms, and appears to endorse the curse in retrospect, he is creating a paradox that invites thought and discussion, the kind of thought that might have enabled the gentleman to fend off Guzmán's deception in the first place.

On this occasion Guzmán seems willing to risk our thinking him heartless and cynical in the interests of provoking thought and ultimately of teaching a complex and difficult lesson. Having cursed the man who gives generously, however, Guzmán goes on to curse those who do not give at all. Again he risks the charge of inconsistency and lack of charity himself, particularly as he makes it clear that his anger is with him still: 'gastábaseme la paciencia y aún hoy se me refresca con ira, embistiéndoseme un furor de rabia en contra dellos, que no sé cómo lo diga' (p. 395) ('I was ready to lose all patience. And even now (me thinkes) whilest I am now speaking of it, my buttons swell; the coales of my choller, revive and quicken afresh, and such a furie of rage assayleth me, and sets me on against them, that I cannot containe my selfe . . .', Mabbe, II, 193). This statement has been taken as evidence of Guzmán's unrepentant attitudes, as inconsistent with the attitudes of a 'convert to a non-materialistic faith'.[107] We should find in him tranquillity, inner peace, resolution of the torments that cause such strong feelings. Instead we find anger and harsh feelings unabated. Two points might be made in reply. Firstly, if we draw up requirements about what a character ought to feel and then criticise him for not feeling like that we must expect constantly to be disappointed. We should be concerned with what he does feel. Secondly, Guzmán in this passage is quite clearly reliving his anger ('aún hoy se me refresca'), precisely so that the reader may experience it as such, even if at second hand. Moreover, if we are to identify with him and be moved by what angered him, may he not also identify with us as an onlooker on his own past?[108]

What Guzmán is demonstrating here and elsewhere throughout the book is that things are a good deal more complex than people like to think, that moral and social questions are intricate and often insoluble, and above all that people are prey to powerful conflicts of character and personality. What emerges from Guzmán's own self-portrait is a complex and problematical picture of a fallible man, a man who is as capable of feeling anger or humiliation now as he was then, who was as capable then of knowing what he should and should not do as he is now. This complexity suggests strongly that the sincerity or otherwise of Guzmán's conversion is not a key point at issue. It makes no sense to enquire, *pace* Johnson,[109] whether Guzmán is a contrite or a nostalgic ex-sinner, because, as the episode with Gracia clearly shows, no man is an ex-sinner. Guzmán is a man who has lived and learned, and who has come to see his life as exemplary. His main concern is to present his life in such a way as to enable the reader to see it as exemplary. Once we begin to think in terms of Guzmán's purpose in telling us all that he does, the sincerity of his repentance becomes relatively unimportant.[110] One does not need to be repentant in order to have a conscience, or to see one's life as exemplary, or to write a book about it. 'Claro entendimiento' is enough. Furthermore, a critic wishing to expose the insincerity of a fictional narrator would need to show how it is possible for a non-existent being to create a false front for a real self which he does not have, and what would be the point of doing so even if he could.

There is a real dichotomy, however, that exists at the heart of Guzmán's account of himself, the dichotomy between the ability to perceive evil and the inability, at times, to prevent oneself from committing, saying or thinking evil acts, words or thoughts. Guzmán's perception of himself as a sinner who is capable of seeing his own error is presented analytically in terms of a distinction based on chronology: because wisdom is popularly associated with age and error with youth, these two sides of his personality are laid out accordingly, with the mature observations written as if from the present intercalated into the narrative of the past. Yet because this is a perception he has of himself now and which we as readers have of him now, the distinction between past and present is often deliberately telescoped. He frequently shows us that he had a conscience *then* and that he remains fallible *now*. There is no one moment in Guzmán's life when everything is suddenly changed. His past and present are of a piece, a continuous battle between reason and passion, error and better judgment.

None of this is to deny the importance of the 'repentance' as a structural turning-point in the book. In the *vaivén* of Guzmán's spiritual life, the constant oscillation between reason and passion, a halt has to be called somewhere, and in the interests of verisimilitude if for no other reason, it clearly made sense for Alemán to cut Guzmán's narrative short when conscience was in the ascendant. Men do not, on the whole, write books, or get them published, after throwing in their lot with the devil, and Guzmán's declarations of exemplary intent will clearly carry more weight if they come at a time of resolution. Joan Arias finds no real change in Guzmán's behaviour or attitude after his repentance (p. 95) but she overlooks the most important point: he has at least written a book. If that is not a change of behaviour then I do not know what is, 'pues no se hace sin trabajo'. That alone should guarantee his seriousness, and it provides us with another example of a man resorting, in an age of printing and increased literacy, to the written word as a warranty of his good standing.

It has to be admitted, nevertheless, that Guzmán's repentance may not last, and in this respect, too, Alemán is consistent with the requirements of verisimilitude. Guzmán's life is full of moments of repentance, but none of these last long. '¡Qué buena resolución si durara!' (p. 559) ('O, what a brave resolution was this, if it would have held!' Mabbe, III, 148), might be his epitaph. As he says himself, he stumbled with every step and often fell. After leaving the French Ambassador, Guzmán resolved to mend his ways, but the resolve soon left him, and the seven years of hard work at Alcalá were ruined in an afternoon. The final repentance may last or it may not; for the purpose of reading the book it does not really matter. This may be a moment of resolution among many, but it was sufficiently strong to inspire the writing of the book, or so it seems. Rather than being the key to interpretation, the most we can say of Guzmán's repentance is that it is a useful structural feature, a hinge between a life and the process of its narration, a partial guarantee of the narrator's earnestness, and that it is consistent with what we know of his character elsewhere. The real key is his purpose in writing, and in the way he goes about his task, and in this respect, as I have tried to show, it is the processes by which he engages the reader's sympathy while at the same time enabling him to see his experience with critical detachment that are the outstanding features of Guzmán's narrative.

Episodes such as that of the card-players demonstrate what the Platonist critics of fiction have been telling us all along: that identification of the reader with the protagonist is relatively easy to achieve, and indeed is so natural as to be virtually inevitable. Alemán shows that there is another, more mature, kind of empathy involving detachment as well as identification, and that this is harder won. It would have been relatively easy for Alemán simply to narrate the traumas of a man struggling to reconcile reason and passion, and let the reader identify with that struggle. But this would not have solved the problem that Guzmán's *conseja* would simply be the reader's *consejo*. The reader must have his own struggle, if only a literary one. As I have suggested, Alemán brings this about by a more circuitous but more satisfying route. He gives the reader access to the ingredients of the struggle, not, for the most part, the struggle itself. He retains the separateness of the narrative and the commentary, encourages identification with the first and acceptance of the second, and while retaining the distinction, skilfully intercalates the commentaries into the narrative so that the reader merges them with the recreated events of Guzmán's past. The result is that he experiences the same kind of *debate espiritual* that Guzmán has lived through, yet one of his own making, recreated in his own mind, not simply relived at second hand.

In 1609, soon after his arrival in Mexico, Alemán had a short polemical work published on Spanish spelling and punctuation, the *Ortografía castellana*. Belying its somewhat restricted theme, the book provides many fascinating insights into the mind of its author, particularly in view of the fact that internal evidence suggests that Alemán had been working on it since well before the publication of *Guzmán de Alfarache*.[111] Many of Alemán's general observations in the *Ortografía* are directed against those who subscribe uncritically to the wisdom of the ancients, even when common knowledge is manifestly wrong, and authorities clearly know nothing of what they talk about. His target is the attitude of 'Fulano lo dize, así se usa, esto me parece' (p. 55) ('So-and-so says so, they all say so, so that's what I think'). The wise man's task is to expose this untruth 'porque la narrativa mentirosa es mundo sin sol i cuerpo sin alma' ('a story without truth is a world without sun and a body without soul'). In this respect Alemán seems to be on the side of the moralists and the neo-Aristotelians, even if he does not have fiction specifically in mind. But he goes further, basing his rejection of received opinion on the primacy of first-hand knowledge: 'La experiencia es madre de las cosas, maestra de costumbres, inventora de leyes, principio de la ciencia y descubridora de las artes' (p. 64) ('Experience is the fount of everything, mistress of custom, inventor of law, first principle of science and discoverer of the arts'). The comprehensiveness of this remark could not be more eloquent: in all aspects of human life, moral, political, artistic, experience is the ultimate source of knowledge. These two opinions from the *Ortografía*, make it clear why Alemán was drawn to the didactic potential of fiction, and in their separate ways they sum up what he was trying to do in *Guzmán de Alfarache*: to make fiction speak the truth and to bridge the gap between first- and second-hand experience and knowledge. Alemán's reply to those who condemned fiction for its untruthfulness and its promotion of vicarious experience would be simply that the experience of reading fiction is not genuinely vicarious since it entails empathy, and the emotions experienced by the reader, though they exist in him, are not predicable of him.[112] What is more, the empathy induced by the *energia* in fiction is valuable since it is a real, first-hand experience and one which can, under the proper conditions, be made to yield knowledge and wisdom. It is those conditions, by which a 'narrativa mentirosa' can become a source of truth, that Alemán set out to investigate in *Guzmán de Alfarache*.

La vida del Buscón llamado don Pablos

In spite of, perhaps because of, the difficulty, complexity and subtlety of Alemán's investigations, most readers do not find *Guzmán de Alfarache* an easy book to read. This is almost certainly because the very nature of Guzmán's approach to narrative means that he is constantly giving with one hand and taking away with the other, feeding his reader's involvement in the events and emotions of the story while bringing him up short by encouraging him to view that involvement with a more critical eye. But there are other factors, apart from these thematic considerations, which make *Guzmán de Alfarache* such astringent as well as compelling reading, and these factors form the strongest link between Alemán's work and Quevedo's essay in the picaresque mode, *La vida del Buscón llamado don Pablos*. One of these factors is the self-conscious literariness of both works, though this self-consciousness manifests itself in different ways, and the other is a certain ambiguity of tone, again different in each case, but ultimately attributable to a strange interweaving of learned and colloquial, particularly oral, language.

Like other Golden-Age prose narratives, and like *Don Quijote* in particular, *Guzmán de Alfarache* is a work of literature in the fullest sense of the phrase: it is a work which draws on a wide literary background, weaving fables, *exempla* and moral apologues into a rich carpet of entertaining and illustrative storytelling. In many respects the book is like a miscellany, situated, as Edmond Cros has put it, 'à un carrefour de l'histoire littéraire, comme un livre bâtard qui recueille avidement un héritage hétérogène'.[113] Guzmán's narrative is in large part composed of literature: its flow is often captivating yet its literariness is inescapable. This effect is undoubtedly deliberate, for while there is nothing at all 'unnatural' about a man who is as compulsive a teller of stories as Guzmán is ('Do you know the one about . . .?'), there is something studied about the encyclopaedic impression given by the work as a whole. To a large part this is attributable to a post-Renaissance taste for large collections of second-hand excerpts from ancient authors and old wives' tales. But Guzmán is conscious of his new-found profession of author and makes sure that the reader is also conscious of his effort: 'Si a mí no se me hiciera vergüenza, no gastara en contarte los pliegos de papel deste volumen' (p. 249) ('if I my selfe had not beene ashamed, I should not have wasted so many sheetes of Paper, as this volume containes . . .', Mabbe, 1, 238).

The literariness of Guzmán's account is not entirely the result of the author's desire to impress with his wide reading. Guzmán, after all, knows his readership and how to engage their interest and attention. To this extent the literary allusions are part of Guzmán's overall strategy, particularly in the case of allusions to tales untold which demand the cooperation of the reader.[114] When, for example, Guzmán writes in shorthand: 'Sucedióme lo que al perro con la sombra de la carne' (p. 146) ('That hapned unto me, which befell the Dogge in the Fable . . .', Mabbe, 1, 93), the reader is drawn into a closer relationship with him on the basis of a shared literary background (though not, it should be noted, a very recondite one: all the allusions are to very well known fables). Tests of this sort form a kind of qualification for admission to a club. By seeing if we know what he means, Guzmán is attempting to establish a 'society of discourse' of which membership implies certain shared assumptions and attitudes, in the same way that a shared appreciation of the work of, say, Giraldi Cinthio or Masuccio is marked by Guzmán's borrowings from the *Hecatommithi* or *Il novellino*. Yet the literary basis of the club rules brings home to us the artificial nature of the institution. As appreciative readers we belong, yet we are not disposed to take our association with Guzmán too seriously. The potential harmfulness of literature is kept at bay by underlining its literariness and its artificiality.

The language that Guzmán uses for his account has a similar kind of ambiguity about it. In spite of Alemán's wide reading and love of literary allusion, he did not on the whole, as George Peale has shown,[115] favour a self-consciously literary style. Indeed, in matters of language he was something of a popularist and a pragmatist. The *Ortografía castellana* is, it should be remembered, a book which argues for the primacy of phonetic over etymological spelling, and represents the author's general view that writing should imitate speech: 'que a la lengua imite la pluma' (p. 26). Prose written for publication should simply be oral language transcribed into printed form. Alemán's style, in consequence, displays many of the major characteristics of oral language: discursiveness coupled with brevity of phrase and sentence, paratactic syntax and a rich and varied vocabulary that avoids logical complexity and abstraction. The result is a style that seems relaxed and conversational, almost casual, and one that takes easily to the many kinds of dialogue, the question-and-answer rhetoric, the thinking aloud that Guzmán so often resorts to. Guzmán's persuasiveness rests less on rational argument than on teasing, cajoling, exhorting the reader, and by example. The directness of the oral style is particularly appropriate for this approach.

If it is the presence of oral language behind the written text that helps to make Guzmán such a captivating speaker, his colloquial style does not mean an easy read. His vocabulary, for one thing, is often very difficult, and if we find ourselves frequently resorting to the dictionary, it is because we cannot at this distance keep up with the range of experience – and the vocabulary associated with it – which Guzmán is attempting to set before us. Similar difficulties arise with other Golden-Age writers who make extensive use of, for example, the language of the criminal classes in their work.[116] But more than this, it is frequently the very directness of Guzmán's language that makes it difficult. A paratactic style is inevitably a highly elliptical one. Speakers who address each other face to face do not need to spell everything out; they have all kinds of paralinguistic clues which they can use to understand each other. Once that supporting structure is removed, and the words have to stand on their own, a much greater strain is placed on the reader's capacity to infer the logical or situational links that are not made explicit in the text. This works at the lowest levels of day-to-day language where one is barely conscious of the difficulties one is constantly coping with, and at levels where the difficulties posed by, say, ambiguous pronoun reference are almost insoluble. Two sentences are sufficient to illustrate the kinds of effect produced by Alemán's inclusion of certain features of oral language in written prose:

Por lo de entonces me acuerdo de las casas y repúblicas mal gobernadas, que hacen los pies el oficio de la cabeza. Donde la razón y entendimiento no despachan, es fundir el oro, salga lo que saliere, y adorar después un becerro.
(p. 149)

(Which did then put me in mind of those ill-governed both houses and Common-wealths, where the feet perform the heads office. Where reason and understanding doe not dispatch businesses; where they have not the command, it is to melt a mans gold, (come of it what may come) and afterwards to adore a calfe.)
(Mabbe, I, 96)

That loose use of 'que' as an adverb is common in colloquial Spanish, then and now; 'es' has no explicit subject; and the allusion to the golden calf is hardly a difficult one, but unless it is grasped the melting of gold makes no sense at all. When the sense is completed, however, the elliptical informality of these two innocuous sentences yields up a good deal of food for thought and takes on an unassuming lapidary quality.

With the advantage of hindsight it is now possible to gauge how definitive a blow the author of *Lazarillo de Tormes* dealt to traditional assumptions about the related hierarchies of style and subject matter. But his own book relies for a good deal of its effect on those assumptions, to provide the norm against which his radicalism is measured, and the authors who followed his example also relied, in various ways and to varying degrees, on a background of expectations brought to the text by the readership for their work to make its full effect. The mixture of informality and sententiousness in Guzmán's narrative results in a style that is challenging and provocative, one which implicitly rebukes the reader for his allegiance to high art in the very act of showing him what riches there are to be found in a narrative of low life. When unashamedly literary ambitions are added to this mix the potential unease created in the mind of the reader, used as he is to finding matters of substance dealt with in a context and a style of fitting elevation, is much increased.

Quevedo's *Buscón* pushes the disturbing potential of these issues to their furthest limits. Self-conscious literary artistry so ostentatiously lavished on non-'literary' topics, the mechanisms of high culture at the service of an almost obsessive interest in the mucky side of life, conspire to produce a work which seems intent on turning everything upside down in its topsy-turvy world, even the very canons of taste and scales of value that give literature the privileged rank that it has. It is as if the moral and social misrule which the book documents[117] has spread to the medium itself, so that one no longer knows what a work of fiction is supposed to be, what purpose it is supposed to serve, or how to judge whether it is any good. On top of this, the central character of the book, a creature drawn from the very dregs of contemporary society, narrates his infamous progress in the unmistakable language of one of the foremost writers of his time. The result is a work which is unashamedly derivative yet brilliantly original,[118] one which feeds off its picaresque antecedents while rejecting nearly every assumption that underlies them, whose characteristic voice is so disconcerting at times as to make reading it almost unbearable.

At first it may seem strange that Quevedo, a nobleman of the old school, known for his political conservatism and his antisemitism, should turn his hand to the picaresque and bother about the ill-fated attempts of a pretentious upstart to escape from the ignominy of his *converso* background and join the ranks of high society. Yet there are several reasons why Quevedo may have shown interest in the new genre. In at least one respect he must have looked on the success of the picaresque as a godsend, even though in so many other ways it held up as objects of interest and inherent worth those elements of contemporary society he most despised. Any writer needs form, and a satirist needs form more than most. Quevedo always seemed to find difficulty with form when writing prose. Verse gave him no trouble and he responded brilliantly to the predetermined structure of the available verse forms, and the sonnet in particular. Verse provided the ideal compression for the brilliant insight or incisive remark. When writing prose, Quevedo tended to rely on the shape determined by his subject, biography, history, biblical exegesis or philosophy. But because satire deals in attitudes of mind rather than coherent arguments, it poses formal problems of a special kind: there is no room for weighty exposition in satire and the sharpness of the satirical eye is liable to become blurred in the unbounded context of prose. The dream format of the *Sueño*, to which he had recourse five times between 1606 and

1621, provided one means of organising the miscellaneous products of his maliciously fertile mind. The fictional autobiographical format of the picaresque can only have been welcomed as another.

Quevedo's interest in the achievements and the potential of the picaresque went, however, considerably beyond the parasitical. It would be unfair to dismiss as plagiarism the fact that, not only did he draw extensively on the structure of the new genre, but he also drew heavily on individual works for characters and situations. These borrowings – from the *Lazarillo*, both *Guzmanes* (Alemán's, and Martí's spurious second part), and possibly *Don Quijote* and the *Pícara Justina* – have been much discussed and need no rehearsal here.[119] Quevedo's creatures are intended not just as copies but as rivals. The literary challenge of the *Lazarillo*, and, in particular, *Guzmán de Alfarache*, was one which Quevedo was unable to resist. Pablos's description of his family background attempts to out-do Guzmán's in its baseness and iniquity; Cabra and don Toribio allude to Lazarillo's second and third masters yet parody even those caricatures unmercifully and almost beyond recognition. Cabra's astonishing miserliness in particular shows how much further Quevedo could take the theme of deprivation and its consequence, hunger, than the author of the *Lazarillo*. The *reductio ad nauseam* of life in Cabra's academy, and elsewhere throughout the book, illustrates, as it was no doubt intended to, Quevedo's literary brilliance and the superiority of his imagination and verbal dexterity over that of other writers. Yet his acerbic misanthropy frequently extends beyond the themes of the book to betray a spiteful jealousy of those authors. We should avoid an uncritical tendency to assume that Quevedo's borrowings are based on admiration for the earlier works: all the evidence suggests that there is nothing friendly about this rivalry.

Quevedo must have found the success of Alemán's book particularly irksome, even if he did not know – as seems unlikely – of Alemán's *converso* background. Like his subject, Alemán must have seemed an upstart: a man of no rank, a public servant frequently imprisoned for debt, yet a literary celebrity, lionised for a work which cannot have appealed greatly to Quevedo's taste. Alemán's prose style evidently met with Quevedo's disapproval;[120] Guzmán's Jewishness and pretentious concern for honour are parodied by Quevedo's own pícaro, and his moral homilies must have seemed intolerably pious, to judge from the fact that Quevedo reverts pointedly to the less discursive structure of the *Lazarillo*,[121] discounts specifically in the 'Carta Dedicatoria' any more serious intention than amusement, and gives

Pablos lines to speak that are of an insufferable priggishness. If Quevedo's social, political and racial views are taken fully into account, it seems likely that he found the picaresque as a genre as dangerous and pretentious, in both literary and social senses, as its protagonists, and in the case of Alemán in particular, as its authors. Quevedo made use of the picaresque in a way which suggests that not only did he wish to outdo the opposition in satire but by parodying them to the point of travesty, he intended to destroy the genre along with the society it depicts.[122] Alongside the attractions of a convenient format and some handy ready-made characters and situations there may have been in Quevedo's mind the feeling that the only way to beat the picaresque was to join it.

None of this would have mattered so much, of course, if it had not been for the fact that, at the time Quevedo wrote the *Buscón*,[123] the picaresque was so intensely fashionable. The negative aspects of this modishness have already been alluded to, but there were positive aspects that could be made to suit Quevedo's purpose. Quevedo could, for example, rely on his readership to pick up references and allusions to other works in the same way that Cervantes relies on his readers to spot the allusions in *Don Quijote*. This kind of literary shorthand both depends on and feeds a sense of community between a writer and his public; it promotes a 'society of discourse' in the same way that a dialect or a jargon does; it binds people together and excludes others; and to an extent it gives the lie to the view that a book cannot choose its readers. Neither the *Buscón* nor *Don Quijote* is wholly dependent on its readers' recognising references and allusions. Both are perfectly intelligible without that intertextual awareness, but there is a strong sense of exclusiveness, of a code within a code, in the *Buscón* and this feeling derives, perhaps, from the social circumstances in which the book was written.

One striking fact about the *Buscón* is that, for all that it is a work of literature steeped in other works of literature, it does not appear to have been conceived as a work of literature in the sense that it was not written for publication in printed form. Quevedo seems to have made no attempt to have it printed at a time when fashion would have ensured its success, and when a pirated version did find its way into print in 1626 Quevedo played no part in the preparation of the text: indeed, on other occasions he complained bitterly about unauthorised editions of his works issued by the same publisher. Quevedo was, it must be remembered, not greatly given to publication until after his return from Italy, no doubt feeling that authorship smacked of labour and was therefore beneath him. This unwillingness to be associated with the growing numbers of professional authors, or at least those who published in the hope of making some money – Alemán being among them – may help to explain why the *Buscón* was not sent to press earlier than it was. Further, it should be remembered that the contemporary fashion for the picaresque, though it seems to have begun in books, was not restricted to them. Marcel Bataillon has shown how manners and entertainment reflected the changing tastes: court masques were abandoning nymphs and shepherds in favour of pícaros, the upper classes were experimenting with bohemianism and, along with other prominent contemporaries, Quevedo himself appears, only lightly disguised as Perlícaro the 'matraquista semiastrólogo', in López de Ubeda's 'book of entertainment', the *Pícara Justina*.[124] And the aspirations towards social mobility which the picaresque enshrined were, to Quevedo's intense annoyance, all around for anybody to see. The picaresque, then, was not confined to books and Quevedo did not need to publish his work for it to become known. In a society in which the picaresque already formed part of the pattern of entertainment the conditions existed in which his work could be made available to the only group of people who mattered to him anyway: those who were like him and thought like him. He could and undoubtedly did circulate the work in manuscript but it is also perfectly possible that the *Buscón* was read, in whole or in part, aloud by its author and that its earliest audience was precisely that.[125]

The fact that the *Buscón* was written primarily for internal consumption by a social group who both responded to the generic allusions and shared Quevedo's attitudes has one important consequence that I wish to stress: whether Quevedo read the work to his circle, or merely circulated it in manuscript, his immediate public, those for whom he wrote and to whom the work was directed, must have known the sound of Quevedo's own voice. If they heard him read it aloud, or if they were close enough to him to have been privileged to see a copy, they would have heard or been able to imagine the words as spoken by their author. Anyone outside that circle, in a sense, does not count: Quevedo did not write for them and if he had, he would have published. I argued in chapter 3 that the sound of the inner voice in reading is an important factor in the way the reader builds up a relationship of empathy with what he is reading. Subvocalising the words of another with the acoustic potential of one's own voice is one way in which the barrier between the self and the text is broken down. Roger Fowler has shown how an implicit intonation is created by the syntax of a text:

A given syntax demands its own proper intonation curve, rises and falls in the pitch of the voice appropriate to the structure and meaning of what is written. Stresses must be in the right places, or meaning is distorted . . . Of course it is *literally* palpable only in reading aloud . . . but the silent reader may also be said to experience the intonational structure of text . . .[126]

Why else would Fowler italicise 'literally' in that passage, or Spaniards preface written questions with inverted question marks, if these typographical cues are not there to show readers what they should be hearing in their inner ear?

I also suggested earlier that the reader's own inner voice can easily be displaced by reminiscence of another voice, another reader's or an actor's, or the author's own. Anyone who has heard Laurie Lee, say, read his own work will find it difficult, if not impossible, to exclude the memory of his accent from subsequent private reading. Those who heard Dickens read his own work can only have had the same difficulty, or derived the same pleasure from the recollection. And the same is true of Quevedo's audience. If he did read the part of Pablos the effect must have been bizarre indeed; if he did not, his friends can have had no difficulty imagining what it would sound like. Either way the effect must have been unsettling and deliberately so. If Quevedo made any attempt at all to hide himself behind the character of Pablos, and all the evidence suggests that he did not, he would have remained wholly visible and audible to his public, like some 'rude mechanical', the worst kind of actor who makes no attempt to get into the part. There would have been much amusement, no doubt, in seeing a nobleman masquerading badly as a pícaro, as a female impersonator relies on an ill-fitting wig, an impossibly large bust or his own unshaven legs to turn outrage into laughter. But the act is wholly at the expense of the impersonated, who has no chance to establish a credible character of his own. Quevedo attempts to throw his voice but succeeds in fooling no one. The effect is as unsettling as a badly synchronised soundtrack: we cease to be under the illusion that the sound is coming from the screen at all. With his voice systematically undermined from within, Pablos's attempts to gain sympathy and attention are doomed from the start. It is small wonder that critics have so often used the language of puppetry and masquerade to characterise Quevedo's relationship to Pablos.[127]

A good deal of this argument is inevitably speculative but not entirely so. We do not know if Quevedo read his work aloud and we do not know if his speaking voice was particularly striking. We can not, nor could anyone, imagine what it sounded like or complain that it was interfering with our reading. We are not members of Quevedo's immediate circle and we only have the text in any case thanks to the chance survival of three manuscripts and the cupidity of Roberto Duport. Yet a modern reader's relationship to the *Buscón* is not perhaps so very different from that of the audience for which it was written. For one thing, modern readers of the *Buscón* have to, and in practice do, belong to a group in much the same way as Quevedo's contemporaries did. We have to have read the other works as closely as they did in order to be alert to the literary allusions and more important still, to the wider cultural and social reverberations that they set in motion. In that sense we have to fulfil certain requirements in order to qualify as worthy members of the readership. This is a further example of the way certain books choose their readers by making demands on them. For another thing, merely being a member of that group makes one a social adversary of Pablos in the same way that Quevedo's circle were the social enemies of Pablos. The implied enmity of the protagonist and the inscribed narratee is, after all, one of the basic tenets of the picaresque. V.M. is Lazarillo's social superior, and rather more than that, since he can call him to account, the dialectic of *Guzmán de Alfarache* implies a debate between adversaries, and the readers of these accounts are placed socially in an age of high illiteracy by being able to buy books, and by having the leisure and the ability to read them. Pablos recognises this fact by his frequent deference and 'hablando con perdón'.[128] The modern reader is by no means alone in his ability to read, yet few people can and do master Quevedo's text and if predictions about the effects of electronic media are correct, that number will not get significantly greater. The modern reader of the *Buscón* is, then, manoeuvred by the text into being a social and intellectual stereotype: if he can and wants to read the book he is likely, *ipso facto*, to be a member of an educated élite, alert, intelligent and above all privileged – the one thing Pablos cannot be.

There is, however, one further sense in which the modern reader is not so very far away from the situation of the *Buscón*'s original audience, and that relates to the question of Quevedo's voice. When Pablos returns to Segovia to collect his inheritance he comes upon a procession of condemned men being driven to the gallows by Pablos's uncle who is beating them with a strap, or as Pablos puts it:

Venía una procesión de desnudos, todos descaperuzados, delante de mi tío, y él, muy haciéndose de pencas, con una en la mano, tocando un pasacalles públicas en las costillas de cinco laúdes, sino que llevaban sogas por cuerdas.

(p. 133)[129]

(then came a procession of hatless wretches stripped to the waist walking ahead of my kinsman, and he, cat-o'-nine-tails in hand, playing a tune with unrestrained violence on the five human violins, whose strings were pinion-ropes.)　　　　　　　　　　　　　　　　　　　　　(Stevens–Duff, p. 59)

Fully to understand and appreciate this sentence the reader needs to pick up several levels of word-play: the basic conceit is a musical one, presumably because these men have confessed their crimes, that is, they have 'cantado', and certainly because they are walking down the street, 'pasando por la calle' or, as he does not quite put it, dancing a passacaglia. As the streets are public thoroughfares and there is a good deal of humiliation involved, he qualifies the term: 'pasacalles públicas'. The performance also has its instrumental backing, for by means of the pun on 'costillas' – 'ribs' anatomical and musicological – the prisoners become transformed into lutes, except that these 'lutes' will not have strings but ropes, by which they will be strung up. They are being struck or – 'tocar' – played by Pablos's uncle with a leather strap or 'penca'. He is not sparing them but is making them shout for mercy, 'haciéndose rogar' or as Pablos puts it, 'muy haciéndose de pencas', not allowing himself easily to be swayed by their pleas. The men are naked and 'descaperuzados, delante de mi tío', their heads uncovered in his presence, and literally, because they are being driven, 'before him'. Other layers of allusion are, no doubt, also to be found by readers more perspicacious than I.[130] What is important about this passage, which is representative of the general level of verbal wit in the *Buscón*, is that there is only one writer in Spanish who could possibly have written it, and that writer is Quevedo. Fortunately for the modern reader, Quevedo has an absolutely unmistakable style, or 'voice', which is just as capable of coming across to the modern reader as it must have done to Quevedo's contemporaries. Anyone who was even a peripheral member of the society of discourse to which the *Buscón* belongs would have no difficulty in recognising any part of it as being the work of Quevedo. The consequences of this recognition on the reading of the book are, I would suggest, considerable: because the language in which it is written is Quevedo's it is, as we have seen in the small example discussed above, and as we should see from an analysis of practically any other sentence of Quevedo in this book or any other, extremely difficult to read. It cannot be skimmed over and it can never, even with familiarity, acquire the transparency that language is capable of in other contexts and which makes it possible for a reader to claim another's words as his own. Quevedo's language, even after we have worked out what it means, remains opaque and other, unmistakably his, not ours. Furthermore, in the specific context of the *Buscón* there is an extra dimension to our sense of estrangement from the words on the page, and this results from the fact that the words which are quite obviously Quevedo's and no one else's are attributed to a character, Pablos, who is nothing like Quevedo at all. This extends not just to the way Pablos speaks, but even embraces what he says. Pablos says things in this book that no one in his right mind would say unless he were suffering from acute schizophrenia. His voice is constantly out of tune with himself; he abases himself, betrays himself, willingly allowing his innermost thoughts and motives to be exposed not just to the light of day but to the vilest ridicule. He humiliates himself for the benefit of his reader, all to get a laugh and provide, as he puts it, 'some light relief for times when the heart is heavy'. The constant sense of self-betrayal that makes such uncomfortable and often unpleasant reading in the *Buscón* arises, then, from the extraordinary archness of its tone. When Pablos speaks, as Francisco Rico has suggestively put it,[131] all we hear is his master's voice. So skilfully has Quevedo built this self-defeating knowingness into Pablos's character that it is still possible for us to come close to the original reader's or audience's experience of seeing Pablos open his mouth and hearing Quevedo's voice emerge from it.

Attempts have recently been made, by Gonzalo Díaz Migoyo in particular,[132] to defend Quevedo from the adverse criticism implicit in the view that Pablos is given little opportunity to establish his identity and is constantly being forced to ridicule his aspirations in the act of voicing them. Above all, Díaz Migoyo has sought to defend Quevedo from the charge that he was not interested in, or incapable of, producing a well-structured work that is anything more than a random collection of anecdotes and satirical sketches. Against this should be set a clear distinction which can and should be made, as in the case of the *Lazarillo* and the *Guzmán*, between the protagonist as actor and as narrator. If this is done it is possible to distinguish two types of relationship, between the narrator and the narratee, and the author and the reader. There emerges in consequence a coherent plot based on the protagonist's failure to achieve his ambition to gain admission to a social order from which he is barred by the circumstances of his birth. Some years after the definitive collapse of these ambitions, and after a spell in America where further attempts also meet with failure, he narrates the course of his life to an unnamed narratee in the manner characteristic of the emergent genre. Whereas we might expect, after a career of such unmitigated failure, that Pablos would have come to terms with the realities of his situation, Gonzalo Díaz Migoyo takes the view that Pablos the narrator is still fundamentally the man he always was. There is a consistency between actor and narrator that is clearly the product of one mind. Pablos's verbal skill, for example, a necessary tool for the cultivation of illusion, is one of the threads that links the young man to his older self and which helps to explain the present purpose of his narrative.[133]

Pablos's loyalty to his long-standing ambition also links his past to the present moment of narrating. Once a pícaro always a pícaro, particularly when it comes to giving an account of himself. In a sense, his act of narration is the climax of his picaresque career, one last chance to pass himself off as what he is not. From coming within an inch of success in the Casa del Campo, to the ignominy of acting, the courtship of nuns and drunken murder, he has now hit rock bottom: he has turned his hand to writing, for writing gives him the chance to succeed where life has only led to failure:

> La narración de Pablos es el último engaño en la cadena de engaños en que ha consistido su vida. La actividad narrativa se incluye así como continuación de las actividades narradas, sin interrupción entre el vivir y el narrar: el relato es el último episodio picaresco de su vida; parte de una misma vida de engaño porque él mismo es engaño: 'ne plus ultra' de la aparencialidad del personaje.
>
> (p. 101)

(Pablos's narrative is the final deception in the chain of deceptions of which his life has been composed. The act of narration is therefore one more of his narrated acts. There is no discontinuity between living and narrating: the story is the ultimate picaresque episode of his life, part of one and the same life of deceit because he himself is a deception, appearance taken to its furthest extreme.)

This approach departs from the assumption that the *Buscón* is the same kind of narrative as the *Lazarillo* and the *Guzmán*, and focusses attention on the relationship of the older narrator to his former self and to his narratee and reader. It also provides a framework for making other distinctions: between the protagonists – actor and narrator – and the author; and between the relationships narrator/ narratee and author/reader. These distinctions may help to explain features of the book which have often been regarded as blemishes or the products of an inconsistent point of view. There are many places in the narrative where Pablos displays an omniscience which is at odds with his supposed ignorance of what is going on behind his back. He describes himself in ways that would only have been apparent to others,[134] falls into traps which he has just told us have been set for him, such as the excrement in the bed at Alcalá, and the beating he receives from Diego's henchmen, with its problematic assertion that he never suspected don Diego's part in the incident.[135] All this, even this last difficulty, could be explained if we posit the separateness of Pablos the actor and Pablos the narrator and assume that the text is speaking with two voices at once. The actor behaves in ignorance of what the narrator knows with hindsight.

What this approach cannot explain, however, is the fact that, in spite of Pablos's extensive apprenticeship in the verbal skills of deception and the creation of false fronts, and in spite of his frequent conscious recognition of the importance of language in his campaign to enter polite society, when it comes to persuasion in writing Pablos is such an abysmal failure. The paradox here is more startling than it might seem at first: even in a work of fiction, where there is no objective reality behind the façade to betray him, Pablos is incapable of passing himself off successfully as a gentleman, and this in spite of the fact that critics of fiction and moralists, as we have seen, consistently argued that the danger of fiction lay in its persuasiveness. In the *Buscón* we have a work of fiction in which a character not only fails to persuade us but does everything he can to prevent us from being taken in by his pretence. When the point of this technique becomes clear, the *Buscón* will emerge as the ultimate reply to the critics of fiction, in spite of the fact that its author may have the last laugh: Pablos's 'real' self, the upstart real self, emerges perhaps all the more strongly from the collapse of his attempts at façade.

Gonzalo Díaz Migoyo has anticipated this objection to an extent with reference to the declared aim of the narrator in his 'Carta Dedicatoria': 'he querido enviarle esta relación, que no le será pequeño alivio para los ratos tristes' ('I have decided to send you this account which will serve as light relief for your heavy heart'). The emphasis on laughter is, of course, in the wider context an attempt to put down the *Lazarillo* and the *Guzmán* for their declarations of serious intent. In the local context the accent on laughter is something of a pre-emptive strike: '¿Qué mejor manera de impedir que los demás se rían de él que empezar por reírse de sí mismo?' ('What better way of preventing others from laughing at him than by laughing at himself from the outset?') The self-abasement, the deliberate sabotaging of his aspirations are, so it seems, not just attempts at ingratiation. His narrative shamelessness is a cover for his inner shame.[136] Pablos's narrative is his last and greatest picaresque act, painting a false self-portrait, 'una autobiografía mentirosa' using words as a veil (p. 161). But there is a major inconsistency here. If we ask Pablos why he is telling us all this we get no more satisfactory answer than is there in the 'Carta Dedicatoria' and if his life story is a pre-emptive strike, why does it succeed in hiding nothing? What is this false front that he offers us? Is it the fact that he was a pretentious upstart, son of a thief and a witch, who tried to beat the world at its own game and failed because the reality of his social and racial origins always came back to haunt him? Is all this, bluntly displayed for all to see, some kind of elaborate double bluff? It seems unlikely. Pablos did have his successes, of course: for years he persuaded critics that don Diego was a model citizen because he himself believed it in defiance of the evidence of his eyes and ears.[137] But if his 'pensamientos de caballero' amount to an attempt at deception then they are, quite simply, a non-starter.

The lesson of Díaz Migoyo's argument is nevertheless an important one: there is no point in trying to treat the *Buscón* as if it were the same kind of picaresque narrative as *Lazarillo de Tormes* or *Guzmán de Alfarache*. To do so is to ask it to display qualities which it does not have, and above all, to require that the protagonist himself should illustrate the purpose of his narrative. The coherence and purposefulness of the *Buscón* are beyond question, but they are not necessarily to be found in the same areas as they are found in *Lazarillo* and *Guzmán*. Defending, along analytical lines laid down by *Lazarillo* criticism, a work which has been compared unfavourably in those respects with its predecessors, does not do it the best service, particularly when Quevedo went to some pains to mark his departure from many of the assumptions which lay behind the picaresque. In theory, and because of the superficial structural similarity of the *Buscón* to the earlier works, the distinction between actor, narrator and author should be there to be made, but Quevedo has telescoped them all into one by the unifying thread of his own unmistakable style. Not for Pablos, not for any other character in the book, does Quevedo bother to disguise his voice.[138] When the young Pablos puts on a display of verbal dexterity for the benefit of doña Ana[139] or for the two ladies he is attempting to cheat,[140] or when he coarsens his speech to gain more success at begging,[141] and when Pablos the narrator nods approvingly at his skill, it is Quevedo's own self-congratulation that provides the element of consistency. Even Pablos's *conceptismo* is subservient to Quevedo's own: when Pablos describes a group of men going to the gallows as musical instruments he is using language conceptually as befits a man who enjoyed 'fama de travieso y agudo', a self-confessed liar who forces language to part company from reality, creating a self-contained world of its own. When it is clear that Quevedo has written his script, Pablos is exposed for the imposter he is: even his 'agudeza' is second-hand.

Quevedo's refusal to give Pablos a voice of his own is not accidental or unplanned. Francisco Rico's much-quoted judgment on the book, 'pésima novela picaresca',[142] has often been maligned and misunderstood. There are reasons to suppose that Quevedo might have been pleased to be regarded as a writer of a very poor picaresque novel, particularly one which is described by the same critic in the same sentence as a work of genius. Quevedo probably scorned the picaresque, especially Alemán's notion of the picaresque, as much as he scorned most other things in life and literature, and his own work both parodies his predecessors and dissociates itself from them in significant ways. In that sense it is a poor example of a picaresque novel and Quevedo would have wanted it that way. As I have argued, Quevedo's most radical departure from the picaresque was his denial of an independent voice to the pícaro. When Pablos tries to explain himself, Quevedo puts words into his mouth that will blurt out his baseness and his fraudulence. Pablos is not a pícaro but a nobleman impersonating a pícaro. That is not a fault in the book, it is a feature of it. It needs explanation; it does not need to be explained away.

Fernando Lázaro has argued vigorously that the originality of the *Buscón* lies in the absence from it of the two outstanding characteristics of the earlier novels, social protest and didacticism.[143] The strength of the book lies, he feels, in the sheer exuberance and inventiveness of its language and in a wit which is fired off almost at random with no particular aim in view. The darts are pointed but pointless: 'El *Buscón* se muestra, así, charla sin objeto, dardo sin meta, fantasmagoría' (p. 136). There is a great deal to be said for this viewpoint. What social

protest there is in the *Buscón* arises, as far as Pablos is concerned, from
the cries of the outsider trying to get in. The didacticism – again, such
as it is – comes from the author's insistence that 'they shall not pass'
and is summed up in the final cliché (time-honoured and of
distinguished classical pedigree, but still a cliché) that going elsewhere
never improved anything.[144] It is questionable, however, if in an
intellectual climate in which the language of fiction was seen as being
as problematical as has been argued in chapters 1 and 2, any author
can stand wholly aside from the issues implicit in such a long-standing
and hard-fought debate. The act of writing fiction in those circumstances entails a degree of commitment, even if, as Quevedo may have
done, the writer reverts to an almost Platonic ideal of dynamic oral
presentation to a select audience with whom he has a relationship of
give and take: conditions which are a long way from the silent private
reading of a print-based culture which so concerned the moralists.
What is said is in some ways less significant than the fact that it is said,
and Cervantes showed in the *Novelas ejemplares* that any writing
inevitably illustrates the system of values within which it is written,
even if it contains no explicit moral.[145] In the context of the Platonist
debate about fiction, any example of fictional language, however it is
delivered, still has to answer the charge of falsehood.

Quevedo, typically, evolves a brilliantly paradoxical solution to
this problem: Pablos, after all, is a self-confessed liar who cannot stop
revealing the truth about himself. Francisco Rico has invoked
Euboulides's riddle to explain how the picaresque sets forth the
problem of language and truth.[146] If a man tells you he always lies
('Jamás se halla verdad en nuestra boca' affirms don Toribio, Pablos's
mentor, at one point: p. 160; 'Never a word of truth crosses our lips',
Stevens–Duff, p. 72) do you believe him? Quevedo's answer is
undoubtedly 'yes'. No one ever speaks the truth under normal
circumstances. In this world appearance is everything, nothing is
substantial; façade, pretence, illusions are the only reality. The only
truth is falsehood. To illustrate this Quevedo turns Pablos into a kind
of Mime and his readers into Siegfrieds who, without recourse this
time to the power of the dragon's blood, are able to hear through the
wheedling and the flattery to the voice of his innermost thoughts. The
result, as in Wagner, is comically grotesque. Pablos tells us how he
sucked up to the school-master and his wife, how he made himself a
teacher's pet, ran errands for 'señora' and deservedly won the envy of
his fellows; he tells us how he paid court to the sons of gentlefolk and

cultivated the grace and favour of don Diego by unequal exchanges of food and toys, loss-leaders in the pathetic commerce of friendship. He acts like a creep, but what is worse he tells us that he acted like one, deliberately to achieve his own ends. At least part of the discomfort that this causes comes from the fact that such frankness is unacceptably outspoken. We expect self-seeking to be wrapped in a protective tissue of hypocrisy and are alarmed when we see it openly displayed. Perhaps, too, we expect to be protected from a consciousness of our own baser motives and find Pablos's self-awareness disarming. There is, it seems, such a thing as too much honesty.

Pablos's mother felt the same: 'esas cosas, aunque sean verdad, no se han de decir' (p. 23) ('Whether they be true or otherwise such things ought not to be spoken', Stevens–Duff, p. 7), yet in spite of this lesson, or perhaps because of it, Pablos progresses through the account of his life as if reeling under the effects of a truth drug, giving all his secrets away. When he wants to impress his landlady, and her daughter, he begins as anyone might by making himself agreeable, telling them stories, bringing them gossip and so on. Once he has caught their interest he is in a position to test their credulity further. He tells them he knows some spells and can make the house appear to collapse and be consumed by fire. He gets friends to call at the house to ask for him, sends one with a fake bill of exchange, and sits up one night counting and recounting the same fifty escudos over and over again till they hear six thousand counted. He plies the daughter with *billets doux* full of standard lover's rhetoric and calls at the house in disguise to ask for 'don Ramiro de Guzmán, señor de Valcerrado y Vellorete'. That finally does the trick and the girl agrees to receive his nocturnal visit. That this tryst does not, in the event, take place does not concern us for the moment.

What is startling here is the frankness with which Pablos reveals his methods. Out they all come, all the tricks of the illusionist's trade, for all to see. And not all of them are a great deal different from the standard seduction techniques practised by those who are more reputable but less frank: pleasantries, care over appearance, earnest declarations of respectability, evidence of prospects, intimations of comfort and prosperity, and so on. It would be easy, and natural, to treat this as simply part of Quevedo's approach to satire, making a man articulate his own sub-text and holding him up for ridicule on the strength of that. Quevedo could simply be saying, 'Look, know him for what he is: he says one thing but really means something quite different.' The fact that what he says and what he means are different only in degree, not in kind, from what we all say and mean gives the satire that extra dimension of universal applicability that we would expect from a writer of Quevedo's quality. There is, however, a further dimension to Pablos's illusionism that is particularly evident in such chapters as that (III, 5) in which he tries to hoodwink the landlady and her daughter. Here and elsewhere Pablos's techniques are not just those of the con-man but those of the writer.

Pablos manipulates the landlady and her daughter in exactly the same way as a writer manipulates his reader, luring them into a position where their propensity to believe what they want to believe will take over and assist him in the creation of ever more unlikely fictitious façades. At first he woos them with words: 'contábales cuentos que yo tenía estudiados para entretener; traíales nuevas aunque nunca las hubiese . . . Díjelas que sabía encantamentos, y que era nigromante' (p. 208) ('told her yarns I had by heart for entertainment purposes, and brought news when nothing happened. . . persuaded them I knew all about enchantments, was a magician', Stevens–Duff, p. 98). There is a very subtle and slippery slope here. From fiction as entertainment he progresses to fiction as lie; from *cuentos* to *nuevas* and the manufacture of non-existent gossip. The next step is enchantment, when fiction intervenes and changes the world in a kind of necromancy. By now they are hooked, but his shabby appearance is still a problem. The obvious thing to do would be to improve it, but Pablos adopts a different approach, setting out to transform his down-at-heel appearance in the minds of his victims. Like Cervantes, he eschews the easy way out. He does not give them a plausible fiction, but an implausible one. He suggests instead that he is a rich man pretending to be a poor one. There are several reasons why he does this and as many consequences of his doing so.

The world of this book is not a place, as we are constantly shown, where simply buying new clothes is enough to establish a credible identity. Pablos joins don Toribio's 'cofradía' with money which he is not allowed to spend. He has to make do, as the others do, with scraps of clothing elaborately arranged into a flimsy veil of respectability. The reason is simple and devastatingly logical: since reality itself is a façade any attempt to reproduce that reality itself must also involve the creation of a façade. Pablos gives the landlady and her daughter just such a dose of illusion, playing with the concepts of appearance and reality in a new and alarming way. He reverses the polarities of riches and poverty and transforms his own poverty into the suggestion of riches, not by pretending to be rich, but by pretending that his poverty is a pretence of poverty. The consequences of this tell us a great deal about the society portrayed in the book; in this society pretence is so deeply rooted that nothing could be more credible than the idea of a rich man attempting to pass himself off as poor. Pablos's tactic is chosen, and is successful up to a point, because it relies on the women themselves to supply the illusory reality by inference. He has only to drop a few hints – the visits from friends, the fake document, a telling display of annoyance at the breach of privacy implied – and they are ready, as 'buenas creedoras', to jump to a conclusion that reveals as much about their rapacity as it does about Pablos. He tricks them with the truth, with nothing, and creates huge voids of potential meaning between a few deftly-placed strokes of suggestion. They fall through these trap doors only because they want to. And like a true artist Pablos is able to sustain their illusion in the face of greater and greater concessions to reality. Three times he mentions his unprepossessing appearance: the women describe him as 'más roto que rico, pequeño de cuerpo, feo de cara y pobre' (p. 209) ('who had more rags than riches, was small in the body, had an ugly face, and was indeed poverty stricken', Stevens–Duff, p. 99); the other two guests, the Catalan and the Portuguese, call him 'piojoso, pícaro, desarropado' and 'cobarde y vil' (p. 212) ('shabby, lousy scoundrel . . . mean coward', Stevens–Duff, p. 100); the daughter again refers to his short stature when Pablos calls to visit himself (p. 212). Several things are interesting here: firstly, the allusions to his physical appearance and poverty reinforce the view that Quevedo is having a joke with his readers at his own expense – the terms of the description recall very strongly those which Quevedo used on other occasions to describe himself.[147] Secondly, Pablos makes his appearance work brilliantly to his own advantage. Once he has sown in their minds the idea that he might be pretending to be poor, then from that moment on, the more unprepossessing he looks the more this can be taken as confirmation of their suspicion. Once the terms of the hypothesis are reversed, everything that would otherwise call his wealth into question serves instead to support their view of him. Once he is known to be pretending, the less he looks like a rich man the better. Pablos himself will become a victim of just such a mistake in the Casa del Campo. Thirdly, Pablos's frankness about his appearance shows that once an illusion has taken root in the victim's mind, there is little that can shift it: the Catalan and the Portuguese can call him what they like and the girl will ignore them; and – a master stroke, this – he can actually call at the house and ask for himself as don Ramiro de Guzmán, señor de Valcerrado y Vellorete, and be told by the girl that, yes, there is a gentleman of that name living there, 'pequeño de cuerpo' ('short in stature', Stevens–Duff, p. 101). The name and the illusion it feeds blind her to the reality that is there in front of her eyes.

This last trick is, of course, not really necessary, but is something of a Cervantine dare, the act of a supreme creative artist playing with the credulity of his audience and showing off his skill. Pablos at all times in this chapter acts with the cool calculation and skill of a great creator of fiction, drawing out his audience, helping them to suspend their disbelief and making sport with them once they are mesmerised. The repertoire of literary and linguistic illusion is impressive throughout, from those seemingly innocent initial *cuentos*, through the judicious play of lovers' rhetoric in the letters, to the final *coup de théâtre* in which Pablos impersonates someone else in order the better to impersonate himself. And this theatre of illusion is set against the real-life backdrop of the short, ugly and somewhat impoverished nobleman who is the impresario of the show. Pablos's success gets the better of him, however, when he slips and falls on his way across the roof to his assignation. So convinced is the girl by his tales of 'burlas y encantamentos' that she refuses to believe that he is not waving but drowning: 'y era lo bueno que ella pensaba que era artificio, y no acababa de reír' (p. 214) ('she concluded that my fall was merely a necromantic turn; and called me to return, for it had pleased her well', Stevens–Duff, p. 101).

Pablos's career as an illusionist, and the skill with which he plies his trade, reveals an important fact about his creator's approach to fiction. For Quevedo, fiction operates exactly as language does: it creates illusions and destroys them at the same time. Like language in general, fiction is one of the most effective ways in which man throws up façades, hiding the truth from himself and from his victims; yet it can also become the single most powerful means of demonstrating its own falsehood. The literary artist, working with language and fiction, is in the best position to exploit this dual potential. Quevedo was always quick to make use of the natural resources of language to this end. He saw it as his task to expose the true meaning of the images men create for themselves when they speak. He drew on the capacity of language for creative ambiguity, using homonyms, false etymologies and figurative language as the basis of puns and conceits, offered strikingly appropriate re-definitions ('buenas creedoras', 'comida eterna') and, above all, demonstrated an unerringly sharp ear for the social use and misuse of language.[148] One of the best examples of this comes in the scene (1, 4) in the Venta de Viveros, in which the characters, particularly Diego and Pablos, become enmeshed in a charade of civility in which the language of courtesy is exposed as a tissue of ritualised hypocrisy. The ruffians act out a subtle parody of good manners with which they manoeuvre don Diego into a position where he is unable to do or say anything which cannot be interpreted as a further offer of hospitality. The only way to break out of this vicious circle of politeness would be to be impolite, yet neither don Diego nor Pablos wishes to appear discourteous. By playing up to don Diego the ruffians have flatteringly created a role for him which he has to live up to or admit that he is not all that they pretend to think he is. To call their bluff would involve loss of face. They have paralysed him with their attentiveness, as a hotel doorman does, and are free to seek their own ends, secure in the knowledge that a refusal on don Diego's part in that context would inevitably appear churlish.

The interest of this scene, apart from its being an excruciatingly awful reminder of the times we have all been similarly trapped in real life, is the difficulty Pablos has telling the story: as a narrator he has the problem of deciding whether he knows what is going on or not. Authorial omniscience abounds: the *venta* is 'siempre maldita' ('ever-accursed'), the inn-keeper, 'morisco y ladrón' ('a Moor – and a shark'), hand-in-glove with the highway patrol who have alerted him of the boys' arrival, and the inn is populated with 'dos rufianes con unas mujercillas, un cura rezando al olor, un viejo mercader y avariento procurando olvidarse de comer' ('two ruffians with some wenches, beside whom a priest was saying his prayers, a miserly old shopman trying to go without supper'). The warning is clearly given, if we needed it, yet Pablos allows their attentions to go to his head and answers the girl's questions in good faith 'creyendo que era así como lo decían' ('Thinking they were honest'). Soon after, however, the inn-keeper is described as 'oliendo la estafa' ('catching the drift') and Pablos, seeing the numbers who were invited or invited themselves comments: 'afligíme, y temí lo que sucedió' (pp. 51–3) ('my heart was in my mouth and I foresaw what came to pass', Stevens–Duff, pp. 19–20). Now there is no problem of point of view here. Pablos begins the story with hindsight, reverts to ignorance once he is embarked and, as the light gradually dawns, he begins to move from innocent protagonist to knowing narrator. The overlapping of the two levels is important, however, in the effectiveness of the scene. Pablos warns us by the very way he describes the characters to be on the alert. From the opening exchange in the inn (don Diego orders food for himself and his servants, and the ruffians, quick as a flash, step forward: 'We are all your servants') the reader knows exactly how to decipher the code. Pablos casts himself and his friend as ironic victims in order to illustrate his point, and although he and, eventually, Diego wake up to what is happening to them, by the time they do so they are as helplessly cornered as the reader has known them to be all along.

The Venta de Viveros scene, then, is another of Quevedo's exquisitely self-destructive fictions, showing the writer's uncommonly acute hearing for hollowness in language, recreated in a way which contrives to ring absolutely true. For the fact is that this fiction is convincing: it persuades the characters, who are successfully en-meshed in the web of language; it persuades the reader, who constantly has to admit 'yes, yes, how true!' Yet throughout the scene neither they nor he are ever less than fully aware that every word the ruffians speak is false. It is this duplicity that has led Edmond Cros to describe the language of the *Buscón* as 'un discours qui masque ou qui démasque'[149] and to speak of two texts in the work which sometimes lie side by side and sometimes cut across each other.[150] Such an overlap frequently exists between a form of expression which acts as a vehicle for prevailing social values, particularly those of the dominant social class, and a form of expression which sets against those values the economic and material realities of life.[151] In the Venta de Viveros the language of good manners is eroded from within by the self-seeking of those in search of a free meal. The effect is double-edged: the ruffians' trick is reprehensible, but it exposes the emptiness of the conventions they manipulate at will.

The two texts of the *Buscón* coincide and coexist, inevitably, in Pablos himself, since he is the nominal origin of both. As we have seen, however, Quevedo is never far behind. Pablos is a mask behind which Quevedo lies barely concealed.[152] It is impossible to think of the two of them except as a comedy routine: puppeteer and puppet, comedian and fall-guy. So often Pablos sets himself up only to knock himself down. Even the phrases are constructed in this rhythm of 'now you see it, now you don't'. Of his father, Pablos remarks, invoking the prevailing social ethic of honourable pedigree, 'Dicen que era de muy buena cepa' (p. 15) only for another, more mischievous voice to interject the cutting gloss 'y, según él bebía, es cosa para creer' ('It was said that he came of good stock, and, to judge by his love for the pot, this can easily be believed', Stevens–Duff, p. 3). The sentence is made for the double-act, or the skilled rhapsode, using all the resources of his oral art – change of voice (the second 'aside'), change of demeanour to indicate ironic detachment – to convey the narrator's self-destruction. The fact that Pablos's words are self-consuming[153] makes him the perfect exemplar of Quevedo's attitude to language and to fiction. Like Lazarillo and Guzmán, Pablos is what Raimundo Lida calls an 'Héroe doble, de la picardía y de la ingeniosidad, [que] llega a ser una figura casi alegórica: la de un pecador fatal, con clara conciencia de serlo.'[154] Pablos's duality, though, is not, like Lazarillo's, a carefully devised means of living in a corrupt world, or, like Guzmán's, an expression of man the irresolute, would-be idealist. Pablos's hypocrisy is thrust on him by his creator to illustrate the fact that fiction, like the language of which it is composed, can be used to conceal and to reveal. Therein lies its justification. Through Pablos, Quevedo gives the Platonists what they said could not be done: a lie that speaks the truth.

I have argued throughout this chapter that the key to the reply given by these writers to the Platonist case against fiction lies in the writer's manipulation of his reader's response to the text. To make the lie – the fiction – effective it must convince, yet it must also be made to demonstrate its own falsehood. The reader must, therefore, be both engaged with the text and detached from it. The major structural principle of the picaresque, autobiography, lies behind the tendency of any reader to identify, to become the 'yo' of the text: 'espejo en que me miro y me conozco . . . el que diga *yo* resuena en mí, imponiéndome su discurso que, quiera que no, se me hace mío'.[155] As Maurice Molho says here, first-person narrative is naturally conducive to the identification of reader and character. But this is what the Platonists particularly abhorred. If the reader is to see himself 'as in a glass'[156] he must see himself also as a third person. I have suggested a number of ways in which the writers of the picaresque bring about this detachment. In the case of Pablos, Quevedo builds the dissociation into the character through the language he speaks. Quevedo, in a sense, imposes 'bad faith' on Pablos: what he says is perfectly acceptable; what he is is totally unacceptable.

There are two main consequences of Quevedo's choosing to portray Pablos in this way: one of them highlights the enmity between them,[157] the other, an unlikely alliance. At first it hardly seems possible that Quevedo could have created Pablos for any reason other than to expose him to ridicule. Through the example of Pablos and his eternally doomed attempts to escape from the ignominy of his background, Quevedo is hitting at the picaresque genre as a whole, and, more particularly, at the social restlessness that he felt underlay it. Pablos could be made to stand for everything that Quevedo most resented and for the very social types – much caricatured, admittedly – that were rising to prominence all around him: 'the non-U on the way up'.[158] By ridiculing Pablos's attempts to get on, and by making Pablos's own words the origin of much of that ridicule, Quevedo is acting as a spokesman for his social group. The humour springs from an assumption of superiority and seems intended to bring comfort to a somewhat beleaguered class. It is intended to reinforce a sense of solidarity, to inspire team spirit in the society of discourse.[159] The language and the allusions in the book help to promote this sense of identity, but more effective even than these shared cultural touchstones, is the sense of relief that comes from seeing a potential rival wreck his chances out of his own mouth.

There is, however, a curious further consequence of this ridicule. In order to expose Pablos Quevedo makes him speak the truth in spite of himself (and in defiance of the unlikelihood that anyone will find anything at all funny in the spectacle of a man telling the truth). What he says becomes thereby in a strange way entirely acceptable. In making Pablos speak the truth Quevedo endows him with his own wit and intelligence, his own mercilessly satirical vision and powers of expression. Pablos gains what successes he does by exploiting the corruption of others who lack his own intelligence and understanding. He is a criminal by design, not by accident, and the nature of his crimes – fraud by deception out of imposture – shows his scorn for the stupidity and gullibility of his victims. The example of his manipulation of the landlady and her daughter, and in particular that outrageously virtuoso trick of paying himself a visit, is enough to show how his crimes feed off the self-delusion of those who enable him to flourish. These women are like the women he meets at the Puerta de Guadalajara (III, 2) who are convinced by Pablos's pretence because he speaks to a passing flunkey. Their eagerness to credit his wealth springs from their eagerness to relieve him of it.

Pablos's mixture of ambition and intelligence should have taken him far, and in real life no doubt would have done. But Quevedo makes frequent and, some would say, excessive use of his authorial prerogative to determine the course of events. Whenever Pablos is on the brink of success some quirk of fate, some coincidence, some misfortune always intervenes to ensure that he is thwarted. These 'desgracias encadenadas' have been seen as a major structural principle of the book,[160] and they often involve the physical discomfiture of Pablos in the form of a fall. When on his way to his assignation with the landlady's daughter, he falls, and this misfortune is attributed to a malevolent agent: 'El diablo, que es agudo en todo, ordenó que . . .' (p. 213) ('the devil, acute in all things, so arranged matters that . . .', Stevens–Duff, p. 101). Quevedo, again, having a joke with his friends at his own expense? The devil certainly left his cruelest trick for the moment when Pablos came close to his greatest success, an advantageous marriage (III, 6–7). For Quevedo at this moment produces his ultimate weapon, don Diego, and in so doing turns all Pablos's illusions against him.

Pablos's relationship to don Diego in the early part of the book had been one of adolescent hero-worship. Diego received all Pablos's advances, his toadying and pathetic one-sided exchanges of toys and food, not, as Pablos imagines, with the hauteur of one whose position would lead him to expect such attention, but with the naked self-interest of the nouveau-riche. This young gentleman is not all that Pablos seems to think.[161] From a Jewish family, like Pablos, his parents cannot have been that different from Pablos's. They lived in the same quarter, the boys went to the same school, and Diego's upbringing was not above getting Pablos into trouble with Poncio de Aguirre. When they go to Cabra's academy and later to Alcalá as master and servant, the true difference between the boys, money, is plain enough. Nevertheless, Pablos is mesmerised by the image he has of Diego, and his 'pensamientos de caballero' are ultimately attributable to this schoolboy crush. Very cleverly Quevedo has saddled Pablos from the outset, not just with an impossible ambition, but with an Achilles heel: an illusion which, for all his clear-headed insight into the illusions of others, Quevedo will be able to turn against him when the need arises.

The opportunity comes one day in the Casa del Campo. Pablos should have seen it coming. He should have known that ladies of quality do not make matches in public parks with strangers and if he had read his *Lazarillo* he would have remembered the *escudero*'s experience by the riverside with the two 'rebozadas mujeres' (3.215–30). But Pablos, masquerading as don Felipe Tristán, is on the scent of victory and his judgment fails him. Like the landlady and her daughter, and like the ladies at the Puerta de Guadalajara, his interest demands that he put faith in his illusions. He fails to hear the warning as the aunt, in the Prado, neatly and quickly trumps his claims. If he is as well off as he says, and can afford to marry a well-bred girl though she be poor, why does the aunt pitch her niece's dowry half as high again as the income Pablos has just boasted of? (p. 223) When they meet again the next day in the Casa del Campo (Pablos, having mislaid his servants, is unable to entertain the ladies, who have omitted to bring their lunch with them – c.f. *Lazarillo*, 3, 218–19 – at their first meeting) don Diego reappears after a long and no doubt well-planned absence from the narrative. Diego recognises Pablos and makes it quite clear with heavily insolent irony that he does so. Once again, a conspiracy of courtesy produces a coded text, one which this time Pablos crucially misreads. Pablos is all but exposed except that the aunt vouches for him with an obvious lie: 'Yo le conozco muy bien al señor don Felipe, que es el que nos hospedó por orden de mi marido, que fue gran amigo suyo en Ocaña' (p. 230) ('Why, I know don Felipe very well – it was he who entertained me at Ocaña, at my husband's request', Stevens–Duff, p. 111). Pablos, catching the drift, plays along with the lie. They are like two exhausted swimmers helplessly clutching at each other to save themselves from drowning. Since Diego's exposure of Pablos also reflects badly on her, the aunt, who cannot risk losing face with Diego, her cousin, steps in to save Pablos. But Pablos should have seen through this rescue attempt: after all, as he tells us, 'entendí la letra'. Here, if only Pablos could see it, is a chance for him to be rid once and for all of his debilitating image of Diego. The aunt and her sister very nearly prompt him: 'dijeron que cómo era posible que a un caballero tan principal se pareciese un pícaro tan bajo como aquél' ('The two old women asked how it was possible that a gentleman of such high quality should be so like that low scoundrel', Stevens–Duff, p. 111). But, in the face of all the evidence, Pablos uses Diego as collateral for his cousins, the 'ladies', when their evident bankruptcy should have made him reconsider Diego's credibility. The illusion remains intact to the end. In spite of the double beating Pablos subsequently receives at Diego's behest and in his stead, he insists that 'nunca sospeché en don Diego ni en lo que era' (p. 241) ('The person I had least expected it from was Don Diego', Stevens–Duff, p. 116). We are not told when the truth dawned, though the account Pablos gives would have been impossible unless it had.

Quevedo's use of this last resort, the destruction of the illusion which had lain behind Pablos's ambition from the outset, brings him victory but at enormous cost. The old devil is at it again ('ordena el diablo', p. 240), busy knocking down upstarts in books when he is powerless to do anything about them in real life. Quevedo's defeat of Pablos shows, as Maurice Molho comments, that Quevedo is living in the past. The *Buscón* is a chimera, 'la pintura de un mundo señorial, que supiera protegerse contra la vertiginosa ascensión de los pícaros' ('a portrait of a ruling class able to defend itself against the dizzy ascent of the pícaros').[162] That comfortable laughter at the pathetic attempts of the pícaro to win an unwinnable battle may in fact be the nervous giggle of a class busy putting out more flags to stave off an unthinkable defeat. But the real cost is not just this admission that the battle is already as good as lost. In order to destroy Pablos, Quevedo has to unmask Diego as well, that is, to pull down the ideal of respectability, of the ordered calm of a society based on nobility and its privileges, to which Pablos, for all his ignominy, nevertheless aspires. In a curious way, the outsider who wants to get in has to uphold the values to which he aspires: those on the inside may end up, even more curiously, finding that the only way they can effectively deny him entry is by denying that there is anything to enter, like the rich man who discourages rivals by stressing the importance of happiness. To cure Pablos of his aspirations, Quevedo has to show him that there is nothing for him to aspire to. In spite of his victory over Pablos, the world Quevedo portrays in the *Buscón* is one in which the pícaros have taken over, one where all values have been eroded away. There is nowhere for Quevedo's own class to take refuge in all this, and nowhere for us, as readers, to retreat to if we do not like what we see. Not for nothing does Pablos, who began by addressing us respectfully as 'señor', end with an insolent 'si fueres pícaro, lector' (p. 273).

5

Conclusion

This book has examined one of the factors which helped to determine the shape and form, the texture and feel of Spanish prose fiction in the Golden Age: the way that, consciously or not, certain writers wrote with half an eye to the critics who contended that fiction had a case to answer. These writers sought to locate the legitimacy of fiction precisely where the Platonist critics found it most wanting, in its ability to convince in spite of its falsehood, and in the complex responses that fiction calls forth from its readership. Where the Platonist critics found an alternative form of reality masquerading confusingly and compellingly as the real thing, the writers found an analogue of the moral and spiritual confusion in which lives are customarily lived. Where the critics saw readers fatally mesmerised, the writers found active participants involved in a degree of dialogue with the text that only silent private reading could have made possible.

If they had cared to look closely at any of the books discussed in chapter 4, or at any of the works of Cervantes – of whom the picaresque so often puts one in mind – critics of fiction would have found a sophisticated and convincing response to their case. They would have found a series of texts in which the practice of falsehood in its many forms becomes one of the major thematic considerations. Characters attempt to deceive each other for gain, for self-aggrandisement, for sport, and narrating protagonists attempt to persuade readers to adopt particular attitudes towards these activi-ties. Such persuasion is carried out by means of a considerable armoury of literary and linguistic strategies of which fictional autobiography and its narrative consequences are the most characteristic. Fictional autobiography exploits all the resources of first-person narrative to lure readers into a relationship of empathy with the text. But autobiography necessarily entails a division of self which undermines the security of the reader's response. Important and unsettling consequences follow: points of view start to shift as the narrator superimposes the present on the past; things start to look different from one moment to the next and values seem less reliable than once they did; the text starts to call itself into question as the narrator's tone oscillates between confidentiality and aggression. The result is a complex experience for the reader who finds that his suspension of disbelief is at issue and his willingness to accept what he is told is being exploited by a disingenuous narrator. Key episodes – the stone bull on the bridge at Salamanca, the *buldero*'s confidence trick, the wooing of the landlady and her daughter – seem to make explicit what is implicit throughout: that, indeed, the literary artist and the liar are one and the same; but that a reader's gullibility is, by the same token, a form of blindness of which he can and must be cured. All three texts discussed in chapter 4 seek to bring about this awakening by the careful control of the reader's ambiguous response. His natural engagement with the text – not, *pace* the Platonists, a source of danger, but a source of strength – is countered by the equal and opposite sense of disengagement that comes with a recognition that he has, as a reader, been made to work hard at his reading, to interpret difficult and conflicting evidence, to judge complex issues and ultimately to submit himself to judgment.

Notes

1. Introduction – first premises

1. E.g. Jacques Monod, *Le hasard et la nécessité*, ch. 7.
2. For two fine examples of what can be done with the analysis of surviving inventories and legal documents see C. Batlle, 'Las bibliotecas de los ciudadanos de Barcelona en el siglo xv', in *Livre et lecture en Espagne et en France sous l'ancien régime*, pp. 15–31 and Ph. Berger, 'La lecture à Valence de 1474 à 1560, évolution des comportements en fonction des milieux sociaux', *ibid.*, pp. 97–107.
3. Denys Hay, Introduction, *New Cambridge Modern History*, vol. i, p. 4; id., *Printing and the Mind of Man*, p. xxii. The evolutionary interpretation of the effects of printing on literary culture is argued by Lucien Febvre and Henri-Jean Martin, *L'apparition du livre*. The revolutionary view is put by Elizabeth L. Eisenstein, *The Printing Press as an Agent of Change*, which should be read in the context of Paul Needham's highly critical review in *Fine Print*, vi, 1 (January, 1980), 23–35. I am grateful to Professor E. J. Kenney for drawing my attention to this review.
4. Febvre and Martin, *Apparition*, pp. 393–6; 420–5. R. R. Bolgar, *The Classical Heritage and its Beneficiaries*, p. 280, makes much the same point but with a different emphasis: that printing helped to preserve the ideals of humanism against a possible conservative reaction.
5. Febvre and Martin, *Apparition*, p. 378.
6. Figures are based on information given in F. J. Norton, *A Descriptive Catalogue of Printing in Spain and Portugal 1501–1520*. The proportion of Latin books to total production for each centre is as follows (percentages are given in statistically significant cases):

Alcalá	54:83	65 per cent
Barcelona	76:153	49.7
Burgos	36:104	34.6
Gerona	2:6	
Granada	4:16	
Lérida	0:1	
Logroño	50:67	74.5
Medina	0:1	
?Monterrey	1:1	
Montserrat	6:9	
Murcia	0:1	
Pamplona	2:2	
Perpignan	6:11	
Salamanca	88:142	62
Saragossa	74:119	62
Seville	58:300	19.3
Toledo	18:139	13
Valencia	36:122	29.5
Valladolid	8:56	
Unknown	0:39	
	519:1372	38

7. F.J. Norton, *Printing in Spain 1501-1520*, p. 134.
8. Maxime Chevalier, *Lectura y lectores en la España del siglo XVI y XVII*, pp. 65-103.
9. *Ibid.*, pp. 25-6, cites examples from Juan Costa and Juan de Arguijo, along with the following observation by Juan de Mal Lara: 'Ha venido la cosa a tales extremos que aún es señal de nobleza de linaje no saber escribir su nombre', *Filosofía vulgar*, vol. II, p. 284. This question is discussed by Nicholas G. Round, 'Renaissance culture and its opponents in fifteenth-century Castile', *Modern Language Review*, LVII (1962), 204-15, and P. E. Russell, 'Las armas contra las letras: para una definición del humanismo español del siglo XV' in *Temas de 'La Celestina'*, pp. 209-39. Ph. Berger's figures for the Valencia nobility suggest, if anything, a decrease in readership among the upper classes during the period he studies, though he does not press the point: 'La lecture à Valence', pp. 101-2.
10. Febvre and Martin, *Apparition*, p. 378.
11. Norton, *Printing*, p. 127.
12. Cf. Malesherbes, on being admitted to the Académie Française: 'Dans un siècle où chaque citoyen peut parler à la nation entière par la voie de l'impression, ceux qui ont le talent d'instruire les hommes ou le don de les émouvoir, les gens de lettres, en un mot, sont au milieu du peuple dispersé ce qu'étaient les orateurs de Rome et d'Athènes au milieu du peuple assemblé', F. M. Grimm, *Correspondance littéraire, philosophique et critique*, vol. XI, p. 36. George Steiner, *Language and Silence*, p. 383: 'Writing and print isolate. There is no collective noun or concept for readers corresponding to "audience". The collective "readership" . . . is a far-gone abstraction. To think of readers as a united group, we have to fall back on calling them an "audience", as though they were in fact listeners.'
13. Josef Balogh, 'Voces paginarum', *Philologus*, 82 (1927), 84-109, 202-40; G. L. Hendrickson, 'Ancient reading', *Classical Journal*, 25 (1929), 182-96; W. P. Clark, 'Ancient reading', *Classical Journal*, 26 (1931), 698-700; H. J. Chaytor, *From Script to Print*, pp. 5-21; Bernard M. W. Knox, 'Silent reading in antiquity', *Greek, Roman and Byzantine Studies*, 9 (1968), 421-35.
14. *The Confessions of Augustine*, VI, III, p. 141: 'sed cum legebat, oculi ducebantur per paginas et cor intellectum rimabatur, uox autem et lingua quiescebant. saepe, cum adessemus . . . sic eum legentem uidimus tacite et aliter numquam sedentesque in diuturno silentio – quis enim tam intento esse oneri auderet? – discedebamus.' *Benedicti Regula*, XLVIII, 5: 'Post sexta autem surgentes a mensa pausent in lecta sua cum omni silentio aut forte, qui uoluerit legere sibi, sic legat, ut alium non inquietet.' The passage from the *Tusculan Disputations* is as follows: 'Et si cantus eos forte delectant, primum cogitare debent, ante quam hi sint inventi, multos beate vixisse sapientes, deinde multo maiorem percipi posse legendis his quam audiendis voluptatem. Tum, ut paulo ante caecos ad aurium traducebamus voluptatem, sic licet surdos ad oculorum' (V, 116).
15. William Nelson, *Fact or Fiction. The Dilemma of the Renaissance Storyteller*, pp. 4-6.
16. Fr. Pedro Malón de Chaide, *La conversión de la Magdalena*, vol. I, pp. 23-8.
17. 'como si no bastaran los ruines siniestros con que nacemos y los que mamamos en la leche, y los que se nos pegan en la niñez con el regalo que en aquella edad se nos hace; y como si nuestra gastada naturaleza, que de suyo corre desapoderada al mal, tuviera necesidad de espuela y de incentivos para despertar el gusto del pecado, así la ceban con libros lascivos y profanos, a donde y en cuyas rocas se rompen los frágiles navíos de los mal avisados mozos, y las buenas costumbres (si algunas aprendieron de sus maestros) padecen naufragios y van a fondo y se pierden y malogran. Porque ¿qué otra cosa son los libros de amores y las *Dianas* y *Boscanes* y *Garcilasos* . . . puestos en manos de pocos años, sino cuchillo en poder del hombre furioso?' (pp. 23-4).

18. '¿Qué ha de hacer la doncellita que apenas sabe andar, y ya trae una *Diana* en la faldriquera? . . . Otros leen aquellos prodigios y fabulosos sueños y quimeras, sin pies ni cabeza, de que están llenos los *Libros de Caballerías*, que así los llaman a los que, si la honestidad del término lo sufriera, con trastocar pocas letras se llamaran mejor de bellaquerías que de caballerías' (pp. 25–7).

19. Gaspar de Astete, *Tratado del gobierno de la familia y estado de las viudas y donzellas*, pp. 179–80: 'hombres desalmados, vanos, habladores, mentirosos, destemplados, deshonestos y sin temor de Dios: cuyas bocas están llenas de maldad, y de blasphemias y torpezas: cuyas gargantas son como sepulchros hediondos, que hechan de sí podredumbre y hediondez, cuyos coraçones son sentina de toda maldad', cited by Edward Glaser, 'Nuevos datos sobre la crítica de los libros de caballerías en los siglos XVI y XVII', *Anuario de Estudios Medievales*, III (1966), 406.

20. Marcel Bataillon, *Erasmo y España*, pp. 609–23; Américo Castro, *El pensamiento de Cervantes*, pp. 60–1; Chevalier, *Lectura*, pp. 155–61; Glaser, 'Nuevos datos', pp. 393–410; Werner Krauss, 'Die Kritik des Siglo de Oro am Ritter- und Schäferroman', *Gesammelte Aufsätze zur Literatur- und Sprachwissenschaft*, pp. 152–76; Marcelino Menéndez y Pelayo, *Orígenes de la novela*, vol. I, pp. 239–40, 440–7; Martín de Riquer, Introduction, *Tirante el Blanco*, vol. I, pp. xxxii–xlviii; id., 'Cervantes y la caballeresca', *Suma cervantina*, pp. 279–84; Henry Thomas, *Spanish and Portuguese Romances of Chivalry*, pp. 146–79; Francisco María Tubino, *El Quijote y la estafeta de Urganda*, pp. 65–80. Wherever possible, sources have been checked from original editions. When this has not been possible reference is made to the anthology from which the quotation is taken.

21. P. E. Russell, 'Spanish Literature (1474–1681)', *Spain. A Companion to Spanish Studies*, p. 271.

22. Benito Arias Montano, *Rhetoricorum Libri IV*, p. 64:

> . . . monstra vocamus
> Et stupidi ingenii partum, faecemque librorum,
> Collectas sordes in labem temporis . . . (ll. 402–4)

23. *Libro del muy esforzado e invencible caballero de la fortuna propiamente llamado Claribalte*, Valencia, 1519.

24. Gonzalo Fernández de Oviedo y Valdés, *Historia general de las Indias*, fol. lxiiiv: 'Mas los hombres sabios e naturales atenderán a esta lección, no con otra mayor cobdicia e desseo que por saber e oyr las obras de natura: e assí con más desocupación del entendimiento aurán por bien de oyrme (pues no cuento los disparates de los libros mentirosos de Amadís ni los que dellos dependen).' Id., *Las quinquagenas de la nobleza de España*, p. 481: 'Razón muy grande es, sancto y prouechoso, de mucha vtilidad, y nesçessario sería dexar de leer esos libros de Amadís: y que esos e ni otros semejantes no se vendiesen, ni los ouiese, porque es vna de las cosas con quel diablo enbauca e enbelesa y entretiene los neçios, y los aparta de las leçiones honestas y de buen exemplo.'

25. Juan de Valdés, *Diálogo de la lengua*, pp. 173–4: 'demás de ser mentirosíssimos, son tan mal compuestos, assí por dezir las mentiras muy desvergonçadas, como por tener el estilo desbaratado, que no hay buen estómago que los pueda leer'.

26. Thomas, *Romances*, pp. 150–1.

27. Juan Luis Vives, *Opera Omnia*, vol. IV, pp. 85–90. 'invaluit consuetudo, quavis gentilia pejor, ut vulgares libri, qui in hoc scribuntur ut ab otiosis, tum viris, tum feminis, legantur, nullam habeant aliam quam de bellis, aut amoribus materiam'.

28. Juan Luis Vives, tr. Richard Hyrde, *The Instruction of a Christian Woman*, fol. 9v. *Opera*, vol. IV, p. 85: 'quid ego quanta sit ea pestis dicam, quum igni stipulae, et arida subjiciuntur ligna?'

29. *Ibid.*, fol. 10r. *Opera*, vol. IV, p. 86: 'non facile animus est pudicus, quem ferri, et lacertorum, et virilis roboris cogitatio occupavit'.

30. *Ibid.*, fol. 10r. *Opera*, vol. IV, p. 86: 'lethalis est hic morbus; nec detegendus tamen a me, sed obruendus, atque opprimendus, ne alias, et odore offendat, et contagio inquinet'.

31. *Ibid.*, fol. 10r. *Opera*, vol. IV, p. 86: 'arma igitur, quum Christianum virum tractare, nisi in acerrima atque inevitabili necessitate, fas non sit, spectare feminam fas erit? et, si non manibus, certe, quod gravius est, animo et corde versare?'

32. *Ibid.*, fol. 10v. *Opera*, vol. IV, pp. 87–8: 'quos omnes libros conscripserunt homines otiosi, male feriati, imperiti, vitiis ac spurcitiæ dediti; in queis miror, quid delectet, nisi tam nobis flagitia blandirentur; eruditio non est expectanda ab hominibus, qui ne umbram quidem eruditionis viderant; jam quum narrant, quæ potest esse delectatio in rebus, quas tam aperte et stulte confingunt? . . . Quæ insania est, iis duci, aut teneri? Deinde argutum nihil est, præter quædam verba ex penitissimis Veneris scriniis deprompta, quæ in tempore dicuntur ad permovendam, concutiendamque, quam ames, si forte sit paullo constantior: si propter hæc leguntur, satius erit libros de arte lenonia (sit honos auribus) scribi; nam in aliis rebus argutæ quæ possunt proficisci ab Scriptore omnis bonæ artis experte? Nec ullum audivi affirmantem illos sibi libros placere, nisi qui nullos attigisset bonos; et ipse interdum legi, nec ullum reperi vel bonæ mentis, vel melioris ingenii, vestigium; nam eis qui ejusmodi laudant, quorum ipse quosdam novi, ita demum fidem habebo, si id dixerint postquam Senecam, aut Ciceronem, aut Hieronymum, aut Sacras litteras degustarint, moribus quoque fuerint non omnino corruptissimi, nam plerunque ea sola est laudandi causa, quod in illis, ceu in speculo, mores suos contemplentur, et approbari gaudeant: Postremo, etsi essent acutissima, si jucunda, nolim tamen voluptatem veneno illitam, nec exacui feminam meam ad flagitium; profecto ridenda est maritorum dementia, qui permittunt suis uxoribus ut ejusmodi legendis libris astutius sint pravæ.'

33. Vives, tr. Thomas Paynell, *The Office and Duetie of an Husband*, fol. o7r–v. *Opera*, vol. IV, p. 363: 'voluptates titillant pleraque Poetarum opera, et Milesiæ fabulæ, ut Asinus Apuleji, et fere Luciani omnia, quales crebræ sunt in linguis vernaculis scriptæ Tristani, Lanciloti, Ogerii, Amadisii, Arturi, et his similes; qui libri omnes ab otiosis hominibus, et chartarum abundantibus, per ignorantiam meliorum sunt conscripti: hi non feminis modo, verumetiam viris officiunt, quemadmodum ea omnia, quibus nutus iste noster ad pejora detruditur, ut quibus armatur astutia, accenditur habendi sitis, inflammatur ira, aut cujuscunque rei turpis atque illicita cupiditas.'

34. Fr. Juan de la Cerda, *Libro intitulado vida política de todos los estados de mujeres*, fol. 41r: 'estos vanos libros gastan el espíritu y ensuzian el alma', cited by Glaser, 'Nuevos datos', p. 406.

35. Russell, *Spain*, p. 271.

36. Fr. Antonio de Guevara, *Libro del emperador Marco Aurelio con relox de príncipes*, fol. VIIv: 'que no pasan tiempo, sino que pierden el tiempo'.

37. Heliodorus, *Historia etiópica*, pp. lxxvii–lxxviii: 'la imbecilidad de nuestra natura no puede sufrir que el entendimiento esté siempre ocupado a leer materias graves y verdaderas, no más que el cuerpo no podría durar sin intermisión al trabajo de muchas obras. Por lo cual, es menester algunas veces, cuando nuestro espíritu está turbado de algunos infortunios, o cansado de mucho estudio, usar de algunos pasatiempos para le apartar de tristes pensamientos y imaginaciones, o, a lo menos, usar de algún descanso y alivio para le tornar después a poner más alegre y vivo en la consideración y contemplación de las cosas de más importancia.'

Amyot's prologue, which originally appeared with his French translation of the *Aethiopica* in 1549, was translated and used to introduce the Spanish version by 'un secreto amigo de su patria' published at Antwerp in 1554.

38. Fr. Agustín Salucio, *Avisos para los predicadores del Santo Evangelio*, cited by Glaser, 'Nuevos datos', p. 397.
39. João de Barros, *Espelho de casados*, fol. 4, cited by Thomas, *Romances*, p. 157.
40. Oviedo y Valdés, *Quinquagenas*, cited by Tubino, *Estafeta*, p. 67; Salucio, *Avisos*, cited by Glaser, 'Nuevos datos', p. 397.
41. Menéndez y Pelayo, *Orígenes*, vol. I, p. 447.
42. Tubino, *Estafeta*, p. 77.
43. Irving A. Leonard, *Romances of Chivalry in the Spanish Indies*, p. 221; id., *Books of the Brave*, p. 83: 'The need to repeat these commands at short intervals is in itself an indication that the prohibition of fictional books in the overseas realms was largely ineffective from the outset.'
44. Menéndez y Pelayo, *Orígenes*, vol. I, 446.
45. P. E. Russell, 'El concilio de Trento y la literatura profana' in *Temas de 'La Celestina'*, pp. 443–78.
46. D. W. Cruickshank, 'Literature and the book trade in Golden-Age Spain', *Modern Language Review*, 73 (1978), 806.
47. *Republic*, III, 397; X, 595–607.
48. Iris Murdoch, *The Fire and the Sun*, p. 9.
49. Bernard Weinberg, *History of Literary Criticism in the Italian Renaissance*, vol. I, p. 250.
50. Vives, *Opera*, vol. IV, p. 89. Fr. Marco Antonio de Camos, *Microcosmia y govierno universal del hombre christiano*, p. 3: 'Ya Platón ordenó se tuuiesse grande cuydado en el sacar a luz libros nueuos, prohibiendo por las leyes de su República sacar los que fuessen dañosos a essa República. Y él mismo desterró de la que instituyó a Homero y a Esiodo por ser poetas con ser de tanta vtilidad y doctrina.'
51. Alonso de Ulloa, *Comentarios de la guerra contra Guillermo de Nausau Príncipe de Oranges*, fol. 69v: 'como cosa contajosa deurían [sc. books of chivalry] ser desterrados de la República por el beneficio común'. E. C. Riley, *Cervantes's Theory of the Novel*, pp. 97–8, points out that Cervantes twice alludes to the expulsion of the poets in *Don Quijote* (I, 47, pp. 481, 482 and II, 38, p. 817). To these instances we might add the Canon's further remark at *DQ*, I, 49 (p. 495) that books of chivalry are 'dañadores e inútiles para la república'. The Canon's persistent use of the word 'república' throughout his debate with don Quixote may well be intended to invest his remarks with the authority of Plato's.
52. Diego Gracián, *Las obras de Xenophon*, cited by Thomas, *Romances*, p. 161. Castro, *Pensamiento*, p. 61 gives the following quotation from Diego Gracián, but does not give a source: 'Nadie puede ni debe imitar lo mentiroso. Que cierto, como dice Platón, ninguna cosa hay tan suave al buen entendimiento como decir y oír verdad.' The sentiments are very similar to those of a passage from Gracián's *Morales de Plutarco* cited by Thomas, *Romances*, pp. 159–60.
53. Juan Huarte de San Juan, *Examen de ingenios*, pp. 69–70; Alonso López Pinciano, *Philosophía antigua poética*, vol. I, p. 222; Luis Alfonso de Carvallo, *Cisne de Apolo*, vol. I, p. 47, vol II, pp. 193, 216–20; Fray Juan de Pineda, *Diálogos familiares de la agricultura cristiana*, vol. III, p. 223.
54. Heliodorus, *Historia etiópica*, p. lxxvii. The allusion is to Plato, *Republic*, II, 377.
55. Diogo Fernandes, Dedication, *Terceira parte da chronica de Palmeirim de Inglaterra*, cited by Glaser, 'Nuevos datos', pp. 398–9: 'os antigos Philosophos . . . em suas feiçoens nos deixaram escondidos os precitos e exemplos dos bõs costumes, como depois de Homero fez Plato nos dialogos . . .'

56. Bolgar, *Classical Heritage*, p. 277, 280; J. V. de Pina Martins, 'Platon et le Platonisme dans la culture Portugaise du XVIe siècle', *Platon et Aristote à la Renaissance*, pp. 421-2; Frances Yates, *The French Academies of the Sixteenth Century*. A search of fourteen sixteenth-century inventories of private libraries in Spain reveals mention of only seven works by, attributed to, or referring to Plato: the library of the Marqués del Cenete (1523), no. 570 (F. J. Sánchez Cantón, *La biblioteca del Marqués del Cenete*, p. 102); the library of Juan de Mal Lara (1571), unnumbered (Francisco Rodríguez Marín, 'Nuevos datos para las biografías de algunos escritores españoles de los siglos XVI y XVII', *Boletín de la Real Academia Española*, v, 1918, 207); the library of Diego Hurtado de Mendoza (1575), nos. 125, 146, 165, 403 (Angel González Palencia and Eugenio Mele, *Vida y obras de don Diego Hurtado de Mendoza*, vol. III, pp. 511, 514, 519, 561); the library of Luis Barahona de Soto (1595), no. 299 (Francisco Rodríguez Marín, *Luis Barahona de Soto*, p. 543). Miguel Angel Ladero Quesada and María Concepción Quintanilla Raso record the presence of Platonic texts in the library of the Marqués de Priego (1518) without specifying numbers or titles ('Bibliotecas de la alta nobleza castellana en el siglo XV' in *Livre et lecture*, pp. 47-59).

57. *Timaeus*, Valencia, 1547; *Symposium*, Salamanca, 1553 and Saragossa, 1559. Other Spanish-printed editions may exist; there is no bibliography of Plato for the sixteenth and seventeenth centuries (C. B. Schmitt, 'L'introduction de la philosophie platonicienne dans l'enseignement des universités à la renaissance', *Platon et Aristote à la Renaissance*, p. 96, n. 10). Sebastián Fox Morcillo's commentaries on the *Timaeus* and the *Republic* were published at Basle in 1554 and 1556 respectively.

58. Fernando de Herrera, *Obras de Garcilaso de la Vega con anotaciones de Fernando de Herrera*, annotation H667, p. 537.

59. Nicholas G. Round, 'The shadow of a philosopher: medieval Castilian images of Plato', *Journal of Hispanic Philology*, III, 1 (Autumn, 1978), 1-36.

60. *Bocados de oro*, p. 71: 'e començó primera mente de aprender el lenguaje e el arte poética, e llegó con ella a grant estado. E estudo un día ante Socrates, e vido-le que denostava la arte poética, e plogo-le lo que oyó dezir d'ella, e aborresció por eso lo que sabíe d'ella.'

61. E. R. Curtius, *Literatura europea y Edad Media Latina*, p. 667.

62. Vernon Hall, Jr, 'Scaliger's defense of poetry', *Publications of the Modern Language Association of America*, LXIII (1948), 1127: 'tamen propter Platonis auctoritatem paucula nobis sunt dicenda'. Scaliger also mentions Plato's expulsion of the poets in the *Poetices Libri Septem*, I, II, 5, a.l.

63. López Pinciano, *Philosophía*, vol. I, pp. 163-87.

64. See below, pp. 34-50.

65. J. E. Spingarn, *A History of Literary Criticism in the Renaissance*, p. 18.

66. *Ibid.*, p. 4.

67. Plato, *Republic*, x, 606: 'if the dramatic poetry whose end is to give pleasure can show good reason why it should exist in a well-governed society, we for our part should welcome it back, being ourselves conscious of its charm'.

2. The case against fiction

1. See p. 14, above.

2. Alonso de Fuentes, *Summa de philosophía natural*, cited by Menéndez y Pelayo, *Orígenes*, vol. I, p. 445.

3. Benito Remigio Noydens, *Historia moral del Dios Momo*, p. 286: 'Yo me acuerdo auer leído de vn hombre sumamente vicioso; que hallándose amartelado de vna,

y sin esperança de conquistarla por fuerça, se resoluió a cogerla con engaño, y maña, y haziéndola poner los ojos en vno destos libros, con título de entretenimiento, le puso en el corazón tales ideas de amores, que componiéndola a su exemplo, descompusieron en ella, y arruynaron el honesto estado de su recato, y de su vergüença.'

4. Pedro Mexía, *Historia imperial y cesárea*, fol. cxliiv: 'que dan muy malos ejemplos y muy peligrosos para las costumbres'.

5. Giovanni Francesco Pico della Mirandola, *Examen vanitatis doctrinae gentium et veritatis disciplinae Christianae*, in *Opera omnia*, vol. ii, p. 938: 'non minores enim malorum occasiones ex poëtis, ad uitia quam ad uirtutes trahunt homines'.

6. In the *Laws* poets are allowed a qualified freedom on sufferance and subject to a rigorous but unspecified censorship (Paul Vicaire, *Platon, critique littéraire*, p. 66), but this does not constitute a fundamental departure from Plato's position in the *Republic*, merely an admission that the banishment was wishful thinking: the *Laws* are, after all, the pragmatic face of the coin of which the *Republic* is the ideal.

7. López Pinciano, *Philosophía*, vol. i, pp. 164–5.

8. Strabo, *Geography*, i, 2, 5, vol. i, pp. 62–3.

9. López Pinciano, *Philosophía*, vol. i, p. 154: 'la obra salida desta abstinencia, sudor y vela ha de ser muy buena'; p. 148: 'tengo por imposible que vno sea buen poeta y no sea hombre de bien'.

10. The dissertation appears as no. 7 in some collections, as it does in the translation of Thomas Taylor quoted here.

11. López Pinciano, *Philosophía*, vol. i, pp. 176–9.

12. Mario Equicola, *Institutioni al comporre in ogni sorte di rima della lingua volgare*, cited by Weinberg, *History*, vol. i, p. 264. Huarte de San Juan, *Examen*, p. 57 gives an analogous argument about the terrestrial paradise: in a perfect world the arts and the sciences are unnecessary.

13. *Republic*, iii, 401.

14. Equicola, *Institutioni*, cited by Weinberg, *History*, vol. i, p. 264.

15. Astete, *Tratado*, in Glaser, 'Nuevos datos', p. 407.

16. Vicaire, *Platon*, p. 233.

17. Murdoch, *The Fire and the Sun*, p. 6.

18. Lodovico Castelvetro, *Chiose intorno al libro del Comune di Platone* (*c.* 1565–71), in *Opere varie critiche*, pp. 215–16, cited by Weinberg, *History*, vol. i, p. 293.

19. Sperone Speroni, *Dialogo sopra Virgilio* in *Opere*, vol. ii, p. 360: 'perciocchè 'l male si dee far male come è, e non far bene come non è'. Cf. Alessandro Lionardi, *Dialogi della inventione poetica*, p. 80: 'non però che quello che è noceuole e da fuggirsi, il poeta narrar non debba, essendoli necessario riferir le cause così de' fatti maluagi, e uitupereuoli, come de' buoni, e laudeuoli'.

20. Castelvetro, *Opere varie*, pp. 215–16, cited by Weinberg, *History*, vol. i, p. 293. Castelvetro is alluding to the phenomenon of catharsis discussed in Aristotle, *Poetics*, 6; 14–15.

21. López Pinciano, *Philosophía*, vol. i, pp. 173–6.

22. Spingarn, *History of Literary Criticism*, pp. 5–6; Sanford Shepard, *El Pinciano y las teorías literarias del siglo de oro*, pp. 12–13.

23. Francesco Patrizi, *De institutione reipublicae*, fol. xxixr: 'Habet enim in se violentiam quandam nimiam mistam desperationi, quae facile ex stultis insanos reddat, et leues in furorem compellat.'

24. *Ibid.*, fol. xxixr–v: 'Corrumpit [comoedia] nanque hominum mores, eosque effoeminatos reddit, et ad libidinem, luxuriamque compellit . . . Comodiarum nanque argumenta, magna ex parte adulteria, et stupra continent, quocirca spectandi consuetudo, mutandi etiam licentiam facit.'

25. Giovanni Francesco Pico della Mirandola, *De studio divinae et humanae philosophiae*, I, VI, in *Opera*, vol. II, p. 18: 'animum et emolliri sentiebam . . . Quare scribit Isidorus ideo christianis prohiberi legere figmenta poetarum quia per oblectamenta fabularum excitant mentem ad incentiua libidinum.'

26. Antonio de Guevara, *Aviso de privados y doctrina de cortesanos*, in *Las obras*, fol. 7.

27. Alejo Venegas, Prologue to Luis Mexía, *Apólogo de la ociosidad y el trabajo*, fol. a7r: 'porque vemos que veda el padre a la hija, que no le venga y le vaya la vieja con sus mensajes, y por otra parte es tan mal recatado, que no le veda, que leyendo Amadises, y Esplandianes con todos los de su vando, le esté predicando el diablo a sus solas, que allí aprende las celadas de las ponçoñas secretas, demás del hábito que haze en pensamientos de sensualidad, que assí la hazen saltar de su quietud, como el fuego a la póluora'.

28. Francisco Ortiz Lucio, *Libro intitulado jardín de amores santos*, fol. 3r–v: 'Y al contrario, es muy inútil y de poco prouecho, la lección de las Celestinas, Dianas, Boscanes, Amadises, Esplandianes, y otros libros llenos de portentosas mentiras. Y del abuso que Satanás con estos libros ha introducido, no se grangea cosa, sino que la tierna donzella, y mancebo, hagan, de tal lección, vn tizón y fuego, y soplo incentivo de torpeza, donde enciendan sus deseos y apetitos de liuiandad, y estos se vayan ceuando poco a poco, hasta experimentar por obra, lo que por palabra leen.'

29. Cerda, *Vida política*, fol. 41v: 'Ay algunas donzellas que por entretener el tiempo, leen en estos libros, y hallan en ellos vn dulce veneno que les incita a malos pensamientos, y les haze perder el seso que tenían', cited by Glaser, 'Nuevos datos', p. 406.

30. Luisa María de Padilla Manrique y Acuña, *Excelencias de la castidad*, p. 599: 'la lectura que debajo de vn dulce y afectado lenguaje tiene encubierta la amargura de la muerte de toda virtud y buenas costumbres, y es diuertimiento mezclado con veneno mortífero', cited by Glaser, 'Nuevos datos', p. 408.

31. Remigio Noydens, *Historia moral*, p. 286: 'píldoras doradas que con capa de vn gustoso entretenimiento lisongean los ojos, para llenar la boca de amargura, y tosigar el alma de veneno'.

32. Juan Sáncnez Valdés de la Plata, *Corónica y historia general del hombre*, fol. 2r: 'mentiras y vanidades, que es lo que mucho el diablo siempre codicia, para que con estas ponçoñas secretas, y sabrosas, las aparte del camino verdadero de Iesu Christo'; Venegas, Prologue to Mexía, *Apólogo*, fol. a7r: 'ponçoñas secretas'.

33. Malón de Chaide, *Conversión*, p. 25: 'Pero responden los autores de los primeros, que son amores tratados con limpieza y mucha honestidad; como si por eso dejasen de mover el afecto de la voluntad poderosísimamente, y como si lentamente no se fuese esparciendo su mortal veneno por las venas del corazón, hasta prender en lo más puro y vivo del alma, a donde, con aquel ardor furioso, seca y agosta todo lo más florido y verde de nuestras obras. Hallaréis, dice Plutarco, unos animalejos tan pequeños como son los mosquitos de una cierta especie, que apenas se dejan ver, y con ser tan nonada, pican tan blandamente que, aunque entonces no os lastima la picadura, de allí a un rato os halláis la parte donde os picó, y os da dolor. Así son estos libros de tales materias que, sin sentir cuándo os hicieron el daño, os halláis herido y perdido.'

34. Francisco Cervantes de Salazar, *Obras que Francisco Cervantes de Salazar ha hecho glosado y traduzido*, III, fol. xiiiv–xivr: 'porque tras el sabroso hablar de los libros de cauallerías beuemos mill vicios como sabrosa ponçoña, porque de allí viene el aborrecer los libros sanctos, y contemplatiuos, y el dessear verse en actos feos . . . guarda el padre a su hija, como dizen tras siete paredes, para que quitada la ocasión de hablar con los hombres: sea más buena, y déxanla vn Amadís en las

manos, donde deprende mill maldades, y dessea peores cosas, que quiça en toda la vida: aunque tratara con los hombres pudiera saber, ni dessear, e vase tanto tras el gusto de aquello, que no querría hazer otra cosa, ocupando el tiempo que auía de gastar en ser laboriosa y sierua de dios, no se acuerda de rezar ni d'otra virtud: desseando ser otra Oriana como allí, e verse seruida de otro Amadís, tras este desseo viene luego procurarlo'.

35. Amyot, Prologue to Heliodorus, *Historia etiópica*, p. lxxviii: 'nuestros corazones . . . naturalmente se apasionan leyendo o viendo los hechos o fortunas de otros'.

36. Fr. Luis de Granada, *Introducción del símbolo de la fe*, p. 92: 'como la muerte sea . . . la última de las cosas terribles, y la cosa más aborrecida de todos los animales, ver vn hombre despreciador y vencedor deste temor tan natural, causa grande admiración en los que esto veen. De aquí nace el concurso de gentes, para ver justas, y toros, y desafíos, y cosas semejantes por la admiración que estas cosas traen consigo . . . Pues esta admiración es tan común a todos y tan grande, que viene a tener lugar no sólo en las cosas verdaderas, sino también en las fabulosas y mentirosas. Y de aquí nace el gusto que muchos tienen de leer estos libros de cauallerías fingidas.'

37. *Ibid.*, 'Pues siendo esto assí, y siendo la valentía y fortaleza de los sanctos mártyres sin ninguna comparación mayor y más admirable, que todas quantas ha auido en el mundo . . . como no holgarán más de leer estas tan altas verdades, que aquellas tan conocidas mentiras?'

38. Astete, *Tratado*, pp. 178-9: 'Vemos que estará . . . vna donzella leyendo vn libro de éstos vn día entero, y vna noche muy larga, y derramará lágrymas, y se enternecerá, leyendo como el otro cauallero auenturero quedó muerto en la batalla, o como el otro loco amador desfalleció en la pretensión de su dama, y no leerá siquiera media hora en vn libro de deuoción, ni derramará vna sola lágrima, o acordándose de sus peccados, o pensando en la amarguíssima passión del Saluador.'

39. *Republic*, x, 607.

40. Murdoch, *The Fire and the Sun*, p. 6.

41. Plutarch, *Life of Solon*, xxix, 4-5 in *Lives*, vol. I, pp. 488-9: 'Solon went to see Thespis act in his own play, as the custom of the ancient poets was. After the spectacle, he accosted Thespis, and asked him if he was not ashamed to tell such lies in the presence of so many people. Thespis answered that there was no harm in talking and acting that way in play, whereupon Solon smote the ground sharply with his staff and said: "Soon, however, if we give play of this sort so much praise and honour, we shall find it in our solemn contracts."'

42. Francisco de Barcelos, *Salutiferae crucis triumphus*, cited by Glaser, 'Nuevos datos', p. 395.

43. Melchor Cano, *De locis theologicis*, p. 657.

44. Francisco de Monzón, *Espejo del príncipe cristiano*, fol. 5v.

45. P. José de Sigüenza, *Historia de la orden de san Jerónimo*, p. 393.

46. Amyot, Prologue to Heliodorus, *Historia etiópica*, p. lxxx: 'sueños de algún enfermo que desvaría con la calentura'.

47. Camos, *Microcosmia*, p. 3: 'andan llenas de mentiras: sin tocar historia verdadera'.

48. Francisco de Vallés, *Cartas familiares de moralidad*: 'se arman sin fundamento en el aire', cited by Castro, *Pensamiento*, p. 61.

49. Sánchez Valdés, *Corónica*, fol. 2r: 'sino hacer hábito en sus pensamientos de mentiras'.

50. Amyot, Prologue to Heliodorus, *Historia etiópica*, p. lxxvii.

51. Valdés, *Diálogo*, p. 177: 'nuestro autor del Amadís . . . dize cosas tan a la clara mentirosas, que de ninguna manera las podéis tener por verdaderas'.

52. Cicero, *De legibus*, I, i, 4, pp. 300–1: 'sed tamen non nulli isti, Tite noster, faciunt imperite, qui in isto periculo non ut a poeta, sed ut a teste veritatem exigent'; Plutarch, *Moralia*, 17, vol. I, pp. 90–1: 'the art of poetry is not greatly concerned with the truth'.

53. Lionardo Bruni d'Arezzo, *De Studiis et Litteris*, in W. H. Woodward, *Vittorino da Feltre and other Humanist Educators*, p. 132.

54. Vallés, *Cartas*, cited by Castro, *Pensamiento*, p. 61: 'La lástima es que aviendo tantos libros de historia y otros de devoción que tienen curiosidad, variedad y verdad . . . haya muchos que desto se cansan'; Malón de Chaide, *Conversión*, p. 28: 'como si no tuviéramos abundancia de ejemplos famosos, en todo linaje de virtud que quisiéramos, sin andar a fingir monstruos increíbles y prodigiosos'.

55. Fr. Pedro de la Vega, *Segunda parte de la declaración de los siete psalmos penitenciales*, p. 194: 'pero ¿quién ay, que siendo bueno y amando sola la virtud, se canse de gana para fauorecer a malos y indignos? Aquí parece que se caen las manos y el coraçón y se entorpecen los pies, y aun la pluma de los que escriuen; fingiendo a su alvedrío, no se atreuieron a fingir tal exageración.'

56. Glaser, 'Nuevos datos', pp. 396–7.

57. Nelson, *Fact or Fiction*, p. 11.

58. Macrobius, *Commentarii in Somnium Scipionis*, I, 2, 17–18: 'de dis autem (ut dixi) ceteris et de anima non frustra se nec ut oblectent ad fabulosa convertunt, sed quia sciunt inimicam esse naturae apertam nudamque expositionem sui, quae sicut vulgaribus hominum sensibus intellectum sui vario rerum tegmine operimentoque subtraxit, ita a prudentibus arcana sua voluit per fabulosa tractari'; Lactantius, *Divinarum Institutionum*, I, XI, col. 171–2: 'cum officium poetae sit in eo, ut ea, quae gesta sunt vere, in alias species obliquis figurationibus cum decore aliquo conversa traducat. Totum autem, quod referas, fingere, id est ineptum esse, et mendacem potius quam poetam.' St Augustine, *Quaestionum Evangeliorum*, II, LI, col 1362: 'Non enim omne quod fingimus mendacium est: sed quando id fingimus quod nihil significat, tunc est mendacium. Cum autem fictio nostra refertur ad aliquam significationem, non est mendacium, sed aliqua figura veritatis.' Augustine is glossing Luke 24.28: 'and he made as though he would have gone further' – 'finxit se longius ire'.

59. Pineda, *Agricultura*, vol. I, p. 73: 'los poetas nunca tuvieron ojo a fingir mentiras, sino a encubrir verdades . . . y que el mentir de los poetas pára en el sonido de las palabras, mas no en el sentido que hacen, so pena que no merecerían el nombre de sapientísimos que todos les dan, sino de pierdetiempo y palabras, como los componedores de libros de caballerías'.

60. Giovanni Battista Pigna, *I romanzi*, p. 31: 'mi penso che ad ognuno no sia vietato il leggere i poeti: ma solo alla gente che ne de i sensi loro è capace, ne intendente de i loro secreti; quale è le plebeia, e la ignorante'.

61. The terms 'true to' and 'true of' are taken from Stein Haugom Olsen, *The Structure of Literary Understanding*, pp. 72–3, although Olsen himself regards the distinction as misplaced.

62. López Pinciano, *Philosophía*, vol. I, pp. 169–70.

63. Keith Whinnom, 'The problem of the "best-seller" in Spanish Golden-Age literature', *Bulletin of Hispanic Studies*, LVII (1980), 196.

64. Mexía, *Historia imperial*, fol. cxliiv: 'al auctor de semejante obra no se le deue dar crédito alguno'.

65. Gracián, *Xenophon*, cited by Thomas, *Romances*, p. 160: 'las patrañas disformes y desconcertadas que en estos libros de mentiras se leen, derogan el crédito a las verdaderas hazañas que se leen en las historias de verdad'.

66. References to the *Sophist* are to the translation of F. M. Cornford, *Plato's Theory of*

Knowledge, pp. 165–331. The term *thaumatopoios* recalls *Republic*, VII, 514b, where Plato expounds the allegory of the cave.

67. W. K. C. Guthrie, *The Sophists*, p. 211.
68. For a fuller discussion of this dialogue see the version of this book submitted as a PhD thesis (University of London, 1984), 'Private Reading and its Consequences for the Development of Spanish Golden-Age Prose Fiction', pp. 96–106, and Paul Seligman, *Being and Not-Being*.

3. Reading and rapture

1. Mexía, *Historia imperial*, fol. cxliiv.
2. Menéndez y Pelayo, *Orígenes*, vol. I, p. 370.
3. Cano, *De locis*, p. 656: 'Nam et aetas nostra sacerdotem vidit, cui persuasissimum esset, nihil omnino esse falsum, quod semel typis fuisset excusum.'
4. In Lope's *La octava maravilla*, *Obras*, vol. VIII, p. 255, Motril meets a sceptical response to an unlikely item in a *pliego suelto* with the words: 'Está de molde, ¿y te burlas?'
5. Chevalier, *Lectura*, pp. 72–3. Chevalier does not make it clear why he rejects this evidence: if the anecdotes are false they were presumably invented to illustrate a point of view. Even if no one ever took fiction literally, the anecdotes show that several people thought that this was what happened.
6. Spingarn, *History of Literary Criticism*, pp. 38–9; Torquato Tasso, *Discorsi dell'arte poetica e del poema eroico*, p. 84: 'dove manca la fede, non può abbondare l'affetto o il piacere di quel che si legge o s'ascolta'; Nicolas Boileau, *L'Art Poétique*, iii, 50: 'L'esprit n'est point ému de ce qu'il ne croit pas.'
7. Horace's warning applies to episodes such as the metamorphosis of Procne or Cadmus that should not be shown by the dramatist but left to be described by the eloquent tongue of a narrator.
8. Alban K. Forcione, *Cervantes, Aristotle, and the 'Persiles'*.
9. Valdés, *Diálogo*, p. 177: 'los que scriven mentiras las deven escrivir de suerte que se lleguen, quanto fuere possible, a la verdad, de tal manera que puedan vender sus mentiras por verdades'.
10. Georges Poulet, 'Phenomenology of reading', *New Literary History*, I (1969), 54.
11. López Pinciano, *Philosophía*, vol. I, pp. 170–2.
12. Cerda, *Vida política*, fol. 41r: 'manchado el entendimiento con mentiras, y turbado el juyzio con embaymientos, está inhábil y ofuscado para las cosas divinas', cited by Glaser, 'Nuevos datos', p. 406.
13. Camos, *Microcosmia*, p. 2: 'todo ello es escriptura, trayda con galano artificio a propósito . . . bien paresce traslado de aquel acendrado entendimiento de su autor'.
14. Spingarn, *History of Literary Criticism*, p. 52.
15. Lodovico Ricchieri, *Lectionum antiquarum libri XXX*, p. 160: 'lectione tanquam exemplo proposito, plerunque concitatior ingerit sese rationi, et illa exculcata latius affectat dominari', cited by Weinberg, *History*, vol. I, p. 259, whose translation is quoted here.
16. Fr. Pedro de la Vega, *Declaración de los siete psalmos penitenciales*.
17. *Ibid.*, fol. 11v: 'No es fácil de hallar la razón porque siendo natural al entendimiento humano abraçarse con la verdad, recibe contento de cosas que sabe él mismo que no lo son, sino ymaginación vana del que las escriuió.' Cited by Glaser, 'Nuevos datos', p. 404.
18. Vallés, *Cartas*: 'esta pasión corre la mayor en las damas, que ponen el gusto en vestir los entendimientos como los cuerpos', cited by Castro, *Pensamiento*, p. 61. C.

Pérez Pastor, *Bibliografía madrileña*, vol II, p. 46 cites the same passage with the variant reading 'el entendimiento'.

19. Plato, *Ion*, 533c–536d; *Phaedrus*, 245a.
20. See chapter 1, n. 53. Pedro Soto de Rojos writes of the role of 'el ardor natural' in poetry in his *Discurso sobre la poética, Obras*, p. 26, and Quevedo's commentary on *Anacreón castellano*, XIII, cites Scaliger, Cicero and Plato (*Phaedrus*, 245a) on divine fury (*Obras completas*, vol. II, pp. 748–9).
21. St Isidore of Seville, *Etymologiarum*, I, xxxix, 4, derives the word *carmen* from the expression *carere mente*: 'Carmen vocatur quidquid pedibus continetur: cui datum nomen existimant seu quod carptim pronuntietur, unde hodie lanam, quam purgantes discerpunt, "carminare" dicimus: seu quod qui illa canerent carere mentem existimabantur.'
22. Vives, *Instruction*, fol. 10v. *Opera*, vol. IV, p. 87.
23. Vega, *Declaración*, cited by Glaser, 'Nuevos datos', p. 404.
24. Heliodorus, *Historia etiópica*, p. lxxxi: 'el entendimiento queda suspenso hasta que viene a la conclusión'.
25. *DQ*, I, p. 21: 'suspender y absortar'.
26. Cervantes, *Obras*, p. 871a: 'se admiraron y suspendieron'.
27. Poulet, 'Phenomenology', p. 55.
28. Forcione, *Cervantes*, p. 253.
29. Gabriel Josipovici, ed., *The Modern English Novel*, p. 7.
30. Cervantes, *Obras*, p. 996a–b: 'otros sucesos me quedan por decir que exceden a toda imaginación, pues van fuera de todos los términos de naturaleza'; 'lo que ahora ni nunca vuesa merced podrá creer, ni habrá persona en el mundo que lo crea'; 'yo oí y casi vi con mis ojos'; 'que si no es por milagro no pueden hablar los animales'; 'yo mismo no he querido dar crédito a mí mismo y he querido tomar por cosa soñada'. Campuzano also makes frequent references at this point to his illness and the delirium brought on by it.
31. Cervantes, *Obras*, p. 996b: 'hasta aquí estaba en duda si creería o no lo que de su casamiento me había contado, y esto que ahora me cuenta . . . me ha hecho declarar por la parte de no creerle ninguna cosa'.
32. Cervantes, *Obras*, p. 997a–b: 'este milagro en que no solamente hablamos, sino en que hablamos con discurso'; 'el decirlo tú y entenderlo yo me causa nueva admiración y nueva maravilla'; etc.
33. Cervantes, *Obras*, pp. 1014–19.
34. Cervantes, *Obras*, p. 997a–b: 'todo lo tomé de coro, y casi por las mismas palabras que había oído lo escribí otro día, sin buscar colores, retóricas para adornarlo, ni qué añadir ni quitar para hacerle gustoso'.
35. Ruth S. El Saffar, *Novel to Romance*, p. 79.
36. Ed. R. K. Sprague, *The Older Sophists*, pp. 50–4.
37. Cervantes, *Obras*, p. 997b: 'púselo en forma de coloquio por ahorrar de "dijo Cipión", "respondió Berganza", que suele alargar la escritura'.
38. Good accounts of the difficulties of distinguishing literary from non-literary language are given by Olsen, *Literary Understanding*, and Mary Louise Pratt, *Toward a Speech Act Theory of Literary Discourse*.
39. Roman Ingarden, *The Cognition of the Literary Work of Art*, p. 63: 'in the literary work of art, the sentences which are predicative sentences in their form and have the external character of assertions are nevertheless only quasi-judgments and should be so read and understood if one does not want to misunderstand the work of art'. Logicians use the assertion sign to distinguish genuine judgments from mere affirmative propositions: writers, too, have certain devices to remind readers that what they are reading has a special quality of affirmation. Some of

these devices are discussed in chapter 4 with reference to Spanish picaresque novels.

40. C. K. Ogden and I. A. Richards, *The Meaning of Meaning*, pp. 14–16.

41. Olsen, *Literary Understanding*, pp. 17–18; Roland Barthes, 'Eléments de sémiologie', *Communications*, 4 (1964), 109, says that the signifier is merely a *relatum*, 'on ne peut séparer sa définition de celle du signifié'.

42. Northrop Frye, *Fearful Symmetry. A Study of William Blake*, pp. 427–8: 'It has been said of Boehme that his books are like a picnic to which the author brings the words and the reader the meaning. The remark may have been intended as a sneer at Boehme, but it is an exact description of all works of literary art without exception.'

43. J. L. Austin, *How to Do Things with Words*.

44. J. R. Searle, *Speech Acts*.

45. H. P. Grice, 'Meaning', *Philosophical Review*, 66 (1957), 377–88. Compare the breakdown of understanding when A asks: 'Can you tell me the time?' and B replies: 'Yes'. (P. N. Johnson-Laird and P. C. Wason, eds., *Thinking*, p. 350.)

46. Stanley E. Fish sounds a note of warning in his article 'How to do things with Austin and Searle: speech-act theory and literary criticism', *Modern Language Notes*, 91 (1976), 983–1025, by citing some notable misuses of speech-act theory. My own use of the theory should not, I trust, incur the same criticisms.

47. Austin, *How to Do Things with Words*, pp. 101–32; Searle, *Speech Acts*, p. 25: 'Correlated with the notion of illocutionary acts is the notion of the consequences or *effects* such acts have on the actions, thoughts, or beliefs, etc. of hearers. For example, by arguing I may *persuade* or *convince* someone, by warning him I may *scare* or *alarm* him, by making a request I may *get him to do something*, by informing him I may *convince him* (*enlighten, edify, inspire him, get him to realize*). The italicised expressions above denote perlocutionary acts.'

48. Cervantes, *Obras*, p. 966a.

49. Marcel Adam Just and Patricia A. Carpenter, eds., *Cognitive Processes in Comprehension*, p. 1.

50. Frank Smith, *Understanding Reading*, pp. 25–42.

51. M. A. Tinker, 'Fixation pause duration in reading', *Journal of Educational Research*, 44 (1951), 471–9; 'The study of eye movements in reading', *Psychological Bulletin*, 43 (1946), 93–120; 'Recent studies of eye movements in reading', *ibid.*, 55 (1958), 215–31; *Bases for Effective Reading*. C. H. Judd and G. T. Buswell, *Silent Reading: a Study of the Various Types*, pp. 21–2: 'Eye movements are as direct measures of the mental state as the rate of the pulse is a measure of the heart beat.' Research on eye movements in reading is summarised by Patricia A. Carpenter and Marcel Adam Just, 'Reading comprehension as eyes see it' in Just and Carpenter, *Cognitive Processes*, pp. 109–39, and by E. J. Gibson and Harry Levin, *The Psychology of Reading*, pp. 351–9.

52. Gibson and Levin, *Psychology of Reading*, p. 356: 'Skilled readers are more adaptive to the nature of the material; their patterns of fixations and pauses are responsive to their comprehension of the materials they are reading. By implication, poor readers use the same oculomotor patterns regardless of the nature of the text'; Carpenter and Just, 'Reading comprehension', p. 109: 'there is a highly systematic relationship between eye fixations and underlying comprehension processes. For example, readers have a tendency to look back to a previous sentence or phrase that is related to the one they are reading. In other words, a semantic relation between two sentences is sometimes manifested as an eye-movement between two sentences. These regressive eye fixations are indicative of the reader's interpretation of the paragraph.'

53. Smith, *Understanding Reading*, pp. 203–4. The general limit on human information processing is 25 bits per second. Random letter uncertainty is almost exactly 4.7 bits, but this falls to about 2.5 bits per letter in random words, an eloquent demonstration of the importance of distributional and sequential redundancy in reducing processing time.

54. Smith, *Understanding Reading*, p. 5.

55. Plato, *Phaedrus*, 274b–275e.

56. Paul Friedländer, *Plato: an Introduction*, pp. 108–25.

57. Smith, *Understanding Reading*, p. 31.

58. Chaytor, *From Script to Print*, pp. 5–10; Ingarden, *Cognition*, p. 21; Roger Fowler, *Linguistics and the Novel*, p. 62: 'A given syntax demands its own proper intonation curve, rises and falls in the pitch of the voice appropriate to the structure and meaning of what is written. Stresses must be in the right place, or meaning is distorted.'

59. A. N. Sokolov, *Inner Speech and Thought*.

60. Gibson and Levin, *Psychology of Reading*, p. 340; D. G. Boyle, *Language and Thinking in Human Development*, pp. 22, 122.

61. E. B. Huey, *The Psychology and Pedagogy of Reading*, pp. 117–18.

62. I owe this phrase, and much else besides, to Pauline Hire of the Cambridge University Press.

63. V. Egger, *La parole intérieure*, p. 67: 'L'individualité de chaque voix humaine, constituée principalment par le timbre, est complétée par d'autres éléments: une certaine intensité habituelle, – des intonations préférées, – une certaine façon de prononcer certaines voyelles ou consonnes, – enfin des mots et des tournures favorites. Tous figurent dans la parole intérieure de chacun de nous; *ma* parole intérieure est l'imitation de *ma* voix.' P. 72: 'Elle [la parole intérieure] est d'ordinaire l'écho affaibli, mais fidèle, de notre voix individuelle; mais elle peut aussi imiter des voix autres que la nôtre; les timbres les plus divers, les prononciations les plus étranges, et, au même titre, tous les sons de la nature, peuvent être intérieurement reproduits.'

64. Bernard Levin, commenting in *The Times*, 10.1.1981, on a radio adaptation of *The Good Soldier Schweik*, says that he dare not listen to it, 'for Schweik is to me a friend so close, so beloved and so intimately known that if Mr Griffiths, or for that matter the actors playing any of the other parts . . . should sound otherwise than I have imagined them all my life, I would be distressed beyond measure'.

65. Richalm of Schönthal, *Liber Revelationum de Insidiis et Versutiis Daemonum Adversus Homines*, col. 390: 'Saepe cum lego solo codice, et cogitatione, sicut soleo, faciunt meo verbotenus, et ore legere, ut tantummodo eo magis auferant mihi internum intellectum, et eo minus vim lectionis intus penetrem, quo magis in verba foris profundor.' The translation is taken from G. G. Coulton, *Five Centuries of Religion*, vol. I, p. 38. The opposite view, that reading aloud promotes greater understanding, is argued, however, by Bruni, *Studiis* in Woodward, *Vittorino da Feltre*, p. 125, by Battista Guarino, *De Ordine Docendi et Studendi, ibid.*, p. 174, and by Vives, *De Tradendis Disciplinis* in Foster Watson, *Vives: On Education*, p. 109: 'What we want to remember must be impressed on our memory while others are silent; but we need not be silent ourselves, for those things which we have read aloud are often more deeply retained.' The contradiction here is more apparent than real, since the humanists are speaking of the retention of a text word for word which is a completely different matter from comprehension of the gist of a text: a text memorised verbatim is not necessarily fully understood.

66. Francisco de Quevedo, *Obra poética*, vol. I, pp. 253–4.

67. T. A. Van Dijk, *Some Aspects of Text Grammars*; *Text and Context*; 'Semantic macro-

structures and knowledge frames in discourse comprehension' in Just and Carpenter, *Cognitive Processes*, pp. 3–32; B. J. F. Meyer, *The Organisation of Prose and its Effects on Memory*; M. A. K. Halliday and R. Hassan, *Cohesion in English*; D. E. Rummelhart, 'Notes on a schema for stories' in D. G. Bobrow and A. Collins, eds., *Representation and Understanding: Studies in Cognitive Science*, pp. 211–36; 'Understanding and summarizing brief stories' in David Laberge and S. Jay Samuels, *Basic Processes in Reading: Perception and Comprehension*, pp. 265–303; Gordon H. Bower, 'Experiments in story comprehension and recall', *Discourse Processes*, 1 (1978), 211–31.

68. Walter Kintsch, 'On comprehending stories' in Just and Carpenter, *Cognitive Processes*, p. 37.
69. Frank Kermode, *The Genesis of Secrecy*, p. 70: R. Rommetveit, 'On the architecture of intersubjectivity' in R. Rommetveit and R. M. Blakar, *Studies of Language, Thought and Verbal Communication*, p. 96.
70. Johnson-Laird and Wason, *Thinking*, pp. 341–54; Umberto Eco, *The Role of the Reader*, pp. 20–2.
71. Marvin Minsky, 'Frame-system theory' in Johnson-Laird and Wason, *Thinking*, pp. 355–76.
72. Eco, *Role of the Reader*, p. 24.
73. John Le Carré, *Smiley's People*, p. 40.
74. The inferences made are: they^2 = they^1; him^2 = him^1; his = him^2 (and thence = him^1); George = him^1 (and thence = him^2 = his); him^3 = body; us = they^1 (and thence = they^2). Herbert H. Clark, 'Inferences in comprehension' in Laberge and Samuels, *Basic Processes in Reading*, pp. 243–63; id., 'Bridging' in Johnson-Laird and Wason, *Thinking*, pp. 411–20.
75. Wolfgang Iser, 'Indeterminacy and the reader's response in prose fiction' in J. Hillis Miller, ed., *Aspects of Narrative*, pp. 1–45; id., *The Implied Reader*; id., *The Act of Reading*.
76. Ingarden, *Cognition*, p. 52.
77. Kermode, *Genesis of Secrecy*, p. 72.
78. J. P. Sartre, 'The work of art' in Harold Osborne, ed., *Aesthetics*, pp. 32–8.
79. Poulet, 'Phenomenology', p. 56.

4. Breaking the illusion

1. Wallace Stevens, *Collected Poems*, p. 358.
2. Clara Reeve, *The Progress of Romance*, p. 11.
3. Matthew Prior, *The Literary Works*, vol. 1, p. 450.
4. Ronald W. Hepburn, 'Aesthetic appreciation of nature' in Osborne, *Aesthetics*, p. 51: 'We might use the word "frame" in an extended sense to cover not only the physical boundaries of pictures but all the various devices employed in different arts to prevent the art object being mistaken for a natural object or for an artefact without aesthetic interest. Such devices are best thought of as aids to the recognition of the formal completeness of the art objects themselves, their ability to sustain aesthetic interest.'
5. Keith Whinnom, 'The *Historia de Duobus Amantibus* of Aeneas Sylvius Piccolomini (Pope Pius II) and the development of Spanish golden-age fiction', in R. B. Tate, ed., *Essays on Narrative Fiction in the Iberian Peninsula in Honour of Frank Pierce*, p. 255: 'It is difficult to think of any narrative device with which Spanish writers of the late fifteenth and sixteenth centuries did not at some time play.'
6. Ong, *Orality and Literacy*, p. 79.
7. Eco, *Role of the Reader*, pp. 47–66.

8. Catherine Belsey, *Critical Practice*, ch. 4.

9. Forcione, *Cervantes*, pp. 122, 258.

10. Cf. Plato, *Republic*, III, 392.

11. Forcione, *Cervantes*, p. 123.

12. Cf. Riley, *Cervantes's Theory of the Novel*, p. 89.

13. C. A. Jones has suggested the appropriateness of the application of this Brechtian term to the Spanish Golden Age in 'Brecht y el drama del siglo de oro en España', *Segismundo*, 5–6 (1969–70), 39–54.

14. Forcione, *Cervantes*, p. 151.

15. Marshall McLuhan, 'The effect of the printed book on language in the sixteenth century' in Edmund Carpenter and Marshall McLuhan, eds., *Explorations in Communication*, p. 127.

16. Cf. Russell, *Spain*, pp. 313, 325.

17. Iser, *The Implied Reader*, p. 294: 'The need to decipher gives us the chance to formulate our own deciphering capacity.'

18. Richard Wollheim, 'On drawing an object' in Osborne, *Aesthetics*, pp. 121–44.

19. Anthony Savile, 'The place of intention in the concept of art' in Osborne, *Aesthetics*, p. 160 and n. 1.

20. Thomas Hooker, *The Application of Redemption . . . The Ninth and Tenth Books*, pp. 53–4. Quoted in Gabriel Josipovici, *The World and the Book*, p. 162.

21. Barbara Hardy, *Tellers and Listeners*, p. 3.

22. Ong, *Orality and Literacy*, p. 176: 'I have to sense something in the other's mind to which my own utterance can relate. Human communication is never one-way. Always, it not only calls for response but is shaped in its very form and content by anticipated response.'

23. William Labov, *Language in the Inner City*, p. 366.

24. David Riesman, 'The oral and written traditions' in Carpenter and McLuhan, *Explorations*, p. 110.

25. Josipovici, *Modern English Novel*, p. 8.

26. Walter J. Ong, *Interfaces of the Word*, pp. 54–81; id., *Orality and Literacy*, pp. 102, 177.

27. References are by line (for the prologue), and *tratado* and line (elsewhere), to the edition of R. O. Jones. Francisco Rico's edition has also been consulted. English versions are from David Rowland's classic translation of 1586, ed. J. E. V. Crofts. This rendering makes up in vividness what it sometimes lacks in accuracy. When Rowland cannot be used, the versions are my own. No attempt has been made in what follows to refer comprehensively to the vast and growing literature on the *Lazarillo*. The following books have been particularly influential in helping me to formulate my views: Francisco Rico, *La novela picaresca y el punto de vista*; A. D. Deyermond, *'Lazarillo de Tormes'. A Critical Guide*; and a book which is frequently infuriating but always provocative, Harry Sieber, *Language and Society in 'La vida de Lazarillo de Tormes'*. A comprehensive bibliography of work published on the picaresque novel is to be found in Joseph V. Ricapito, *Bibliografía razonada y anotada de las obras maestras de la picaresca española*.

28. Donald McGrady, 'Social irony in *Lazarillo de Tormes* and its implications for authorship', *Romance Philology*, XXIII (1970), 557; Frank Durand, 'The author and Lázaro: levels of comic meaning', *Bulletin of Hispanic Studies*, XLV (1968), 90.

29. Bruce W. Wardropper, 'El trastorno de la moral en el *Lazarillo*', *Nueva Revista de Filología Hispánica*, XV (1961), 445; id., 'The strange case of Lázaro Gonzales Pérez', *Modern Language Notes*, 92 (1977), 202–12. See also A. D. Deyermond, 'Lazarus and Lazarillo', *Studies in Short Fiction*, 2 (1964–5), 351–7.

30. Claudio Guillén, 'La disposición temporal del *Lazarillo de Tormes*', *Hispanic*

Review, XXV (1957), 271: 'el *Lazarillo* . . . más que un relato puro, es una "relación" o informe hecho por un hombre sobre sí mismo'. See also Edward H. Friedman, 'Chaos restored: authorial control and ambiguity in *Lazarillo de Tormes*', *Crítica Hispánica*, 3 (1981), 59–73.

31. Labov, *Language in the Inner City*, pp. 366–75.
32. Rico, *La novela picaresca*, pp. 15–25.
33. Douglas M. Carey, '*Lazarillo de Tormes* and the quest for authority', *Publications of the Modern Language Association of America*, 94 (1979), 39, suggests that 'the structure of the novel in some ways parallels the format of a legal interrogation', and quotes private correspondence with Bruce W. Wardropper who also suggests that the novel is a kind of deposition: 'Lázaro is giving written evidence that could be used in a court of enquiry.'
34. Claudio Guillén, 'Toward a definition of the picaresque' in *Literature as System*, p. 97: 'Disposición temporal', p. 270; Raymond S. Willis, 'Lazarillo and the pardoner: the artistic necessity of the fifth *tractado*', *Hispanic Review*, XXVII (1959), 271.
35. Horace, *Ars Poetica*, 148–9:
'semper ad eventum festinat et in medias res
non secus ac notas auditorem rapit . . .'
36. R. W. Truman, 'Lázaro de Tormes and the *Homo novus* tradition', *Modern Language Review*, LXIV (1969), 62–7.
37. Fernando Lázaro Carreter, 'La ficción autobiográfica en el *Lazarillo de Tormes*' in '*Lazarillo de Tormes*' *en la picaresca*, pp. 13–57.
38. Sieber, *Language and Society*, pp. 4–6, offers a rather different, though related, interpretation of this incident from a more strictly psychoanalytical point of view.
39. Emile Benveniste, *Problems in General Linguistics*, p. 226: 'And so it is literally true that the basis of subjectivity is in the exercise of language.'
40. Guillén, 'Disposición temporal', p. 268.
41. Durand, 'The author and Lázaro', p. 94, notes that Lázaro refers to himself as a third person, 'el pobre Lázaro', when the blind man is about to smash the wine jug into his face (1.205). 'The first-person narrator thus assumes the role of audience at a telling of his own story' (p. 95).
42. B. W. Ife, ed., *La vida del Buscón llamado don Pablos*, p. 5.
43. Stephen Gilman, 'The death of Lazarillo de Tormes', *Publications of the Modern Language Association of America*, LXXXI (1966), 153.
44. Wardropper, 'El trastorno de la moral', p. 442.
45. Howard Mancing, 'The deceptiveness of *Lazarillo de Tormes*', *Publications of the Modern Language Association of America*, XC (1975), 430.
46. There are many examples of this generalising formula, e.g. 'le hacía burlas endiabladas, de las cuales contaré algunas' (1.138–9). See F. Courtney Tarr, 'Literary and artistic unity in the *Lazarillo de Tormes*', *Publications of the Modern Language Association of America*, XLII (1927), 413, and Francisco Rico, 'Problemas del *Lazarillo*', *Boletín de la Real Academia Española*, XLVI (1966), 287.
47. Didier T. Jaén, 'La ambigüedad moral del *Lazarillo de Tormes*', *Publications of the Modern Language Association of America*, LXXXIII (1968), 132, has noticed particular stress placed on the adjectives 'mezquino' and 'avariento'.
48. Mancing, 'Deceptiveness', p. 426.
49. Ife, ed., *Buscón*, pp. 13–14.
50. Critics are divided in their views of Lazarillo's behaviour towards the squire. Most find that his attitude is one of compassion: Dámaso Alonso, 'El realismo psicológico en el *Lazarillo*' in *De los siglos oscuros al de oro*, p. 228; Douglas M.

Carey, 'Asides and interiority in *Lazarillo de Tormes*', *Studies in Philology*, XLVI (1969), 131; Jaén, 'Ambigüedad', pp. 131–2; Norma Louise Hutman, 'Universality and unity in the *Lazarillo de Tormes*', *Publications of the Modern Language Association of America*, LXXVI (1961), 472. Against this must be set the views of L. J. Woodward, 'The author–reader relationship in the *Lazarillo de Tormes*', *Forum for Modern Language Studies*, I (1965), 49, and Derek W. Lomax, 'On re-reading the *Lazarillo de Tormes*', *Studia Iberica. Festschrift für Hans Flasche*, p. 373, that Lazarillo behaves here as elsewhere as a 'shifty wideboy'.

51. This remark, in view of its tone, might be interpreted as an example of an aside. C.f. Carey, 'Asides and interiority'.

52. See J. E. Gillet, 'The squire's dovecote' in *Hispanic Studies in Honour of I. González Llubera*, pp. 135–8.

53. Rico, 'Problemas', p. 291: 'el inciso condicional garantiza la existencia de la propiedad'.

54. Carey, 'Asides and interiority', pp. 129–30: 'the Squire refuses to admit his poverty and to abandon the role which he plays for Lázaro. Lázaro in his turn acts out his part. As a consequence the pretence is maintained as the two characters stage scenes for each other, creating a dialogue filled with lies and conventions – the need for which have both been learned – while at the same time subtly understanding each other. There is an unspoken agreement . . .'

55. Jean Ricardou, *Problèmes du nouveau roman*, p. 13, points out that the word 'knife' cannot cut anything. The problem of literary realism arises, though, from the fact that the word 'knife' can 'cut' 'bread'.

56. Willis, 'Lazarillo and the pardoner', p. 271.

57. Guillén, 'Disposición temporal', p. 271: 'El hombre maduro, Lázaro, reúne en sí las conclusiones que el muchacho, Lazarillo, sacó de sus experiencias.'

58. D. W. Harding, 'Psychological processes in the reading of fiction', *British Journal of Aesthetics*, 2 (1962), 133–47.

59. R. K. Elliot, 'Aesthetic theory and the experience of art' in Osborne, *Aesthetics*, p. 147.

60. Wollheim, 'On drawing an object', p. 139.

61. Lomax, 'On re-reading', pp. 372, 380.

62. Gilman, 'Death', p. 153.

63. Mancing, 'Deceptiveness', p. 431; A. Marasso, *Estudios de literatura española*, p. 184: 'La diferencia en Lázaro del simpático niño y del adulto repulsivo en que se convierte, está perfectamente establecida.'

64. Hutman, 'Universality and unity', p. 473.

65. Carey, 'Asides and interiority', p. 133.

66. Woodward, 'Author–reader relationship', p. 44.

67. C. B. Morris, 'Lázaro and the Squire: *hombres de bien*', *Bulletin of Hispanic Studies*, XLI (1964), 238–41.

68. Albert A. Sicroff, 'Sobre el estilo del *Lazarillo de Tormes*', *Nueva Revista de Filología Hipánica*, XI (1957), 166, notes that the *buldero* episode relegates Lazarillo to the 'segundo término, convirtiéndolo en mero narrador de las hazañas de su amo'.

69. Willis, 'Lazarillo and the pardoner', p. 277.

70. Sicroff, 'Estilo', p. 168: 'En todo esto, Lázaro no ha sido más que un espectador. Sus aventuras se han dejado a un lado para dar cabida a un suceso que, si no se relaciona con él, sí tiene que ver, al menos, con el resto del libro, puesto que ofrece un ejemplo más de la ilusoria realidad en que viven los hombres.'

71. *Canterbury Tales*, VI, 398–404. See Josipovici, *The World and the Book*, p. 92.

72. Eisenstein, *Printing Press*, vol. I, p. 375.

73. Woodward, 'Author–reader relationship', p. 43.

74. Sieber, *Language and Society*, pp. 79–80; Mancing, 'Deceptiveness', p. 429; Morris, 'Lázaro and the Squire', pp. 238–41.

75. Claudio Guillén, Introduction to his edition of *Lazarillo de Tormes*, p. 27: 'He does not simply espouse "evil" in the end, for his judgment does not surrender to such simplifications. His conduct may become corrupted but not his mind.'

76. Durand, 'The author and Lázaro', p. 100.

77. *Pace* Carey, 'Asides and interiority', p. 133.

78. Harry Sieber, in attempting to make a related point, ruins a good punch-line in his *Language and Society*, p. 97: 'Hoc est meum liber.' Leaving aside the grammatical solecism – books are masculine – what I take Sieber to mean is: 'Hoc est vita mea': 'this book is my life'. Lázaro is prepared to stand or fall by the quality of his insight and his artistry.

79. M. J. Woods, 'Pitfalls for the moralizer in *Lazarillo de Tormes*', *Modern Language Review*, 74 (1979), 597. Georgina Sabat de Rivers, 'La moral que Lázaro nos propone', *Modern Language Notes*, 95 (1980), 251, concludes that the ultimate moral of the novel is 'No juzgues'. I would prefer to say something slightly different: the author assumes that we will judge, indeed, encourages us to do so, in order that we may see that our judgment is at fault. Then, as M. J. Woods says, we can laugh at ourselves on the basis of our failure.

80. See the paper read at the 1983 Conference of the Association of Hispanists of Great Britain and Ireland by Dr G. A. Longhurst: 'The narrator in *Guzmán de Alfarache*: repentant or unrepentant?' I am grateful to Dr Longhurst for allowing me to see a copy of the paper before publication. After comparing Guzmán's change of heart with the conversions of St Augustine and Mary Magdalene, Dr Longhurst questions whether Alemán had a conversion in mind at all, genuine or simulated: 'Guzmán's so-called conversion is totally circumstantial. He has neither discovered the truth by the power of his intellect as St Augustine did, nor is answering the direct call of God as Malón de Chaide's Mary Magdalene did. At best, all that can be said is that Guzmán evinces a desire for spiritual regeneration, but not out of a newly-found religious conviction, more as a recognition that this time he has no alternative.'

81. The relationship of the narrative and commentary was first seriously discussed by Enrique Moreno Báez, *Lección y sentido del 'Guzmán de Alfarache'*. His conclusions are endorsed in large part by A. A. Parker, *Literature and the Delinquent*, Francisco Rico, 'Consejos y consejas de *Guzmán de Alfarache*' in *La novela picaresca*, pp. 59–91, Angel San Miguel, *Sentido y estructura del 'Guzmán de Alfarache' de Mateo Alemán*, and J. A. Jones, 'The duality and complexity of *Guzmán de Alfarache*' in C. Whitbourn, ed., *Knaves and Swindlers*, pp. 25–46. Guzmán's repentance is questioned by Joan Arias, *Guzmán de Alfarache: The Unrepentant Narrator*, Carroll Johnson, *Inside Guzmán de Alfarache*, and Benito Brancaforte, *Guzmán de Alfarache: ¿Conversión o proceso de degradación?*.

82. The text is quoted from the edition of Francisco Rico, *La novela picaresca española*, vol. 1. The edition of Benito Brancaforte has also been consulted. The English versions are from the translation of James Mabbe (1623).

83. The use of the preterite recalls a similar use of a past tense by Lazarillo de Tormes: 'Pues en este tiempo estaba en mi prosperidad' (7.80). Guzmán's 'gasté' is not, however, supported by the same epistolary convention as Lazarillo's. See Rico, *La novela picaresca*, p. 22, n. 19.

84. The inconsistency is one plank of the argument put forward by Arias and Brancaforte against the genuineness of Guzmán's conversion. Francisco Rico, however, sees the release of Guzmán as a last-minute change of plan and one that does not alter the narrator's viewpoint: 'a efectos de la estructura la obra debe suponerse compuesta en la galera.' See *La novela picaresca*, p. 65, n. 8.

85. There are still problems, nevertheless. The prologue to Part II, though it reports the theft of the original Part II, makes no further allusion to the enforced publication of the first two parts separately. Further, Alemán announces that Part III is complete, though this was never published. It is just possible that the announcement of Parts II and III was premature in both cases, and reflected Alemán's intentions rather than his achievements. He would not be the only author to announce the imminent publication of books that were never in the event written.

86. 'Malo y lascivo, escribo cosas honestas; y lo que más siento es que han de perder por mí su crédito', Dedication to Tomás Tamayo de Vargas of *La cuna y la sepultura*. See also the letter to Margarita de Espinosa dated 3 June 1613 in Quevedo, *Obras completas*, vol. II, p. 821a.

87. Ovid, *Metamorphoses*, 7.20–1. Benito Brancaforte also makes clear the importance in the structure of *Guzmán de Alfarache* of the contradiction between theory and practice, between 'acción novelística y reflexión' (see his edition, vol. I, pp. 28, 30).

88. Cicero, *Cael*. 53: 'possum omnis latebras suspicionum peragrare dicendo', where the association with the arts of rhetoric is particularly interesting. C.f. *de Orat*. I. 222.

89. Gaspar Ens, *Proscenii vitae humanae Pars Tertia*, fol. 5r.

90. C.f. Carlos Blanco Aguinaga, 'Cervantes y la picaresca', *Nueva Revista de Filología Hispánica*, XI (1957), 326: '[la forma autobiográfica] permite que la vida, narrada naturalmente *a posteriori*, esté concebida *a priori* como ejemplo de desengaño'. This is precisely not what *Guzmán de Alfarache* is designed to do, to turn life into a sermon. By intermixing autobiography and contemplation, Alemán recreates a truly complex moral life to be lived in the moment of reading.

91. Marcel Bataillon, *Novedad y fecundidad del 'Lazarillo de Tormes'*, p. 104: 'El narrador se ve siempre dividido, en mayor o menor grado, entre el amoralismo de las acciones que cuenta y la moralidad de las enseñanzas recibidas o de la experiencia adquirida.'

92. Quoted by Stanley E. Fish, *Surprised by Sin: the Reader in 'Paradise Lost'*, p. 21.

93. Maurice Molho, *Introducción al pensamiento picaresco*, p. 68: 'Guzmán, al modo de los predicadores, se mete con cada uno según su condición, de tal forma que el lector será alternativamente el escribano, el alguacil, el médico, el ministro, el comerciante o el mesonero.'

94. See George Craig, 'Reading: who is doing what to whom?' in Josipovici, *The Modern English Novel*, p. 25.

95. See Edmond Cros, *Mateo Alemán: Introducción a su vida y a su obra*, pp. 157–62.

96. Arias, *Unrepentant Narrator*, pp. 13, 36–7, 41–2.

97. Gonzalo Sobejano, 'De la intención y valor del *Guzmán de Alfarache*', *Romanische Forschungen*, 71 (1959), 267–311. Reprinted in *Forma literaria y sensibilidad social*.

98. Rico, 'Consejos y consejas' and 'Estructuras y reflejos de estructuras en el *Guzmán de Alfarache*', *Modern Language Notes*, LXXXII (1967), 171–84.

99. Rico, 'Consejos y consejas', pp. 75–6: 'En las meditaciones de Guzmanillo, el uso más pertinente (aunque no exclusivo) del *tú* es plasmar con economía de medios la escisión de una conciencia, atormentada por la necesidad de optar entre las llamadas del instinto y las mociones de la gracia.'

100. M. J. Woods has illustrated something of the quality and subtlety of the opening chapters in 'The teasing opening of *Guzmán de Alfarache*', *Bulletin of Hispanic Studies*, LVII (1980), 213–18.

101. 'Dice la señora Doña como es su gracia: – Yo sería buena y honesta; sino que la

necesidad me obliga más de cuatro veces a lo que no quisiera . . . No son ya las manos de las mujeres tan largas, que puedan a tanto, comer, vestir, y pagar una casa. – Téngalas Vuestra Merced largas para querer servir y daránle casa, de comer y dineros con que se vista. – ¡Bueno es eso! ¿Pues decís vós que no queréis entrar a servir y téngolo yo de hacer, que soy mujer?' (p. 599)

102. Fish, *Surprised by Sin*, p. 1.

103. Cros, *Mateo Alemán*, pp. 152–4.

104. Brancaforte, edition of *Guzmán de Alfarache*, vol. i, p. 35: 'Ese movimiento de atracción y repulsión a la vez corresponde al modo de reaccionar de los lectores y estriba en el papel del narrador, quien toma una doble postura, la del juez y la del penitente.' As I suggest in this section, Guzmán recreates himself as 'impenitente' rather than 'penitente'.

105. Arias, *Unrepentant Narrator*, p. 54.

106. Johnson, *Inside Guzmán de Alfarache*, esp. chapter 3, 'The cash nexus'.

107. Arias, *Unrepentant Narrator*, p. 80.

108. Molho, *Introducción*, p. 72: 'todos leen en el corazón de Guzmán al mismo tiempo que Guzmán lee en los suyos'.

109. Johnson, *Inside Guzmán de Alfarache*, p. 43.

110. See Milagros Ezquerro, 'Le roman en première personne: *Pedro Páramo*' in *L'autobiographie dans le monde hispanique*, p. 67: 'Dans cette perspective l'inévitable question de la "sincérité" de l'auto-biographie peut être posée dans des termes qui ni soient pas moraux. En effet si l'on accepte l'hypothèse qui fait de l'acte d'auto-engendrement du sujet d'écriture le noyau générateur de l'auto-biographie, il s'ensuit que l'image du MOI qui se construit n'est pas celle de la personne que les contemporains de l'auteur ont pu connaître, mais bien une instance symbolique ou imaginaire qui n'a d'existence que dans et par l'écriture ou elle s'est réellement auto-engendrée. Ainsi les événements de la vie seront non pas l'objet, la finalité de l'écrit autobiographique, mais bien plutôt matériaux, matière narrative qui sera utilisée dans la mesure où elle sera pertinente au projet fondamental. Il faut aussi préciser que dès lors que des événements de la vie d'un homme deviennent matière narrative – c'est-à-dire qu'ils changent de nature –, l'exactitude objective des faits compte moins que la fonction qui leur est départie par leur insertion et leur fonctionnement dans l'ensemble où ils sont inscrits.'

111. The *Ortografía* has recently been discussed in some depth by Michel Cavillac, 'Mateo Alemán et la modernité', *Bulletin Hispanique*, LXXXII (1980), 380–401, and it is edited by J. Rojas Garcidueñas.

112. Elliott, 'Aesthetic theory', p. 147.

113. Edmond Cros, *Protée et le gueux*, p. 61; see also the evidence of the same author's *Contribution à l'étude des sources de 'Guzmán de Alfarache'*, n.p., n.d.

114. Cros, *Protée*, p. 229.

115. C. George Peale, '*Guzmán de Alfarache* como discurso oral', *Journal of Hispanic Philology*, 4 (1979), 25–57.

116. C.f. Monique Joly, *La bourle et son interprétation*.

117. Edmond Cros, *L'aristocrate et le carnaval des gueux*; the revised Spanish version, *Ideología y genética textual*, makes no substantial change to the author's thesis that the *Buscón* is inspired by the conventions of carnival.

118. Raimundo Lida, 'Pablos de Segovia y su agudeza' in *Homenaje a Joaquín Casalduero*, pp. 285–98, reprinted in revised form in *Prosas de Quevedo*, p. 242: 'El libro de Quevedo supone esos modelos [*Lazarillo*, *Guzmán*]: los imita, los parodia y se aleja de ellos espectacularmente.'

119. Fernando Lázaro Carreter, 'Originalidad del *Buscón*' in *Homenaje a Dámaso*

Alonso, vol. II, pp. 319-38, reprinted in *Estilo barroco y personalidad creadora*, pp. 109-41; Molho, *Introducción*, p. 130; Cros, *Aristocrate*, pp. 16-25; id., *Ideología*, pp. 11-13.

120. Lázaro Carreter, 'Originalidad' in *Estilo barroco*, p. 123, n. 26.

121. Maurice Molho, 'Cinco lecciones sobre el *Buscón*' in *Semántica y poética*, p. 95.

122. Molho, *Introducción*, p. 135.

123. Gonzalo Díaz Migoyo, 'Las fechas en y de *El Buscón* de Quevedo', *Hispanic Review*, 48 (1980), 171-93, summarises the arguments in favour of a date around 1604 for the first draft, and proposes, not wholly convincingly since his argument does not take account of the time Pablos claims to have spent in America, a date of composition nearer 1608.

124. Marcel Bataillon, *Pícaros y picaresca*.

125. The existence of several MSS and the number of variants apparent from Lázaro Carreter's critical edition suggest a wide and active circulation, but it should be borne in mind that MS copying is time-consuming, and therefore expensive if a professional is employed. A printed version would undoubtedly have been cheaper and more convenient if Quevedo had sought a wide circulation. Some details of the text suggest that it was written rather like a script, with indications about intonation and timing of delivery: Lida, 'Pablos de Segovia' in *Prosas*, p. 259, n. 58. It would be typical of Quevedo the conservative to revert, in the process of defending fiction in the context of the printed word, to a form of publication – oral performance – which prevailed before the age of printing.

126. Fowler, *Linguistics and the Novel*, pp. 62-3. C.f. Walter J. Ong, 'Voice as summons for belief' in *The Barbarian Within*, p. 51: 'silent reading is a form of speaking, as silent reading is a form of hearing'.

127. E.g. Molho, *Introducción*, pp. 132-3: 'personajes . . . desprovistos de interioridad . . . exterioridades caricaturescas . . . seres, tomados en sus posturas, un poco a manera de marionetas, cuyo interior está vacío para que el presentador pueda introducir la mano . . .'

128. Gonzalo Díaz Migoyo, *Estructura de la novela*, p. 128.

129. References are to the critical edition of Fernando Lázaro Carreter. English versions are from the translation of John Stevens (1709), revised by Charles Duff (1926).

130. As an indication of the fact that no reading of a text can ever be assumed to be exhaustive, compare the now inadequate comments on this passage in my own edition, p. 240.

131. Rico, *La novela picaresca*, pp. 114-29.

132. Díaz Migoyo, *Estructura*.

133. *Ibid.*, pp. 107-16.

134. E.g. the description of himself as a tortoise, p. 62, or as a dog with cramp, p. 69, both of which instances recall the passage from *Portnoy's Complaint* quoted above.

135. Pablos's words, 'nunca sospeché en don Diego ni en lo que era' (p. 241), are not as problematical as it may be thought. C.f. the English sentence, 'I never knew you had written a book on the picaresque (i.e. until I found out).'

136. Díaz Migoyo, *Estructura*, p. 101: 'esa contradictoria pareja que tanto se cuida el texto de realzar: la vergüenza del actor y la desvergüenza del narrador'.

137. The view that don Diego is Pablos's alter ego and a symbol of goodness and true nobility is shared by T. E. May, 'Good and evil in the *Buscón*', *Modern Language Review*, XLV (1950), 319-35, and Parker, *Delinquent*. Don Diego's Jewish background and his less than chivalrous behaviour is discussed by Carroll B. Johnson, '*El Buscón*: d. Pablos, d. Diego y d. Francisco', *Hispanófila*, 51 (1974), 1-26, and Agustín Redondo, 'Del personaje de don Diego Coronel a una nueva

interpretación del *Buscón'* in *Actas del V Congreso Internacional de Hispanistas (1974)*, vol. II, pp. 699–711. See also the discussion of the implications of the scene in the Casa del Campo in Ife, ed., *Buscón*, pp. 25–6 and below.

138. Lida, 'Pablos de Segovia' in *Prosas*, p. 263: 'Ni siquiera el matón (Mata, Matorral, Matorrales) se expresa con voz personal y autónoma, sino con la del "filólogo" Quevedo, la del entusiasta de Teofrasto y sus caracteres o tipos . . . Quevedo, el gran bululú, apenas se molesta en mudar la voz de sus personajes.'

139. Lázaro Carreter, ed., *Buscón*, pp. 222–3: 'Yo dije lo ordinario: que las viesen colocadas como merecían; y agradóles mucho la palabra *colocadas*.'

140. 'Yo empecé luego, para trabar conversación, a jugar del vocablo' (p. 182).

141. 'No dije más *Jesús*, sino quitábale la *s*, y movía a más devoción. Al fin, yo mudé de frasecicas, y cogía maravillosa mosca' (p. 251).

142. Rico, *La novela picaresca*, p. 120. Díaz Migoyo, 'Fechas', p. 193, goes so far as to misquote the phrase as 'pésima novela' which completely falsifies the meaning. Only Cros, *Aristocrate*, has given Rico's, admittedly provocative, description its proper due.

143. Lázaro Carreter, 'Originalidad' in *Estilo barroco*, p. 199: 'Estas dos últimas ausencias – protesta social y didactismo – confieren ya a la historia del tacaño una evidente originalidad.'

144. 'Pues nunca mejora su estado quien muda solamente de lugar, y no de vida y costumbres' (p. 280). The phrase is an allusion to Horace, *Epist.* I, II, 27: 'Caelum non animum mutant qui trans mare currunt.' See Dale B. J. Randall, 'The classical ending of Quevedo's *Buscón*', *Hispanic Review*, XXXII (1964), 101–8.

145. B. W. Ife, 'From Salamanca to Brighton Rock: names and places in Cervantes's *La ilustre fregona*', in Richard A. Cardwell, ed., *Essays in Honour of Robert Brian Tate*, pp. 46–52.

146. Euboulides's riddle is that 'Epimenides the Cretan said all Cretans are liars. Does he speak truly?' Rico alludes to the riddle in *La novela picaresca*, p. 50.

147. In particular, the *Carta a la rectora del Colegio de las Vírgenes*, *Obras completas. Prosa*, p. 90, and the *Memorial a una academia*, ed. Luisa López Grigera, in *Homenaje a la memoria de don Antonio Rodríguez Moñino*, pp. 389–404. C.f. Michèle Gendreau-Massaloux, 'Quevedo et la déviation de l'autobiographie: *Je* est un autre' in *L'autobiographie*, pp. 205–15. The phrase 'más roto que rico' recalls the joke 'hijo de algo, señor de nada' and the ugliness and short stature are recalled in phrases like 'quebrado de color y de piernas . . . falto de pies y de juicio' (*Memorial*, p. 401, ll. 18–19). Molho, 'Cinco lecciones' in *Semántica*, p. 111 suggests that Quevedo's description of don Toribio could be a self-portrait.

148. For further discussion of this and following points see Ife, ed., *Buscón*, pp. 20 ff.

149. Cros, *Aristocrate*, p. 63.

150. *Ibid.*, p. 63: 'Il n'est donc pas excessif de prétendre que le *Buscón* est fait de deux textes qui, dans certains cas, se juxtaposent et, dans d'autres cas, se recoupent.'

151. *Ibid.*, pp. 66–7: '. . . une expression lexicalisée qui, à un premier niveau de décodage, connote de valeurs sociales telles que la piété et la noblesse, tandis que prise dans le réseau sémantique allusif du second texte, elle éclate et se délexicalise . . . La délexicalisation nous fait passer ici du plan idéal de l'abstraction (la honte, la justice) au plan des réalités les plus matérielles (le sexe, les exécutions de justice, les gestes lubriques).'

152. *Ibid.*, p. 100: 'Le *yo* est un dernier masque derrière lequel se cache, mal, Quevedo.'

153. The allusion to Stanley E. Fish, *Self-Consuming Artifacts: the Experience of Seventeenth-century Literature*, is deliberate.

154. Raimundo Lida, 'Sobre el arte verbal del *Buscón*', *Philological Quarterly*, LI (1972), 255–69, reprinted in revised form in *Prosas*, p. 303.

155. Molho, 'Cinco lecciones' in *Semántica*, p. 131.

156. C.f. chapter 1, n. 32.

157. Edwin Williamson, 'The conflict between Author and Protagonist in Quevedo's *Buscón*', *Journal of Hispanic Philology*, 2 (1977), 45–60.

158. M. C. Bradbrook, 'The image of the delinquent in literature, 1955–1960' in *Metaphor and Symbol*, ed. L. C. Knights and Basil Cottle, p. 28. Quoted in Parker, *Delinquent*, p. 5.

159. Molho, 'Cinco lecciones' in *Semántica*, pp. 97–102: 'lenguaje lúdico, codificado y deseifrable, destinado a funcionar como el vehículo semiológico de una conciencia de grupo . . . libro concebido para dar al grupo hegemónico, y en especial a la casta dominante, la conciencia de su dominación.'

160. C. B. Morris, *The Unity and Structure of Quevedo's 'Buscón': Desgracias Encadenadas*.

161. C.f. Johnson, 'El *Buscón*'; Redondo, 'Diego Coronel'; Ife, ed., *Buscón*, p. 27: 'Pablos sets out to be like his friend, but his friend turns out to be like him.'

162. Molho, 'Cinco lecciones' in *Semántica*, p. 104.

Bibliography

Only works cited in the notes are included in this bibliography.

Primary sources

Alemán, Mateo. *Guzmán de Alfarache*. Ed. Francisco Rico, *La novela picaresca española*, vol. I. Barcelona, 1967
    Guzmán de Alfarache. Ed. Benito Brancaforte. 2 vols. Madrid, 1981
    The Rogue. Tr. James Mabbe, London, 1623. The Tudor Translations. Second Series. 4 vols. London, 1924
    Ortografía castellana. Ed. J. Rojas Garcidueñas. Mexico, 1950
Amyot, Jacques. Prologue to Heliodorus, *Historia etiópica*
Anon. *La vida de Lazarillo de Tormes*. Ed. R. O. Jones. Manchester, 1963
    La vida de Lazarillo de Tormes. Ed. Claudio Guillén. New York, 1966
    La vida de Lazarillo de Tormes. Ed. Francisco Rico. Barcelona, 1976
    The Pleasaunt Historie of Lazarillo de Tormes, translated by David Rowland. London, 1586. Ed. J. E. V. Crofts. Oxford, 1924
Arias Montano, Benito. *Rhetoricorum libri IV*. Antwerp, 1569
Aristotle. *Poetics*. Tr. T. S. Dorsch in *Classical Literary Criticism*. Harmondsworth, 1965
Astete, Gaspar de. *Tratado del gobierno de la familia y estado de las viudas y donzellas*. Burgos, 1603
Augustine, St. *The Confessions of Augustine*. Ed. John Gibb and William Montgomery. Cambridge, 1927
    Quaestionum Evangeliorum Libri II. Ed. J. P. Migne, *Patrologiae Cursus Completus Series Prima*, vol. XXXV. Paris, 1845
Barcelos, Francisco de. *Salutiferae crucis triumphus*. Coimbra, 1553
Benedict, St. *Benedicti Regula*. Ed. R. Hanslik. Corpus Scriptorum Ecclesiasticorum Latinorum, vol. LXXV. Vienna, 1960
Bocados de oro. *Bocados de oro*. Ed. Mechtild Crombach. Romanistische Versuche und Vorarbeiten, vol. 37. Bonn, 1971
Boileau, Nicolas. *L'art poétique*. Ed. August Buck. Munich, 1970
Bruni d'Arezzo, Lionardo. *De Studiis et Litteris* (*c.* 1405), in Woodward, *Vittorino da Feltre*, pp. 123–33
Camos, Fr. Marco Antonio de. *Microcosmia y govierno universal del hombre christiano*. Madrid, 1595
Cano, Melchor. *De locis theologicis* (1563). Louvain, 1564
Carvallo, Luis Alfonso de. *Cisne de Apolo*. Ed. A. Porqueras Mayo. 2 vols. Madrid, 1958
Castelvetro, Ludovico. *Opere varie critiche*. Lione, 1727
Cerda, Fr. Juan de la. *Libro intitulado vida política de todos los estados de mujeres*. Alcalá, 1599

Cervantes Saavedra, Miguel de. *Obras completas.* 14th edn. Madrid, 1965
Don Quijote de la Mancha. Ed. Martín de Riquer. 2 vols. Barcelona, 1958
Cervantes de Salazar, Francisco. *Obras que Francisco Cervantes de Salazar ha hecho glosado y traduzido.* Alcalá, 1546
Cicero. *De legibus.* Ed. and tr. C. W. Keyes. London, 1928
Tusculanarum Disputationum. Ed. and tr. J. E. King. London, 1927
Ens, Gaspar. *Proscenii vitae humanae Pars Tertia . . .* Danzig, 1652
Equicola, Mario. *Institutioni al comporre in ogni sorte di rima della lingua volgare.* Milan, 1541
Fernandes, Diogo. *Terceira parte da chronica de Palmeirim de Inglaterra.* Lisbon, 1587
Fernández de Oviedo y Valdés, Gonzalo (tr.). *Libro del muy esforzado e invencible caballero de la fortuna propiamente llamado Claribalte.* Valencia, 1519
Historia general de las Indias. Seville, 1535
Las quinquagenas de la nobleza de España. Madrid, 1880
Fuentes, Alonso de. *Summa de philosophía natural.* Seville, 1547
Gracián, Diego. *Las obras de Xenophon.* Salamanca, 1552
Morales de Plutarco. Alcalá, 1548
Granada, Fr. Luis de. *Introducción del símbolo de la fe.* Saragossa, 1583
Guarino, Battista. *De Ordine Docendi et Studendi* (1459), in Woodward, *Vittorino da Feltre,* pp. 161–78
Guevara, Fr. Antonio de. *Libro del emperador Marco Aurelio con relox de príncipes.* Valladolid, 1529
Las obras. Valladolid, 1539
Heliodorus. *Historia etiópica de los amores de Teágenes y Cariclea,* tr. Fernando de Mena. Ed. Francisco López Estrada. Biblioteca Selecta de Clásicos Españoles, series II, vol. XV. Madrid, 1954
Herrera, Fernando de. *Obras de Garcilaso de la Vega con anotaciones de Fernando de Herrera.* Ed. Antonio Gallego Morell, in *Garcilaso de la Vega y sus comentaristas.* Madrid, 1972
Hooker, Thomas. *The Application of Redemption . . . The Ninth and Tenth Books.* London, 1659
Horace. *Ars Poetica.* Ed. Augustus S. Wilkins. London, 1960
Huarte de San Juan, Juan. *Examen de ingenios* (Baeza, 1575). 2nd edn. Buenos Aires, 1946
Isidore of Seville, St. *Etymologiarum sive Originum.* Ed. W. M. Lindsay. Oxford, 1911
Lactantius. *Divinarum Institutionum Libri Septem.* Ed. J. P. Migne, *Patrologiae Cursus Completus Series Prima,* vol. VI. Paris, 1844
Le Carré, John. *Smiley's People.* London, 1979
Lionardi, Alessandro. *Dialogi della inventione poetica.* Venice, 1554
López Pinciano, Alonso. *Philosophía antigua poética.* Ed. Alfredo Carballo Picazo. 3 vols. Madrid, 1953
Macrobius. *Commentarii in Somnium Scipionis.* Ed. J. Willis. Bibliotheca Scriptorum Graecorum et Romanorum Teubneriana. Leipzig, 1970
Mal Lara, Juan de. *Filosofía vulgar* (Seville, 1568). Ed. A. Vilanova. 4 vols. Barcelona, 1958–9

Malón de Chaide, Fr. Pedro. *La conversión de la Magdalena* (Barcelona, 1588). Ed. P. Félix García. 3rd edn. 3 vols. Madrid, 1959

Maximus of Tyre. *The Dissertations of Maximus Tyrius*. Tr. Thomas Taylor. 2 vols. London, 1804

Mexía, Luis. *Apólogo de la ociosidad y del trabajo*. Alcalá, 1546

Mexía, Pedro. *Historia imperial y cesárea* (Seville, 1545). Seville, 1547

Monzón, Francisco de. *Espejo del príncipe cristiano*. Lisbon, 1544

Ortiz Lucio, Francisco. *Libro intitulado jardín de amores santos*. Alcalá, 1589

Padilla Manrique y Acuña, Luisa María de. *Excelencias de la castidad*. Saragossa, 1642

Patrizi, Francesco. *De institutione reipublicae*. Paris, 1518

Pez, Bernard. *Thesaurus anecdotorum novissimus*. Augustae Vindelicorum et Graecii, 1721

Pico della Mirandola, Giovanni Francesco. *Opera omnia*. 2 vols. Basle, 1573

Pigna, Giovanni Battista. *I romanzi*. Venice, 1554

Pineda, Fr. Juan de. *Diálogos familiares de la agricultura cristiana* (Salamanca, 1589). Ed. P. Juan Meseguer Fernández. 5 vols. Biblioteca de Autores Españoles, vols. 161–3, 169–70. Madrid, 1963–4

Plato. *Ion*. Tr. B. Jowett. Oxford, 1871

Phaedrus. Tr. R. Hackforth. Cambridge, 1972

The Republic of Plato. Tr. Francis Macdonald Cornford. Oxford (1941), 1975

Sophist. Tr. F. M. Cornford, as *Plato's Theory of Knowledge*. London (1935), 1973

Plutarch. *Lives*. Tr. Bernadotte Perrin. 11 vols. London, 1914–26

Moralia. Tr. F. C. Babbitt, *et. al.* 16 vols. London, 1927–

Prior, Matthew. *The Literary Works*. Ed. H. Bunker Wright and Monroe K. Spears. 2 vols. Oxford, 1959

Quevedo Villegas, Francisco Gómez de. *Memorial a una academia*. Ed. Luisa López Grigera, in *Homenaje a la memoria de don Antonio Rodríguez Moñino*, Madrid, 1975, pp. 389–404

Obras en verso in *Obras completas*. Ed. Felicidad Buendía. 6th edn. 2 vols. Madrid, 1967

Obra poética. Ed. J. M. Blecua. 4 vols. Madrid, 1969–81

La vida del Buscón llamado don Pablos. Ed. Fernando Lázaro Carreter. Salamanca, 1965

La vida del Buscón llamado don Pablos. Ed. B. W. Ife. London, 1977

The Choice Humorous and Satirical Works. Ed. Charles Duff. London, 1926

Reeve, Clara. *The Progress of Romance*. Colchester, 1785

Remigio Noydens, Benito. *Historia moral del Dios Momo*. Madrid, 1666

Ricchieri, Lodovico. *Lectionum Antiquarum*. Venice, 1516

Richalm of Schönthal. *Liber Revelationum de Insidiis et Versutiis Daemonum Adversus Homines*, in Pez, *Thesaurus*, i, ii

Salucio, Fr. Agustín. *Avisos para los predicadores del Santo Evangelio* (1573). Ed. A. Huerga. Barcelona, 1959

Sánchez Valdés de la Plata, Juan. *Corónica y historia general del hombre*. Madrid, 1598

Scaliger, J. C. *Contra Poetices Calumniatores Declamatio* in *Epistolae et Orationes nunquam ante hac excusae*. Leyden, 1600. Ed. Vernon Hall Jr, 'Scaliger's defense of poetry', *Publications of the Modern Language Association of America*, LXIII (1948), 1125–30
Poetices Libri Septem (Lyons, 1561). Facsimile edn. Stuttgart, 1964
Sigüenza, P. José de. *Historia de la orden de san Jerónimo* (Madrid, 1600, 1605). 2 vols. Nueva Biblioteca de Autores Españoles, vols. VIII, XII. 2nd edn. Madrid, 1907–9
Soto de Rojas, Pedro. *Obras*. Ed. Antonio Gallego Morell. Madrid, 1950
Speroni, Sperone. *Opere*. 5 vols. Venice, 1740
Stevens, Wallace. *Collected Poems*. London, 1959
Strabo. *Geography*. Tr. H. L. Jones. 8 vols. London, 1917–32
Tasso, Torquato. *Discorsi dell'arte poetica e del poema eroico*. Ed. L. Poma. Bari, 1964
Ulloa, Alonso de. *Comentarios de la guerra contra Guillermo de Nausau Príncipe de Oranges*. Venice, 1569
Valdés, Juan de. *Diálogo de la lengua* (*c*. 1533–5). Ed. José F. Montesinos. Madrid, 1953
Vallés, Francisco de. *Cartas familiares de moralidad*. Madrid, 1603
Vega, Fr. Pedro de la. *Declaración de los siete psalmos penitenciales*. Alcalá, 1599
Segunda parte de la declaración de los siete psalmos penitenciales. Salamanca, 1607
Vega Carpio, Lope Félix de. *Obras*. 13 vols. Madrid, 1916–30
Venegas, Alejo. Prologue to Mexía, *Apólogo*
Vives, Juan Luis. *Opera Omnia*. 8 vols. Valencia, 1783–90
De Institutione Christianae Feminae. Antwerp, 1524. Tr. Richard Hyrde, *The Instruction of a Christian Woman*. London, 1541. Tr. Juan Justiniano, *Instrucción de la mujer cristiana*. Valencia, 1528
De Officio Mariti. Bruges, 1529. Tr. Thomas Paynell, *The Office and Duetie of an Husband*. London, *c*. 1558
De Tradendis Disciplinis. Tr. Foster Watson, *Vives: On Education*. Cambridge, 1913

Secondary sources

Alonso, Dámaso. 'El realismo psicológico en el *Lazarillo*' in *De los siglos oscuros al de oro*. Madrid, 1958, pp. 226–34
Arias, Joan. *Guzmán de Alfarache: the Unrepentant Narrator*. London, 1977
Austin, J. L. *How to Do Things with Words*. Oxford (1962), 1978
L'autobiographie dans le monde hispanique. Actes du Colloque International de la Baume-Lès-Aix, 11–13 Mai 1979. Aix-en-Provence, 1980
Balogh, Josef. 'Voces paginarum', *Philologus*, 82 (1927), 84–109, 202–40
Barthes, Roland. 'Eléments de sémiologie', *Communications*, 4 (1964), 91–135
Bataillon, Marcel. *Erasmo y España*. Tr. Antonio Alatorre. 2nd edn. Mexico, 1966
Novedad y fecundidad del 'Lazarillo de Tormes'. Salamanca, 1968
Pícaros y picaresca. Madrid, 1969

Batlle, C. 'Las bibliotecas de los ciudadanos de Barcelona en el siglo XV' in
    Livre et lecture, pp. 15–31
Belsey, Catherine. *Critical Practice*. London, 1980
Benveniste, Emile. *Problems in General Linguistics*. Miami, 1971
Berger, Ph., 'La lecture à Valence de 1474 à 1560, évolution des
    comportements en fonction des milieux sociaux' in *Livre et lecture*, pp. 97–
    107
Blanco Aguinaga, Carlos. 'Cervantes y la picaresca. Notas sobre dos tipos de
    realismo', *Nueva Revista de Filología Hispánica*, XI (1957), 313–42
Bobrow, D. G. and Collins, A., eds. *Representation and Understanding: Studies in
    Cognitive Science*. New York, 1975
Bolgar, R. R. *The Classical Heritage and its Beneficiaries*. Cambridge (1954),
    1977
Bower, Gordon H. 'Experiments in story comprehension and recall',
    Discourse Processes, I (1978), 211–31
Boyle, D. G. *Language and Thinking in Human Development*. London, 1971
Bradbrook, M. C. 'The image of the delinquent in literature, 1955–1960' in
    Metaphor and Symbol, ed. L. C. Knights and Basil Cottle. London, 1960
Brancaforte, Benito. *Guzmán de Alfarache: ¿Conversión o proceso de degradación?*
    Madison, 1980
Carey, Douglas M. 'Asides and interiority in *Lazarillo de Tormes*', *Studies in
    Philology*, XLVI (1969), 119–34
    '*Lazarillo de Tormes* and the quest for authority', *Publications of the Modern
    Language Association of America*, 94 (1979), 36–46
Carpenter, Edmund and McLuhan, Marshall, eds. *Explorations in Communi-
    cation*. Boston, 1960
Carpenter, Patricia A. and Just, Marcel Adam. 'Reading comprehension as
    eyes see it' in Just and Carpenter, *Cognitive Processes in Comprehension*, pp.
    109–39
Castro, Américo. *El pensamiento de Cervantes*. Ed. Julio Rodríguez-Puértolas.
    Barcelona, 1972
Cavillac, Michel. 'Mateo Alemán et la modernité', *Bulletin Hispanique*, LXXXII
    (1980), 380–401
Chaytor, H. J. *From Script to Print*. Cambridge, 1945
Chevalier, Maxime. *Lectura y lectores en la España del siglo XVI y XVII*. Madrid,
    1976
Clark, Herbert H. 'Inferences in comprehension' in Laberge and Samuels,
    Basic Processes in Reading, pp. 243–63
    'Bridging' in Johnson-Laird and Wason, *Thinking*, pp. 411–20
Clark, W. P. 'Ancient reading', *Classical Journal*, 26 (1931), 698–700
Coulton, G. G. *Five Centuries of Religion*. 4 vols. Cambridge, 1923–50
Craig, George. 'Reading: who is doing what to whom?' in Josipovici, *The
    Modern English Novel*, pp. 15–36
Cros, Edmond. *Protée et le gueux*. Paris, 1967
    Mateo Alemán: Introducción a su vida y a su obra. Salamanca, 1971
    Contribution à l'étude des sources de 'Guzmán de Alfarache'. n.p., n.d.
    L'aristocrate et le carnaval des gueux. Montpellier, 1975
    Ideología y genética textual. Madrid, n.d. (1981?)

Cruickshank, D. W. 'Literature and the book trade in golden age Spain', *Modern Language Review*, 73 (1978), 799–824

Curtius, E. R. *Literatura europea y Edad Media latina*. Buenos Aires, 1955

Deyermond, A. D. 'Lazarus and Lazarillo', *Studies in Short Fiction*, 2 (1964–5), 351–7

'Lazarillo de Tormes'. A Critical Guide. London, 1975

Díaz Migoyo, Gonzalo. *Estructura de la novela*. Madrid, 1978

'Las fechas en y de *El Buscón* de Quevedo', *Hispanic Review*, 48 (1980), 171–93

Durand, Frank. 'The author and Lázaro: levels of comic meaning', *Bulletin of Hispanic Studies*, XLV (1968), 89–101

Eco, Umberto. *The Role of the Reader*. Bloomington, 1979

Egger, Victor. *La parole intérieure*, 2nd edn. Paris, 1904

Eisenstein, Elizabeth L. *The Printing Press as an Agent of Change*. 2 vols. Cambridge, 1979

Elliot, R. K. 'Aesthetic theory and the experience of art' in Osborne, *Aesthetics*, pp. 145–57

El Saffar, Ruth S. *Novel to Romance. A Study of Cervantes's 'Novelas ejemplares'*. Baltimore and London, 1974

Ezquerro, Milagros. 'Le roman en première personne: *Pedro Páramo*' in *L'autobiographie dans le monde hispanique*, pp. 63–74

Febvre, Lucien and Martin, Henri-Jean. *L'apparition du livre*. Paris, 1958. Tr. David Gerard, *The Coming of the Book. The Impact of Printing 1450–1800*. London, 1976

Fish, Stanley E. *Surprised by Sin: the Reader in 'Paradise Lost'*. London and New York, 1967

Self-Consuming Artifacts: the Experience of Seventeenth-century Literature. Berkeley, 1972

'How to do things with Austin and Searle: speech-act theory and literary criticism', *Modern Language Notes*, 91 (1976), 938–1025

Forcione, Alban K. *Cervantes, Aristotle and the 'Persiles'*. Princeton, 1970

Fowler, Roger. *Linguistics and the Novel*. London, 1977

Friedländer, Paul. *Platon: Seinswahrheit und Lebenswirklichkeit*. Berlin, 1954. Tr. Hans Meyerhoff, *Plato: an Introduction*. London, 1958

Friedman, Edward. 'Chaos restored: authorial control and ambiguity in *Lazarillo de Tormes*', *Crítica Hispánica*, 3 (1981), 59–73

Frye, Northrop. *Fearful Symmetry. A Study of William Blake*. Princeton, 1967

Gendreau-Massaloux, Michèle. 'Quevedo et la déviation de l'autobiographie: *Je est un autre*' in *L'autobiographie dans le monde hispanique*, pp. 205–15

Gibson, E. J. and Levin, Harry. *The Psychology of Reading*. Cambridge, Mass. and London, 1975

Gillet, J. E. 'The squire's dovecote' in *Hispanic Studies in Honour of I. González Llubera*, Oxford, 1959, pp. 135–8

Gilman, Stephen. 'The death of Lazarillo de Tormes', *Publications of the Modern Language Association of America*, LXXXI (1966), 149–66

Glaser, Edward. 'Nuevos datos sobre la crítica de los libros de caballerías en los siglos XVI y XVII', *Anuario de Estudios Medievales*, III (1966), 393–410

González Palencia, Angel and Mele, Eugenio. *Vida y obras de don Diego Hurtado de Mendoza*. 3 vols. Madrid, 1941–3

Grice, H. P. 'Meaning', *Philosophical Review*, 66 (1957), 377–88. Reprinted in Steinberg and Jakobovits, *Semantics*

Grimm, Friedrich Melchior. *Correspondance littéraire, philosophique et critique par Grimm, Diderot, Raynal, etc.* Ed. Maurice Tourneux. 16 vols. Paris, 1877–82

Guillén, Claudio. 'La disposición temporal del *Lazarillo de Tormes*', *Hispanic Review*, xxv (1957), 264–79

'Toward a definition of the picaresque' in *Literature as System*, Princeton, 1971, pp. 71–106

Guthrie, W. K. C. *The Sophists. A History of Greek Philosophy*, vol. III, pt 1. Cambridge (1969), 1977

Hall, Vernon, Jr. 'Scaliger's defense of poetry', *Publications of the Modern Language Association of America*, LXIII (1948), 1125–30

Halliday, M. A. K., and Hassan, R. *Cohesion in English*. London, 1976

Harding, D. W. 'Psychological processes in the reading of fiction', *British Journal of Aesthetics*, 2 (1962), 133–47

Hardy, Barbara. *Tellers and Listeners*. London, 1975

Hay, Denys. Introduction, *New Cambridge Modern History*, vol. I. *The Renaissance, 1493–1520*. Ed. G. R. Potter. Cambridge, 1957, pp. 1–19

Introduction, *Printing and the Mind of Man: the Impact of Print on the Evolution of Western Civilization During Five Centuries*. Ed. J. W. Carter and P. H. Muir. London, 1967

Hendrickson, G. L. 'Ancient reading', *Classical Journal*, 25 (1929), 182–96

Hepburn, Ronald W. 'Aesthetic appreciation of nature' in Osborne, *Aesthetics*, pp. 49–66

Huey, E. B. *The Psychology and Pedagogy of Reading*. New York (1908), 1968

Hutman, Norma Louise. 'Universality and unity in the *Lazarillo de Tormes*', *Publications of the Modern Language Association of America*, LXXVI (1961), 469–73

Ife, B. W. 'From Salamanca to Brighton Rock: names and places in Cervantes's *La ilustre fregona*', in *Essays in Honour of Robert Brian Tate*, ed. Richard A. Cardwell, Nottingham, 1984, pp. 46–52

'Private Reading and its Consequences for the Development of Spanish Golden-Age Prose Fiction', University of London PhD thesis, 1984

Ingarden, Roman. *The Cognition of the Literary Work of Art*. Evanston, 1973

Iser, Wolfgang. 'Indeterminacy and the reader's response in prose fiction' in Miller, *Aspects of Narrative*, pp. 1–45

The Implied Reader. Baltimore and London, 1974

The Act of Reading. London, 1978

Jaén, Didier T. 'La ambigüedad moral del *Lazarillo de Tormes*', *Publications of the Modern Language Association of America*, LXXXIII (1968), 130–4

Johnson, Carroll B. '*El Buscón*: d. Pablos, d. Diego y d. Francisco', *Hispanófila*, 51 (1974), 1–26

Inside Guzmán de Alfarache. Berkeley and Los Angeles, 1978

Johnson-Laird, P. N. and Wason, P. C., eds. *Thinking. Readings in Cognitive Science*. Cambridge, 1977

Joly, Monique. *La bourle et son interprétation*. Toulouse, 1982

Jones, C. A. 'Brecht y el drama del siglo de oro en España', *Segismundo*, 5–6 (1969–70), 39–54

Jones, J. A. 'The duality and complexity of *Guzmán de Alfarache*: some thoughts on the structure and interpretation of Alemán's novel' in Christine Whitbourn, ed. *Knaves and Swindlers: Essays on the Picaresque Novel in Europe*. Oxford, 1974, pp. 25–46

Josipovici, Gabriel. *The World and the Book*. London, 1971

ed. *The Modern English Novel*. London, 1976

Judd, C. H. and Buswell, G. T. *Silent Reading: a Study of the Various Types*. Supplementary Educational Monographs, 23. 1922

Just, Marcel Adam and Carpenter, Patricia A., eds. *Cognitive Processes in Comprehension*. Hillsdale, New Jersey, 1977

Kermode, Frank. *The Genesis of Secrecy*. Cambridge, Mass., and London, 1979

Kintsch, Walter. 'On comprehending stories' in Just and Carpenter, *Cognitive Processes*, pp. 33–62

Knox, Bernard M. W. 'Silent reading in antiquity', *Greek, Roman and Byzantine Studies*, 9 (1968), 421–35

Krauss, Werner. 'Die Kritik des Siglo de Oro am Ritter- und Schäferroman', *Gesammelte Aufsätze zur Literatur- und Sprachwissenschaft*. Frankfurt, 1949, pp. 152–76

Laberge, David and Samuels, S. Jay. *Basic Processes in Reading: Perception and Comprehension*. Hillsdale, New Jersey, 1977

Labov, William. *Language in the Inner City*. Philadelphia, 1972

Ladero Quesada, Miguel Angel and Quintanilla Raso, María Concepción, 'Bibliotecas de la alta nobleza castellana en el siglo xv' in *Livre et lecture*, pp. 47–59

Lázaro Carreter, Fernando. 'Originalidad del *Buscón*' in *Homenaje a Dámaso Alonso*, Madrid, 1961, vol. ii, pp. 319–38. Reprinted in *Estilo barroco y personalidad creadora*, Salamanca, 1966, pp. 109–41

'La ficción autobiográfica en el *Lazarillo de Tormes*' in '*Lazarillo de Tormes*' en la picaresca. Madrid, 1972, pp. 13–57

Leonard, Irving A. *Romances of Chivalry in the Spanish Indies*. University of California Publications in Modern Philology. Vol. 16, no. 3, pp. 217–371. Berkeley and Cambridge, 1933

Books of the Brave. Cambridge, Mass., 1949

Lida, Raimundo. 'Pablos de Segovia y su agudeza' in *Homenaje a Joaquín Casalduero*. Madrid, 1972, pp. 285–98. Reprinted in revised form in *Prosas de Quevedo*, Barcelona, 1981, pp. 241–76

'Sobre el arte verbal del *Buscón*', *Philological Quarterly*, li (1972), 255–69. Reprinted in revised form in *Prosas de Quevedo*, Barcelona, 1981, pp. 279–304

Livre et lecture en Espagne et en France sous l'ancien régime. Colloque de la Casa de Velázquez, Paris, 1981

Lomax, Derek W. 'On re-reading the *Lazarillo de Tormes*' in *Studia Iberica. Festschrift für Hans Flasche*, Bern, 1973, pp. 371–81

Mancing, Howard. 'The deceptiveness of *Lazarillo de Tormes*', *Publications of the Modern Language Association of America*, xc (1975), 426–32

Marasso, A. *Estudios de literatura española*. Buenos Aires, 1955

May, T. E. 'Good and evil in the *Buscón*', *Modern Language Review*, XLV (1950), 319–35

McGrady, Donald. 'Social irony in *Lazarillo de Tormes* and its implications for authorship', *Romance Philology*, XXIII (1970), 557–67

McLuhan, Marshall. 'The effect of the printed book on language in the sixteenth century' in Edmund Carpenter and Marshall McLuhan, eds. *Explorations in Communication*, Boston, 1960, pp. 125–35

Menéndez y Pelayo, Marcelino. *Orígenes de la novela*. 4 vols. Madrid-Santander, 1943

Meyer, B. J. F. *The Organisation of Prose and its Effects on Memory*. Amsterdam, 1975

Miller, J. Hillis, ed. *Aspects of Narrative*. New York and London, 1971

Minsky, Marvin. 'Frame-system theory' in Johnson-Laird and Wason, *Thinking*, pp. 355–76

Molho, Maurice, *Introducción al pensamiento picaresco*. Salamanca. 1972
'Cinco lecciones sobre el *Buscón*' in *Semántica y poética*, Barcelona, 1977, pp. 89–131

Monod, Jacques. *Le hasard et la nécessité*. Paris, 1970

Moreno Báez, Enrique. *Lección y sentido del 'Guzmán de Alfarache'*. Madrid, 1948

Morris, C. B. 'Lázaro and the Squire: *hombres de bien*', *Bulletin of Hispanic Studies*, XLI (1964), 238–41
The Unity and Structure of Quevedo's 'Buscón': Desgracias Encadenadas. Hull, 1965

Murdoch, Iris. *The Fire and the Sun. Why Plato Banished the Artists*. Oxford, 1977

Needham, Paul. Review of Elizabeth L. Eisenstein, *The Printing Press as an Agent of Change* in *Fine Print*, VI, 1 (January 1980), 23–25

Nelson, William. *Fact or Fiction. The Dilemma of the Renaissance Storyteller*. Cambridge, Mass., 1973

Norton, F. J. *Printing in Spain 1501–1520*. Cambridge, 1966
A Descriptive Catalogue of Printing in Spain and Portugal 1501–1520. Cambridge, 1978

Ogden, C. K. and Richards, I. A. *The Meaning of Meaning*. London, 1923

Olsen, Stein Haugom. *The Structure of Literary Understanding*. Cambridge, 1978

Ong, Walter J. 'Voice as summons for belief' in *The Barbarian Within*, New York, 1962, pp. 49–67
Interfaces of the Word. Ithaca and London, 1977
Orality and Literacy. London, 1982

Osborne, Harold, ed. *Aesthetics*. Oxford, 1972

Parker, A. A. *Literature and the Delinquent*. Edinburgh, 1967

Peale, C. George. '*Guzmán de Alfarache* como discurso oral', *Journal of Hispanic Philology*, 4 (1979), 25–57

Pérez Pastor, C. *Bibliografía madrileña*. 3 vols. Madrid, 1891–1907

Pina Martins, J. V. de. 'Platon et le Platonisme dans la culture Portugaise du XVIᵉ siècle' in *Platon et Aristote à la Renaissance*, Paris, 1976, pp. 421–37

Poulet, Georges. 'Phenomenology of reading', *New Literary History*, I (1969), 53–68

Pratt, Mary Louise. *Toward a Speech Act Theory of Literary Discourse*. Bloomington, Indiana, 1977

Randall, Dale B.J. 'The classical ending of Quevedo's *Buscón*', *Hispanic Review*, XXXII (1964), 101–8

Redondo, Agustín. 'Del personaje de don Diego Coronel a una nueva interpretación del *Buscón*' in *Actas del V Congreso Internacional de Hispanistas (1974)*, Bordeaux, 1977, vol. II, pp. 699–711

Ricapito, Joseph V. *Bibliografía razonada y anotada de las obras maestras de la picaresca española*. Madrid, 1980

Ricardou, Jean. *Problèmes du nouveau roman*. Paris, 1967

Rico, Francisco. 'Problemas del *Lazarillo*', *Boletín de la Real Academia Española*, XLVI (1966), 277–96

'Estructuras y reflejos de estructuras en el *Guzmán de Alfarache*', *Modern Language Notes*, LXXXII (1967), 171–84

La novela picaresca y el punto de vista. Barcelona, 1970

The Spanish Picaresque Novel and the Point of View. Tr. Charles Davis. Cambridge, 1984

'Consejos y consejas de *Guzmán de Alfarache*' in *La novela picaresca*, pp. 59–91

Riesman, David. 'The oral and written traditions' in Carpenter and McLuhan, *Explorations*, pp. 109–16

Riley, E. C. *Cervantes's Theory of the Novel*. Oxford (1962), 1964

Riquer, Martín de. Introduction, *Tirante el Blanco*. Barcelona, 1947, pp. ix–lviii

'Cervantes y la caballeresca' in *Suma Cervantina*, ed. J. B. Avalle-Arce and E. C. Riley, London, 1973, pp. 273–92

Rodríguez Marín, Francisco. *Luis Barahona de Soto*. Madrid, 1903

'Nuevos datos para las biografías de algunos escritores españoles de los siglos XVI y XVII', *Boletín de la Real Academia Española*, V (1918), 192–213

Rommetveit, R. 'On the architecture of intersubjectivity' in Rommetveit and Blakar, *Studies of Language, Thought and Verbal Communication*, pp. 93–107

Rommetveit, R. and Blakar, R. M. *Studies of Language, Thought and Verbal Communication*. London, 1979

Round, Nicholas G. 'Renaissance culture and its opponents in fifteenth-century Castile', *Modern Language Review*, LVII (1962), 204–15

'The shadow of a philosopher: medieval Castilian images of Plato', *Journal of Hispanic Philology*, III, I (Autumn, 1978), 1–36

Rummelhart, D. E. 'Notes on a schema for stories' in Bobrow and Collins, *Representation and Understanding*, pp. 211–36

'Understanding and summarizing brief stories' in Laberge and Samuels, *Basic Processes in Reading*, pp. 265–303

Russell, P. E., ed. *Spain. A Companion to Spanish Studies*. London, 1973

'Las armas contra las letras: para una definición del humanismo español del siglo XV' in *Temas de 'La Celestina'*, Barcelona, 1978, pp. 209–39

'El concilio de Trento y la literatura profana' in *Temas de 'La Celestina'*, Barcelona, 1978, pp. 443–78

Sabat de Rivers, Georgina. 'La moral que Lázaro nos propone', *Modern Language Notes*, 95 (1980), 233–51

San Miguel, Angel. *Sentido y estructura del 'Guzmán de Alfarache' de Mateo Alemán*. Madrid, 1971

Sánchez Cantón, F. J. *La biblioteca del Marqués del Cenete, iniciada por el cardenal Mendoza (1470–1523)*. Madrid, 1942

Sartre, J. P. 'The work of art' in Osborne, *Aesthetics*, pp. 32–8

Savile, Anthony. 'The place of intention in the concept of art', in Osborne, *Aesthetics*, pp. 158–76

Schmitt, C. B. 'L'introduction de la philosophie platonicienne dans l'enseignement des universités à la renaissance' in *Platon et Aristote à la Renaissance*, Paris, 1976, pp. 93–104

Searle, J. R. *Speech Acts*. Cambridge (1969), 1980

Seligman, Paul. *Being and Not-Being: an Introduction to Plato's 'Sophist'*. The Hague, 1974

Shepard, Sanford. *El Pinciano y las teorías literarias del siglo de oro*. 2nd edn. Madrid, 1970

Sicroff, Albert A. 'Sobre el estilo del *Lazarillo de Tormes*', *Nueva Revista de Filología Hispánica*, XI (1957), 157–70

Sieber, Harry. *Language and Society in 'La vida de Lazarillo de Tormes'*. Baltimore and London, 1978

Smith, Frank. *Understanding Reading*. 2nd edn. New York, 1978

Sobejano, Gonzalo. 'De la intención y valor del *Guzmán de Alfarache*', *Romanische Forschungen*, 71 (1959), 267–311. Reprinted in *Forma literaria y sensibilidad social*. Madrid, 1967, pp. 9–66

Sokolov, A. N. *Inner Speech and Thought*. New York, 1972

Spingarn, J. E. *A History of Literary Criticism in the Renaissance*. 2nd edn. New York (1908), 1924

Sprague, R. K., ed. *The Older Sophists*. South Carolina, 1972

Steinberg, D. D. and Jakobovits, L. A., eds. *Semantics*. Cambridge, 1971

Steiner, George. *Language and Silence: Essays on Language, Literature and the Inhuman*. New York. 1967

Tarr, F. Courtney. 'Literary and artistic unity in the *Lazarillo de Tormes*', *Publications of the Modern Language Association of America*, XLII (1927), 404–21

Thomas, Henry. *Spanish and Portuguese Romances of Chivalry*. Cambridge, 1920

Tinker, M. A. 'The study of eye movements in reading', *Psychological Bulletin*, 43 (1946), 93–120

'Fixation pause duration in reading', *Journal of Educational Research*, 44 (1951), 471–9

'Recent studies of eye movements in reading', *Psychological Bulletin*, 55 (1958), 215–31

Bases for Effective Reading. Minneapolis, 1965

Truman, R. W. 'Lázaro de Tormes and the *Homo novus* tradition', *Modern Language Review*, LXIV (1969), 62–7

Tubino, Francisco María. *El Quijote y la estafeta de Urganda*. Seville, 1862

Van Dijk, T. A. *Some Aspects of Text Grammars*. The Hague, 1972

Text and Context. London, 1977

'Semantic macro-structures and knowledge frames in discourse comprehension' in Just and Carpenter, *Cognitive Processes*, pp. 3–32

Vicaire, Paul. *Platon, critique littéraire*. Paris, 1960

Wardropper, Bruce W. 'El trastorno de la moral en el *Lazarillo*', *Nueva Revista de Filología Hispánica*, xv (1961), 441–7

'The strange case of Lázaro Gonzales Pérez'. *Modern Language Notes*, 92 (1977), 202–12

Weinberg, Bernard. *History of Literary Criticism in the Italian Renaissance*. 2 vols. Chicago, 1961

Whinnom, Keith. 'The problem of the "best-seller" in Spanish Golden-Age literature', *Bulletin of Hispanic Studies*, LVII (1980), 189–98

'The *Historia de Duobus Amantibus* of Aeneas Sylvius Piccolomini (Pope Pius II) and the development of Spanish golden-age fiction' in R. B. Tate, ed., *Essays on Narrative Fiction in the Iberian Peninsula in Honour of Frank Pierce*, Oxford, 1982, pp. 243–55

Williamson, Edwin. 'The conflict between Author and Protagonist in Quevedo's *Buscón*', *Journal of Hispanic Philology*, 2 (1977), 45–60

Willis, Raymond S. 'Lazarillo and the pardoner: the artistic necessity of the fifth *tractado*', *Hispanic Review*, XXVII (1959), 267–79

Wilson, Arthur M. *Diderot. The Testing Years, 1713–1759*. New York, 1957

Wollheim, Richard. 'On drawing an object' in Osborne, *Aesthetics*, pp. 121–44

Woods, M. J. 'Pitfalls for the moralizer in *Lazarillo de Tormes*', *Modern Language Review*, 74 (1979), 580–98

'The teasing opening of *Guzmán de Alfarache*', *Bulletin of Hispanic Studies*, LVII (1980), 213–18

Woodward, L. J. 'The author–reader relationship in the *Lazarillo de Tormes*', *Forum for Modern Language Studies*, 1 (1965), 43–53

Woodward, W. H. *Vittorino da Feltre and other Humanist Educators: Essays and Versions*. Cambridge, 1897

Yates, Frances. *The French Academies of the Sixteenth Century*. London, 1947

Index